English-Only Europe?

Challenging Language Policy

Robert Phillipson

Routledge
Taylor & Francis Group

LONDON AND NEW YORK

First published 2003
by Routledge
11 New Fetter Lane, London EC4P 4EE

Simultaneously published in the USA and Canada
by Routledge
29 West 35th Street, New York, NY 10001

Routledge is an imprint of the Taylor & Francis Group

© 2003 Robert Phillipson

Typeset in Bembo by M Rules
Printed and bound in Great Britain by
Biddles Ltd, Guildford and King's Lynn

British Library Cataloguing in Publication Data
A catalogue record for this book is available from the British
Library

Library of Congress Cataloging in Publication Data
A catalog record for this book has been applied for

ISBN 0 415 28806-1 (hbk)
ISBN 0 415 28807-x (pbk)

English-Only Europe?

'Globalization and EU enlargement mean that languages from the whole of Europe are coming into even closer contact. This perceptive book makes a sweeping Grand Tour of the political, cultural and economic issues that we all consequently face, and I hope that those who frame language policy will be influenced by it.'

Neil Kinnock, Vice-President of the European Commission

'An important and timely book, containing a rich and wide-ranging set of ideas about the "on the ground" reality of language policy in Europe. The book is very engaging, and will appeal to a wide range of readers.'

Joseph Lo Bianco, Director, Language Australia, The National Languages and Literacy Institute of Australia

'Absolutely essential reading if we are to prevent a linguistic catastrophe in a rapidly anglicizing Europe.'

Dafydd ap Fergus, Secretary General of the European Esperanto Union

Languages are central to the development of an integrated Europe. The way in which the European Union deals with multilingualism has serious implications for both individual member countries and international relations.

In this timely and provocative book, Robert Phillipson considers whether the current expansion of English represents a serious threat to other European languages.

The book explores the role of languages in the process of European integration. After looking at the implications of current policies, Phillipson argues the case for more active language policies to safeguard a multilingual Europe. Drawing on examples of countries with explicit language policies, such as Canada and South Africa, the book sets out Phillipson's vision of an inclusive language policy for Europe, and describes how it can be attained.

English-Only Europe? is essential reading for anyone with an interest in the future of the European Union.

Robert Phillipson is Research Professor in the Department of English, Copenhagen Business School, Denmark. His publications include *Rights to Language, Equity, Power and Education* (2000), *Linguistic Human Rights: Overcoming Linguistic Discrimination* (1994) and *Linguistic Imperialism* (1992).

Contents

Appendices

Illustrations

Boxes

Tables

Acknowledgements

My very sincere thanks are due to numerous people who have helped significantly in the genesis of the book:

- those who generously made many suggestions for improving the manuscript: David Ferguson, Jennifer Jenkins, Joe Lo Bianco, Barbara Seidlhofer, Tove Skutnabb-Kangas, Ruth Wodak;
- those who were very welcoming and informative when I visited EU institutions, particularly Emma Wagner, Brian McCluskey, Robert Rowe and Preben Saugstrup;
- those who have made me aware of developments in European language policy: Neville Alexander, Hugo Baetens Beardsmore, Detlev Blanke, Birgit Brock-Utne, Michael Clyne, Niels Davidsen-Nielsen, Bessie Dendrinos, Ina Druviete, François Grin, Hartmut Haberland, Leena Huss, Markku Jokinen, John Kirk, Miklós Kontra, Normand Labrie, Ole Henrik Magga, Virginie Mamadouh, Björn Melander, Dónall Ó Riagáin, Mart Rannut, Giridar Rao, Carol Tongue, Theo van Els;
- those many colleagues who make the English Department of Copenhagen Business School a congenial professional base, particularly the Head, Lise-Lotte Hjulmand;
- special thanks to David Ferguson, Secretary General of the European Esperanto Association, who is a cumulative archive of information about developments throughout Europe;
- loving thanks to Tove Skutnabb-Kangas, who is not only a constant support as a professional colleague, but who follows Voltaire's advice about cultivating one's garden literally, metaphorically and intellectually, and who cared for me lovingly in a protracted hour of medical need in the spring of 2002.

The Federal Trust for Education and Research, London has granted permission to reproduce the tables on pages 283 and 285 of *The Treaty of Nice explained*, edited by Martyn Bond and Kim Feus, 2001, which appear as Appendix 3.

Except in the case of published translations, the texts in translation are my own renderings.

Robert Phillipson
Trønninge, Denmark, June 2002

Chapter 1

The risks of *laissez faire* language policies

The most serious problem for the European Union is that it has so many languages, this preventing real integration and development of the Union.

The ambassador of the USA to Denmark, Mr Elton, 1997[1]

No-one pays attention to what you say unless you speak English, because English is the language of power.

Ombudsperson for Human Rights in Bosnia and Herzegovina, Gret Haller, 1999[2]

The Union shall respect cultural, religious and linguistic diversity.

Article 22, Charter of Fundamental Rights of the European Union, 2000[3]

I asked Voltaire whether he still spoke English. He replied, 'No. To speak English one must place the tongue between the teeth, and I have lost my teeth' . . . When he talked our language he was animated with the soul of a Briton. He had bold flights. He had humour. He had extravagance . . . He swore bloodily, as was the fashion when he was in England.

James Boswell, 1764[4]

Language policy challenges for Europe

Many profoundly important language policy questions need addressing:

* How does English as the key language of globalization impact on national economic, cultural, and educational policies in continental Europe, on job qualifications, mobility, and personal freedoms?
* Do the procedures followed in conducting European Union (EU)

affairs give native speakers of the 'top' languages, particularly English and French, unfair privileges, and if so, what can be done to remedy the problem?

- If speakers of Catalan, Welsh, and other minority languages have no right to use their languages in EU institutions, does this mean that only certain languages are being used to create 'Europe'? If so, does 'Strength in diversity' (an EU mantra) apply only to the privileged languages? Can Europeanness and European citizenship be expressed in any European language? Is European linguistic identity multilingual?
- Practical solutions are needed to the multiple communication needs of cross-European communication in the political, business, cultural, and many other fields, but are pragmatic solutions compatible with principles of equity, language rights, and human rights?
- Can English, and other influential foreign languages, be learned and used in ways that do not threaten other languages?
- Are the language policy issues of European integration being seriously addressed at the national and EU levels? Is there constructive dialogue between key constituencies, politicians and bureaucrats, the corporate world, academics in relevant fields, particularly education, political science, international law, economics, language, and minority rights, and grassroots public opinion?
- What can be done to bring about more informed and more inspired language policies?

This book is a general introduction that situates language policy, language use, language learning, and language rights within broader European political, economic, and social changes. The opening chapter introduces some of the major language policy challenges, clarifies what language policy is, and provides examples of when it becomes newsworthy. The historical background is covered in Chapter 2, the contemporary impact of globalization on European languages in Chapter 3. Chapter 4 is devoted to the institutions of the European Union. Chapter 5 goes through many of the factors that impinge on language policy and the ecology of language, and considers whether some form of English as a lingua franca can replace the traditional view of English as a British or North American language. This is one aspect of the search for an international language which is a genuinely egalitarian means of communication among speakers of different languages. Specific recommendations, within a vision of how language policy could be revitalized, are made in Chapter 6.

The book describes how the influence of English is much profounder than that of Latin and French in earlier periods. It assesses whether the contemporary expansion of English represents a serious threat to all the other languages of Europe. Languages are central to the processes leading to a more deeply integrated Europe, in commerce and the media, and in the activities of the institutions of the EU. With electronic communication and service industries playing an increasingly significant role, the role of languages is even more important than in earlier historical periods. But in the copious literature on European integration and globalization, the language dimension tends to be absent, except in specialist works on the sociology of language and nationalism. Through analysis of how languages are expanding and contracting in processes of European integration, the book will suggest ways in which a more active language policy, nationally and internationally, can ensure that all languages can flourish. The way the EU deals with multilingualism has significant implications, both for international relations and for what happens in each member country. It is important to clarify what sort of Europe current policies are leading towards, and the criteria that could guide policies that permit speakers of different languages to communicate on a basis of equality. The book argues a case for more active language policies that can serve to ensure the continued vitality of all the languages of Europe.

It would have been tempting to call the book 'From Babel to Eurobabble'. However, to do so would have reinforced the notion that a multiplicity of languages is a curse, both in history and at the present. Babel is historical myth rather than fact (see Chapter 2 on the Bible also endorsing 'speaking in tongues'). Multilingualism, in the sense of an individual or an institution operating effectively in more than one language, is an everyday reality for the majority of the world's inhabitants. It is a source of richness and joy for us, facilitating access to a range of cultures and cosmologies. If Babel and Eurobabble are understood as meaning that people who come from different language backgrounds cannot communicate, then the EU institutions, with their elaborate translation and interpretation services, are living proof of the opposite. The British Minister for Europe, Peter Hain, used 'Eurobabble' as a way of rubbishing official EU texts written in impenetrable language, as part of a campaign in 2001 to make the EU more comprehensible to British people.[5] However, neither the EU nor the English language has a monopoly of such texts, and the Eurobabble smear has more to do with the British government distancing itself from what the EU is perceived as representing. Much is at stake in communication at the EU, and the use of English is increasing in Europe. We need to explore whose interests are being served by this trend, and how it impacts on other languages.

English to unite or divide Europe?

For the American ambassador to Denmark who claims that a multiplicity of languages is thwarting the unification of Europe, the solution would be for the EU to eliminate all languages other than English. It is unthinkable that any political leader in Europe would endorse such a scenario. To do so would run counter to the endorsement of diversity that is enshrined in many key EU texts. Thus the Charter of Fundamental Rights of the EU that was approved by the European Parliament and the European Council and Commission in December 2000 commits the EU to respect linguistic diversity (in Article 22). Article 21 also seeks to prevent discrimination on grounds of language, nationality, or membership of a national minority:

> Any discrimination based on sex, race, colour, ethnic or social origin, genetic features, language, religion or belief, political or any other opinion, membership of a national minority, property, birth, disability, age or sexual orientation shall be prohibited. . . .
> Any discrimination on grounds of nationality shall be prohibited.

Nevertheless, the forces of globalization and americanization may be moving language policy in the direction of monolingualism. English may be seen as a kind of linguistic cuckoo, taking over where other breeds of language have historically nested and acquired territorial rights, and obliging non-native speakers of English to acquire the behavioural habits and linguistic forms of English. The EU Charter of Rights is a political declaration that does not have the force of law. According to the EU Ombudsman, 'this seems to imply that European citizens should understand that even the most solemn promises made by politicians are not intended to be taken seriously'.[6]

Things are moving fast in the world of commerce. The cover of the European edition of *Business Week* of 13 August 2001 asked in a banner headline: 'Should everyone speak English?' The inside story was flagged as 'The Great English divide. In Europe, speaking the lingua franca separates the haves from the have–nots'. The cover drawing portrays twin business executives: one communicates successfully, the English speaker; the other is mouthless, speechless. Competence in

English is here projected as being imperative throughout Europe in the commercial world. By implication, proficiency in other languages gets you nowhere. The article describes how more and more continental European companies are switching over to English as the in-house corporate language. It also describes how English for business is big business for English language schools.

Business Week's uncritical celebration of the way English is impacting on continental Europe fails to note that many businesses in Europe are becoming aware that proficiency in English will in future be so widespread that proficiency in other languages will be essential for commercial success. It is arguable that it is monolingual English-speakers who will lose out in the future, and that the high fliers will be multilingual, as is often the case today.[7]

The contemporary power of English makes itself felt in many fields. In international gatherings, there is a pecking order of languages. English has the sharpest beak, one that inflicts wounds on speakers of other languages. Discrimination against speakers of other languages is widespread, often without the users of English being aware that there is a problem. At a Council of Europe conference in 1999 on *Linguistic Diversity for Democratic Citizenship in Europe*, the Ombudsperson for Human Rights in Bosnia and Herzegovina, Gret Haller, who comes from Switzerland, noted that she had 'frequently come across situations where you are not taken seriously unless you speak English. This has been in Bosnia, not in my own country. No-one pays attention to what you say unless you speak English, because English is the language of power.'[8] She warned that going along with this state of affairs could be dangerous for Europe, and pleaded for language policy not to be left to *laissez faire* market forces.

Languages have expanded and contracted throughout history, and there are many languages that are currently expanding at the expense of other languages, but the way English is impacting globally is unique. Its advance has major implications for speakers of all other languages, for education systems and professional qualifications, for the economy, and for the vitality of cultures big and small. Languages are the medium through which communication takes place in politics, commerce, defence, academia, the media, technology, the internet, and most aspects of life. Languages are therefore central to our increasingly international world, to globalization and the accelerating processes of European unification.

In different historical periods, voices have protested against an excessive reliance on English. In the struggle for Indian independence,

Mahatma Gandhi warned that English represented cultural alienation. Nehru, the first Prime Minister of India (educated at Cambridge University and imprisoned by the British before independence), was 'convinced that real progress in India can only be made through our own languages and not through a foreign language. I am anxious to prevent a new caste system being perpetuated in India – an English knowing caste separated from the mass of our public.'[9] In fact, an English-using caste has emerged, because the management of multi-lingualism in India has largely been left to market forces. These strengthen the position of users of English, here as elsewhere. Roughly 30 million Indians are fluent users of English, but they account for under 5 per cent of the population.[10]

The French have long been concerned about their language being corrupted by an invasion from English, by *franglais* and *anglomania*. Successive French governments have invested substantially in the promotion of their language internationally, and in the establishment of a counterpart to the British Commonwealth, a global 'Francophonie' organization.[11] They have also legislated to ensure that French is given priority in France in commerce, education, public life, and the media. The Body Shop, and an American university operating in France, have been prosecuted for failing to use French in their information to customers. However, such sanctions and protective measures may well not prove very successful, because they represent limited treatment of a disease that has multiple causes and symptoms.

To regard the stand taken by the French as a waste of time, as is often done, is misguided. Governments *are* responsible for language policy in their countries. Many act vigorously to promote a single national language. Several are concerned about the impact of English on their own languages. The Polish and Hungarian governments have legislated to restrict the spread of English. A Swedish parliamentary committee has recommended legislation aimed at ensuring that Swedish remains a 'complete language' serving all purposes in Swedish society.[12] It stresses the need for more proactive language policy work so as to maintain the position of Swedish in EU institutions, to build on the diversity of languages in use in present-day Sweden, and to ensure that Swedes in higher education and research can use Swedish and English equally well.

These examples show that the advance of English, while serving the cause of international communication relatively well, and often bringing success to its users, can represent a threat to other languages and cultures. English is influential and popular worldwide because this brand of language connotes pleasure, employment, influence, and prestige.[13] English opens doors, it facilitates mobility. English is often referred to as a 'global' language, but even if many decisions affecting the entire world's population are taken in English, the vast majority of the world's population have no proficiency in the language. In many African states that are often loosely referred to as 'English-speaking countries', such as Nigeria or Kenya, under 10 per cent of the population speak the language well. The same is also broadly true in former colonies in Asia. The hierarchy of languages of colonial times has been maintained, with English as the key medium for prestigious purposes, and proficiency in English correlating with socio-economic privilege. This has serious adverse effects on civil society and democratic participation in the political process.[14] English is the language of the powerful. For the majority, lack of proficiency in English closes doors. Acquiring proficiency in English is therefore seen as desirable by and for marginalized populations, whose prospects often suffer from absence of a coherent national policy for ensuring a balance between competence in, and education in, English and in local languages.

Could a similar hierarchy of languages be evolving in Europe? Language policy in each EU member state largely continues along well-established lines, at the national and sub-national levels. In some countries, the constitution and legislation are explicit about language policy, but many aspects tend to remain implicit and deeply entrenched in traditions and values. It is likely that such national policies are inappropriate in a rapidly changing, internationalizing world in which technology and communication do not respect national borders. It is certainly questionable whether the language policies in place at the national and international levels will ensure that cultural and linguistic diversity are maintained and will flourish. The pressures of globalization and europeanization may be strengthening English at the expense of all the other languages of Europe. It is unclear to what extent this will occur, but many of the factors that will influence the outcome can be identified. These are what an informed language policy must be based on.

The EU and languages: does a common market need a common language?

In theory the eleven official languages of the fifteen EU member states have equal status and equal rights in EU institutions. These languages are Danish, Dutch, English, Finnish, French, German, Greek, Italian,

Portuguese, Spanish, and Swedish. Such EU institutions as the Commission in Brussels, the European Council (not to be confused with the Council of Europe), the European Parliament, and the European Court of Justice are serviced by the largest and most complex translation and interpretation services in the world, so as to facilitate communication between speakers of the different official languages. The language services are a vital link in the many communication chains that connect the shared concerns of the member states. There are regulations on which languages can be used in documents going to and from EU institutions, but the management of multilingualism in the many internal procedures of EU institutions is rather less clear, and the principle of complete equality is affected by constraints of time and funding. The operation of these services will be explored in Chapter 4.

Box 1.1   Speakers of the eleven EU languages

EU Eurobarometer data on percentages of the population of the EU speaking the official languages of the EU as a mother tongue or as a second or foreign language[15]:

	Mother tongue (%)	Foreign or second language (%)
German	24	8
English	16	31
French	16	12
Italian	16	2
Spanish	11	4
Dutch	6	1
Greek	3	0
Portuguese	3	0
Swedish	2	1
Danish	1	1
Finnish	1	0

Notes:

1   This information has been compiled on the basis of a Eurobarometer report (54, 15 February 2001) in which people (15,900 across the member states) reported on

their use of languages, using very broad categories of proficiency. They are therefore crude measures. Exact, reliable data on numbers of speakers of languages is notoriously elusive.

2 For the total population of member and applicant states, see Appendix 3.

3 The survey presumably ignores the widespread bilingualism of those who speak at home a regional minority language (one-sixth of the 378 million citizens of the EU), or an official but demographically small language (300,000 speakers of Swedish as a mother tongue in Finland), or an immigrant language (for instance, there are 400,000 Finnish-speaking immigrants in Sweden).

4 On the basis of the information in this study, the EU website proudly announces that 'Half of Europe is already multilingual', the evidence being

  • '45% of European citizens can take part in a conversation in a language other than their mother tongue
  • there are large variations between the Member States
  • in Luxembourg, nearly everyone speaks another language well enough to hold a conversation
  • this is also true for more than 8 people in 10 living in the Netherlands, Denmark and Sweden
  • people in the UK, Ireland and Portugal are least likely to speak another language, with less than a third of these populations saying they can do this'.[16]

In principle, what happens to languages in each member state is exclusively their own concern. This follows the *subsidiarity* principle that decisions should be taken locally rather than centrally, that is, in member states rather than in EU institutions.[17] The Danes have adopted a more user-friendly term for subsidiarity, '*nærhedsprincippet*', the nearness or proximity principle. However, it would be naive to assume that each EU state is a linguistic island, and that EU policies do not impact on all European languages. The EU has become an immensely complex and influential forum for policy throughout Europe. A common EU policy means that national policies and interests are coordinated, negotiated, and agreed on at the supranational EU level. The label *supranational* is more restricted than *international*, and refers to the EU level that merges the concerns of member states. The EU has exclusive responsibility for policies on agriculture, fishing, and foreign trade. The EU shares with member states responsibility for the environment, consumer protection, employment, food safety, research, energy, and development assistance. Foreign policy and defence were added in the late 1990s to the lengthening list of topics with which the EU is concerned. Financial and economic policy were streamlined with the introduction of the euro in twelve states in 2002. The Maastricht Treaty of 1992 brought in some collaboration in matters of language, culture, and education, though the EU is not mandated to harmonize national legislation on education.

The EU allocates funds to various activities that can contribute to maintaining linguistic diversity, building intercultural understanding, and facilitating lifelong learning. Some examples:

- Schemes such as LINGUA and SOCRATES, referred to as 'actions' in Eurospeak, seek to strengthen foreign language learn- ing, and the international mobility of young people and researchers.
- The year 2001 was proclaimed, jointly by the EU and the Council of Europe, as the 'European Year of Languages', which resulted in a budget of 6 million euros being distributed to 185 activities aimed at making the general public more confident in language learning, with a very wide range of topics represented.[18]
- Regional minority languages such as Breton, Frisian, and Gaelic are supported through schemes administered by the European Bureau for Lesser Used Languages,[19] 45 languages in the fifteen member states currently qualifying for some EU support.
- Under earlier schemes there was funding for the translation of creative writing from one EU official language to another, and many of the existing EU actions in the field of culture represent support for activities in a given national language.

Many aspects of national, sub-national, and supranational language policy have been of concern to the Commission and Parliament. The following examples are followed up in more depth in later chapters:

- The activities of EU institutions in using eleven official languages ensure that these evolve in parallel in terminological development. The extensive production of texts in parallel in eleven languages has led to a convergence of the language of the law in each state.

- The European Trade Mark Office in Alicante operates primarily in the five 'big' EU languages (English, French, German, Italian, and Spanish), and there was considerable debate and uncertainty in 2002 about plans for a European Patent system that conflicts with the principle of the equality of the eleven languages.
- A White Paper on *Teaching and learning: towards the learning society*[20] in 1995 recommends that education should serve to make all EU citizens competent in three (of the official) EU languages.
- In December 2001, the Council of the EU, meaning the Ministers of Education of member states and the division of the Commission with responsibility for education, considered a draft 'resolution on the promotion of linguistic diversity and language learning in the framework of the implementation of the objectives of the European Year of Languages 2001', which states in the preamble that 'all European languages are equal in value and dignity from the cultural point of view'. The resolution (see Appendix 2) also proclaims that member states should take measures 'to offer pupils, as far as possible, the opportunity to learn two, or where appropriate, more languages in addition to their mother tongues'. It is unclear whether these endorsements apply to minority languages in member states, indigenous and immigrant, or only to the eleven official languages.[21] The text is explored in more depth in Chapter 3, which analyses ongoing trends in education.

A firm commitment to the learning of two foreign languages is unlikely to be supported by the United Kingdom, where only 10 per cent of schoolchildren continue learning a single foreign language after age 16.[22] The government lowered this age to 14 in 2002, and simultaneously made a vague promise of an 'entitlement' to foreign language learning in the primary school.

In effect, the European Union is a test case for the maintenance of linguistic diversity, in its institutions and in member states,[23] but language policies in the EU reflect many unresolved and interlocking paradoxes and tensions:

- a legacy of 'nation' states, 'national' interests and languages, BUT supranational integration, and the internationalization of many domains, commerce, finance, education, science, politics, and civil society in EU member states;
- the formal equality of EU member states and their languages, BUT a pecking order of states and languages, currently visible in

the shift from French to English as the primary working language in EU institutions;

- the onward thrust of americanization, cultural homogenization ('McDonaldization'), and the hegemony of English, BUT the celebration of European linguistic diversity, multilingualism, cultural and linguistic hybridity, and support for minority and national language rights;

- languages seen as purely technical, pragmatic tools, BUT languages as existential identity markers for individuals, cultures, ethnic groups, and states;

- Germany as a demographically and economically dominant force in Europe, BUT German progressively marginalized in scholarship, commerce, youth culture, and in the global linguistic marketplace, in similar ways to a reduction in the power of French internationally;

- English being promoted as a linguistic panacea, BUT of the 378 million citizens of the member states, only 61 million speak English as a mother tongue, less than half of the rest are proficient in English as a foreign language, and the proportion speaking it confidently varies greatly from country to country[24] (see Box 1.1).

The contexts within which these tensions and paradoxes are being worked through are unstable and constantly evolving. As well as the myriad ongoing EU activities, there are competing visions of what the EU is for (ranging from a federal Europe with a constitution, to a limited intergovernmental affair), and where increased integration is leading. Popular support for the European project is very limited, as referenda in several countries show. The 'democratic deficit' of the EU refers to the lack of political accountability of EU institutions, and the absence of a shared, open, active political culture throughout the EU over and above national political culture.[25] Many of these intractable political issues have been handed to the EU Convention on the future of Europe, in function from March 2002, with a mandate for its 100 members (plus representatives of applicant countries as observers) to produce within a year a blueprint for reform of the EU, and a unified vision of how activities at the supranational level should best be organized.

Languages are the medium through which these political and cultural options will be clarified. There is now a common market, a common commercial policy, and a common defence and security policy. There is a common agricultural policy of long standing (admittedly one that is likely to be modified, partly because it absorbs nearly half of the EU budget, and is a luxury that current members are unwilling to extend to new ones, quite apart from the indefensibility of such a system of subsidy globally). Are we moving towards a common language policy? And if so, does this mean that a single language will be given a special status? If the EU is to move towards more explicit language policies, agreed on supranationally, and coordinated across member states, the unresolved tensions listed above need to be addressed.

In discussing such issues, great care is needed in distinguishing between language policy and practice in supranational EU institutions and in member states. Uncertainty about supranational language policy reflects uncertainty about the type of political entity that the EU is evolving into, and the relative fragility of channels of communication uniting people and civil society beyond national borders. At the level of the state, political unity builds on relatively strong bonds of identification, often mediated through a single dominant national language. If Europe is in a process of uniting politically and culturally, the role of its languages in supranational affairs is clearly a central, sensitive issue, especially if a single common language is emerging.

What is language policy?

According to a commentator in the German paper *Die Zeit*,[26] language policy is

> a kind of preventive treatment of wounds at places that hurt or that might become painful. Switzerland, which has to juggle with four mother tongues, maintains itself largely free of pain, whereas Belgium is plagued by the severe incompatibility of those who speak French and Flemish. In Macedonia the present language compromise represents urgent treatment that might be able to hinder fatal consequences.

Language policy is manifestly an integral part of social policy. All states engage in it, when creating societal conditions that permit some languages to thrive and cause others to die off, and when ratifying human rights instruments in which language rights are specified.

As the examples of Switzerland, Belgium, and Macedonia referred to in *Die Zeit* suggest, language issues may, like medical problems, be well under control, or in a state of chronic or acute pathology. Proper diagnosis, consultation with those affected, and the existence of well-tried remedies are essential for progress and linguistic health.

Language policy decisions that a state is typically concerned with include the following:

- identification of one or more languages as official or as working languages in a state or region, laws or measures specifying the rights of speakers of majority or minority languages to use their languages in education, public services, or other functions, and legislation on the use of particular languages in commercial activities, in the media, and in publications;
- the production and publication of authoritative reference works (grammars, dictionaries, etc.) that stipulate which forms of a language are appropriate, correct, or 'proper';
- regulations and policy statements prescribing the learning of particular languages in education, whether as first, second, or foreign languages.

The first type of language policy measures is referred to as *status planning*, as they are concerned with attributing particular functions to a given language. Constitutions and laws can serve to strengthen multilingualism or monolingualism. Thus the Welsh Language Act aims to promote the learning and use of Welsh in Wales, alongside English, whereas Turkish legislation has since the 1920s aimed at stamping out Kurdish, such measures being in conflict with human rights law[27].

Some states require private companies operating within their territory to employ a particular language, for instance French in business operations and advertising in Québec.

Absence of explicit status policy measures does not imply that no language policy is in force. The dominant language of a state has often not been designated in legal documents as being 'official' or 'national', terms that are used in a variety of ways. There are many implicit and covert ways of regulating the relative status of languages.[28]

The second type is generally referred to as *corpus planning*, since it refers to the building blocks of a language, the codification of permissible words and forms of a standard language. Institutions have been established in many countries, along the lines of the Accademia della Crusca in Italy (1584), the Académie Française in France (1635), and the Real Academia de la Lengua Española in Spain (1713), to determine norms for a language. In Denmark, corpus planning has been assigned to a language board by Act of Parliament. One of their functions is to produce periodically an authorized version of correct Danish vocabulary, grammar, punctuation, and spelling. All state employees (including academics like myself) are expected to follow these pre-scriptions in any official correspondence or documents.

The third type is referred to as *acquisition planning*, since it refers to the way the learning of languages is organized in education, from pre-school to university, typically under the supervision of a ministry of education. This is responsible for implementing policies on which languages should be used as the medium of education (the language or languages through which the subjects in the curriculum are taught), including, for instance, whether any minority languages have this right. So far as the learning of foreign languages is concerned, a government may select a particular language and make learning it obligatory. English is overwhelmingly the most widely learned foreign language in continental Europe, but is often in fact not obligatory.

Status, corpus, and acquisition planning are the main concerns of *language planning,* a specialization in the sociology of language requiring input from economics, demography, education, and linguistics.[29] Language planning is a term that was popularized at the time of post-colonial states confronting the complexities of running and educating multilingual societies. The processes involved in ordering and recon-ciling the competing rights of languages are complicated, not least because there are just over 200 states in the world, and around 6800 spoken languages,[30] quite apart from Sign languages, which now have official recognition in some states. Language policy is decisively influ-enced by our attitudes to languages, to beliefs about their power, beauty, or utility, and their role in national, ethnic, or religious identity.

Language policies permeate and interconnect with many of the concerns of government. Most European countries do not allocate responsibility for language policy to a specific government depart-ment, but many of these are involved in decisions that affect language policies, among them:

- *culture:* such policy issues as maintaining and fostering the national heritage, and creativity in local languages in films, music, and lit-erature, in the face of change, internationalization, and increasing commercialization;
- *commerce:* ensuring that the business world is equipped to use a range of languages for exports to and imports from a variety of language areas;
- *foreign affairs:* policies to ensure that diplomats, civil servants, and experts are able to function in foreign languages in international affairs and regional links, not least in the EU, policies for the

promotion of national languages abroad, and legal and political aspects of international covenants and charters in which language rights are specified;

• *education:* providing citizens with competence in a range of languages and an understanding of diverse cultures, both in general education and in specialist higher education;

• *research:* ensuring that the scientific community is competent in international languages of communication (in collaborative projects, at conferences, in journals, etc.) and also that scientific findings are communicated in relevant local languages.

Language policies will be in place in all these areas *de facto*, but there may or may not be an infrastructure in the academic and bureaucratic worlds that ensures competent activities in corpus, status, and acquisition planning, implementation, and monitoring. Where language issues have a high priority and political profile, resources are allocated for particular language policy purposes. This has taken place in Finland, which is officially bilingual, for over a century, in Canada since the early 1970s, particularly at the federal level and in Québec, and in post-Fascist Spain, particularly Catalonia and the Basque country.

The language policy measures introduced in France, Poland, Hungary, and Sweden to halt the advance of English represent an attempt to manage a threatening condition through applying various types of preventive action, and sanction. English has acquired a narcotic power in many parts of the world, an addiction that has long-term consequences that are far from clear. As with the drugs trade, in its legal and illegal branches, there are major commercial interests involved in the global English language industry. The dividing-line between the private sector and the public interest is in any case an unclear and shifting one.

The medical analogy has been taken further by Joshua Fishman, a key figure in the sociology of language, who has analysed ways in which the tide against threatened languages worldwide has sometimes been turned. Attrition of the minority language can be reversed by three types of language policy for threatened languages: *permissive* language defence (for instance, tolerating use of particular languages, or ensuring freedom of speech), *active* language defence (therapeutic measures for disadvantaged languages), and *preventive*, proactive language defence (such as legally enforceable measures to ensure use of a particular language in education and public services).[31]

In the fifteen member states of the EU, it is estimated that one in six citizens speaks at home a language other than the dominant language of the state. In addition to these local, regional languages, there are the many languages that are more recent arrivals, for example the diaspora languages of refugees and labour migrants, as well as non-territorial languages like Romani, spoken by Roma/Sinti (this is how they refer to themselves, rather than as 'gypsies').

There is invariably a pecking order of languages, and a class-, gender-, and regionally based hierarchical system of preferred variants of a language, some of which are prestigious and others stigmatized. In the internationalizing world of the EU, issues of linguistic identity and rights, and proficiency in mother tongues and foreign languages, make the language policy options at both the national and the supra-national levels even more complicated.

The analysis of *language policy* is, like most social science, messy in the sense that it is difficult to do justice to the complexity of an ongoing, dynamic scene and to identify a multi-faceted, shifting object unam-biguously. There is also the theoretical problem of effectively integrating the approaches of various scientific traditions, such as political science, sociology, linguistics, general education, and language pedagogy. There is a clear risk, if one concentrates on one particular aspect and approach, of falling victim to the academic Humpty Dumpty syndrome.[32] Taking a topic apart is much easier than putting it together again. However, the field is progressively taking shape in academic circles and is generating an imposing flow of books and journals.[33]

It is likely that in contexts where the term 'language policy' is in active use, it is understood in a specific, focused sense. The Language Policy Unit in the European Commission's Directorate-General for Education and Culture is concerned with the promotion of foreign language teaching and learning in the member states, support for regional and minority languages, and educational innovation that can strengthen multilingualism. In the translation and interpretation ser-vices of EU institutions, language policy refers to 'the policy of multilingualism laid down by the Treaty for legislation and communi-cation with citizens (which is fixed and non-negotiable), and the various ways we cope with language needs in-house and in commu-nication with Member States (where some pragmatic choices have to be made)'.[34]

Many explicit and implicit language policies filter into such activi-ties. In view of the varied cultural backgrounds of EU citizens, the potential for conceptual confusion in this area is considerable. Basic terms such as 'language', 'dialect', and 'language policy' may simply be used and understood differently. Most continental languages use a single word – '*politik*', '*politique*' – for what in English corresponds to both *policy* and *politics*. A Swedish or French context may reveal clearly which meaning is intended, but the terminological obscurity tends to blur the distinction between what is happening on the one hand in the politics of language, which invariably has to do with politics, and on the other in the formation or implementation of policies for particular languages and their use. There is of course a political dimension to many issues of language policy, which merely reinforces the need to ensure conceptual rigour and precision when analysing language issues.

A typical example of this blurring of the distinction between 'politics' and 'policy', generally at the expense of policy, when English is being used as a foreign language, can be seen in a job announcement by a Danish university.[35] The text was in English, as the advertisement aimed at recruitment internationally. After explaining all the details about the post and how to apply, the ad ended with the statement: 'As a link in the university's equality politics, we invite both women and men to apply for a position at the university.' What the university is referring to is its gender equality policy.

In my experience, even very advanced and sophisticated users of English as a foreign language tend sometimes to refer to 'language politics' in contexts where native speakers of English would use 'language policy'.[36] This occurs in both speech and writing. The (political!) question of whether it is fair to expect users of English as a second or foreign language to use English in precisely the same way as native speakers will be considered in Chapter 5.

A further complicating factor that makes for fuzziness in many discussions about language policy is the fact that membership of the EU blurs the traditional line between the domestic and the foreign. The EU is a new type of political structure that is neither a state, nor a federation, but a complex hybrid of the two. The national and supranational systems are being progressively merged, with sovereignty pooled and shared between the two. The EU coordinates and legislates on every conceivable aspect of citizens' lives, whether people are aware of this or not. It is estimated that between 60 and 80 per cent of national legislation is concerned with enacting policies agreed on in the EU. As languages are the channel through which these arrangements are agreed on and implemented, language policies permeate the entire EU system. I will argue for much more attention to be paid to language policy. A *laissez faire* policy, leaving matters to the laws of the linguistic market, entails serious dangers and risks.

When is a language policy issue newsworthy?

Language matters typically erupt in the press when there is a crisis of some kind.

- In Denmark, Germany, and Norway, impassioned debate was triggered in recent years by plans to change spelling and punctuation conventions. Beliefs about correctness tend to be deep-seated and emotionally charged.
- The lead story in the British newspaper *The Independent* of 11 February 2002 was 'Europe tells UK: improve teaching of our languages', followed up by the main editorial 'The ambassadors are right: the British approach to languages is hopeless'. 'Europe' in this case was the ambassadors of Germany, Italy, and Spain to the United Kingdom, with the support of France, jointly pleading for a strengthening of foreign language learning in Britain.
- There was front-page coverage in *The Scotsman* in October 2001, when a report entitled 'Language and Literacy Policy', published by the Scottish Centre for Information on Language Teaching, was published.[37] It was written by Joseph Lo Bianco, a distinguished Australian language policy-maker. The press coverage focused less on the foreign language policy issues and multilingualism, where Scotland differs considerably from England, and more on a crisis in adult literacy.
- Minority languages hit the headlines when a society is polarized along linguistic lines, for instance speakers of Hungarian as a minority language in Romania and Slovakia, and speakers of Russian in the newly independent Baltic states. As in ex-Yugoslavia and many post-communist states, there is a close link between language and political rights.

The summer of 2001 saw two EU language issues get substantial press coverage. One was a dispute between various members of the European Parliament about a report on preparations for the enlargement of the EU.[38] There are major logistic and financial challenges when increasing the number of official languages from eleven to sixteen, let alone twenty-two, as new states join (see Chapter 4). There are practical matters such as the number of interpreters' booths, and how to manage interpretation between all the possible combinations of language pairs. There appears to be universal agreement that the right of all MEPs to address the Parliament in their own language is of paramount importance. The legitimacy of the Parliament depends on MEPs being voted in for their qualities as politicians, rather than for their skill in functioning in foreign languages (though multilingual MEPs in reality have a distinct advantage over others). There is far less agreement about what the financial implications of enlargement are, what the characteristics of good practice are in the organization of the interpretation services (for the spoken word) and translation services (for the written word) in the Parliament, and how raising and administering a substantially increased budget should be tackled. To judge by the press, 'debate' easily degenerates into linguistic mud-slinging with acrimonious accusations about preferential treatment for one or more languages.

The second language policy issue to surface was a proposal to change one of the internal translation procedures in the Commission in Brussels, as part of a cost-saving exercise. The plan was leaked to the French government, as a result of which a joint letter was sent by the Ministers of Foreign Affairs of France and Germany, Hubert Védrine and Joschka Fischer, to Romano Prodi, the President of the Commission, on 2 July 2001. The letter accused the Commission of attempting to introduce 'monolingualism' in EU institutions, which was a coded reference to English being installed as the sole in-house working language, and that this represented an unacceptable departure from the current system (see Chapter 4). Prodi's reply, dispatched in French and German, asserts that multilingualism is of cardinal importance to the EU, that nothing had been decided, but that efficiency and savings in the language services need to be looked into. The impending enlargement of the EU made action even more important. By this stage, press coverage had identified a 'plot to impose English on the EU' (*Irish Times*), 'Fischer and Védrine against more English' (*Frankfurter Allgemeine Zeitung*), 'Kinnock's language plan riles the French' (*The Independent*), and so on.

Much of the press coverage contained inaccurate statements about the present system and its costs, and engaged in fanciful and nationalistic interpretation.[39] The exchange of letters and the press reports clearly reveal that an existential nerve had been touched. The two newsworthy disputes are perfect examples of the recurrent underlying tension between national interests and supranational ones, and the absence of adequate procedures and principles for resolving the issues.

Clear analysis is muddied by the contemporary irrelevance of the notion of 'one language, one nation, one state'. This principle seldom applied to the historical facts (Iceland is probably the only monolingual country in Europe), although it was fundamental to the way states have been established and consolidated over the past 200 years (see Chapter 2). There is now no straightforward correlation between a specific language and a particular state's national interests. French and German are official languages in several countries. English is the main language of the United Kingdom and Ireland, but is also intimately connected to globalization and the influence of the United States, and countless links outside Europe.

The lack of a close fit between language and state does not imply that mother tongue speakers of French and English are not in an advantageous position when their languages are widely used. They definitely are, and this is one reason why the countries whose languages are at the top of the linguistic hierarchy are keen for this position to continue.

One of the paradoxes of language policy in the EU institutions is that languages are often regarded as purely practical, technical matters, while at the same time they are fundamental to personal, group, and national identity, and national interests. Books on 'Europe' are written by political scientists and sociologists that make no reference to the language dimension of European integration. One of the few to do so assesses whether civil society, a forum for working through political issues democratically, will ever exist across the entire EU unless a single language unites people.[40] The language services of the EU are seen as servicing decision-makers in all fields of collaboration, so that in principle it should make no difference which language or languages are used. On the other hand, language is so politically sensitive that warning bells start ringing as soon as issues of language rights are raised, especially if there is a proposal to restrict the rights traditionally attached to a given language or set of languages. This is what happened when the French, during their presidency of the EU in 1995, proposed a change in the language system in the Commission, a formal reduction of the number of working languages. Nothing came of it, because several states perceived that their languages would be deprived of rights and influence.

The last time EU meetings were boycotted was when the German government refused to attend informal ministerial meetings during the Finnish presidency of the EU in 1999.[41] The rule of thumb for such meetings is that they take place in the host country's language, plus English and French, and interpretation is provided between the three languages. The Germans insisted that their language should also be used. The Finns initially refused, and then caved in to pressure. The political problem was solved by concessions being made to speakers of German, a language that is demographically important (German is the mother tongue of a quarter of EU citizens), and financially influential (Germany foots a large part of the EU bill). This left speakers of other 'big' languages, Spanish and Italian, in limbo, in the company of the 'small' languages.[42] The way this political crisis was solved, or buried, exemplifies the point that language problems are fixed pragmatically, instead of the issues of principle, of language rights, or criteria for organizing democratic equality of communication being explored (see Chapter 5).

The Finnish Prime Minister summarized this unsatisfactory state of affairs in an interview with a German newspaper:[43] 'I also hold the view that German in principle should have the same rights as other large languages. It is only a practical problem, because the language problem of the Union has evolved without any planning. We have to solve this question together'. This statement begs the question of what a 'large' language is, and why speakers of large languages should have more rights than others. The tone of his comments is clearly conciliatory, but the second sentence can be interpreted in several ways. Why should lack of any plan cause 'only' a practical problem? This obscurity may be a good example of a politician trying to please everyone; it may also be due to a Finn giving the interview in German, a foreign language which it is unreasonable to expect him to use unambiguously.

The solution agreed on in this case is likely to widen the gap between powerful member states and the rest, a principle enshrined in the voting principles agreed on in the Nice Treaty,[44] and to confirm fears about EU institutions being undemocratic and unaccountable. Speakers of some languages have *de facto* more rights than speakers of other languages. As in George Orwell's world, some are more equal than others, and language plays a decisive role in upholding inequality.[45] Many important policy decisions in the EU are taken late at night after protracted negotiations. It would be a tragedy if the rights of some EU languages are treated as bargaining chips, and sacrificed in exchange for, say, an economic concession on agriculture.

In 1898, when Otto von Bismarck was asked what he felt had been the determining event of the modern history of his time, he replied: 'The fact that North America speaks English.'[46] If the determining event of a century later was the fall of the Berlin wall, it would be a tragedy if the result of this was a single European market economy with *monolingualism* as its medium and ultimate goal. George Bernard Shaw,

born in 1856, observed presciently in 1912: 'What has been happening in my lifetime is the Americanization of the world.'[47] English is
central to ongoing processes of europeanization and globalization.
National autonomy in language policy, as in economic policy, is a
thing of the past. Language policy for the Europe of the future needs
to be based on an understanding of our languages in the past – the
topic of Chapter 2 – prior to assessing current pressures and constraints.

European languages
Families, nations, empires, states

Who the first inhabitants of Britain were, whether natives or immigrants, remains obscure: one must remember we are dealing with barbarians.

Tacitus, Agricola, AD 97[1]

I am always sorry when any language is lost, because languages are the pedigree of nations.

Samuel Johnson, 1773

Every gentleman who took his education seriously
Only put pen to paper in Latin,
Spoke French to the ladies,
German to his dog,
and Danish to his servants.

Christian Wilster, 1827[2]

Familiarity with German, English, Spanish, French, and Italian is no longer sufficient for anyone wanting to keep abreast of modern civilisation . . . The tendency is for the world to have a single civilisation; but there is a multitude of languages of civilisation.

Antoine Meillet, 1918[3]

What the World needs most is about 1000 more dead languages – and one more alive.

C. K. Ogden, 1934[4]

At long last, Europe is on its way to becoming one big family.
The future of the European Union, the Laeken Declaration, 2001[5]

Babel: blessing or curse?

The purpose of this chapter is to identify some of the unifying traits of European culture and languages historically, and to probe into the role of internationally dominant languages. This involves identifying the interlocking of languages with cultural, religious, and political aspects of our identities at the European, national, and local levels.[6]

The epigraphs above, from a Roman historian, an English lexicographer in the eighteenth century, a Danish poet who was the first person to translate Homer's *Iliad* and *Odyssey* from Greek into Danish in the early nineteenth century, and from a French linguist and an English philosopher in the twentieth, demonstrate that since the Age of Enlightenment, proficiency in one or more languages has been associated with perceptions of varying degrees of culture or 'civilization'. Languages serve a variety of purposes, multilingualism has been widespread, and some languages are more prestigious than others.

Distinct cultural cosmologies operate at all levels, from the most abstract to the most mundane and concrete. Each language influences the different ways in which we see, verbalize, create, and influence our reality.

Languages can be deployed so as to unite or divide people, to promote or impede communication. Each of us is extremely sensitive to nuances of language that serve as key markers of group identity. The Bible (the Book of Judges, chapter XII) narrates how mispronunciation of the Hebrew 'shibboleth' resulted in the ethnolinguistic cleansing of 42,000 people. A few centuries later, the Greeks distinguished themselves from barbarians, a term (originally from Sanskrit) which brands foreigners as speakers of meaningless sounds, a non-language.

Language thus plays a major role in distinguishing Us from Them, in shaping group loyalty, and in marking distance from others. States have tended to consolidate their political power by codifying and standardizing a single language within their territory, although worldwide, there are far more languages than states.[7]

The utility of establishing a single language to unite disparate peoples under a single political power has been understood since the start of the post-medieval period. In 1492 an influential plan was presented to Queen Isabella of Spain for establishing Castilian as 'a tool for conquest abroad and a weapon to suppress untutored speech at home'.[8]

A number of factors converged in the late Middle Ages to consolidate the emergence of modern European languages. The Reformation and the invention of printing, combined with new forms of mercantilism, the concentration of capital, and urbanization led to the translation of the Bible into local idioms. This reinforced notions of the distinctness of different peoples.

The establishment of a single dominant, 'national' language has often been accompanied by systematic efforts to eliminate other languages and dialects within the territory. Blindness to the value of these was influenced by the Biblical myth of the curse of Babel, the multiplicity of languages being seen as God's punishment on humanity.[9] However, the extinction of a language represents loss of 'a total vision of life, of reality, of consciousness – a vision like no other . . . Far from being a curse, "Babel" has, in fact, been the very foundation of human creativity, the richness of the mind as it maps different models of being'.[10]

The Babel myth of the Book of Genesis is counterbalanced in the New Testament, firstly when the centrality of language to our cultures and belief systems is stressed: 'In the beginning was the Word, and the Word was with God, and the Word was God' (John I, 1). Multilingualism is endorsed by the miracle of Pentecost, the empowering of the apostles to spread the Christian God's word in diverse languages. The apostles 'began to speak with other tongues, as the Spirit gave them utterance'. They were understood as speaking all the relevant languages of the Middle East and North Africa: Mesopotamia, Asia, Egypt, Libya, Arabia, Crete, and Rome are all listed (Acts of the Apostles II, 8–11).

In our largely secularized modern world, it might appear passé or irrelevant to make so much of Biblical texts. However, there is no doubt that throughout history the Bible has had more influence than any other book on European beliefs and values. The Babel myth sees multilingualism as a curse, whereas the New Testament endorses cultural and ethnic diversity. The complexity of different languages and conceptual universes can be glimpsed in Box 2.1, in the concept 'bread' in the Bible and in the contemporary world. The European Union is committed to maintaining diversity, to seeing a variety of languages and cultures as a blessing rather than a curse. It is therefore important to know what kind of linguistic diversity it is that we are dealing with in Europe.

Europe, holding it in the mind

Europe is currently being actively shaped and created by EU leaders. When the euro was launched as the currency of twelve EU states on

Box 2.1   Our daily bread

In each EU country, bread is a vital food, whatever it is called: *pain, brot, brød, bread, leipä* . . . and whatever its distinct characteristics, which result from how it is produced, marketed, prepared for the table, and eaten. In each culture, bread varies depending on the types of flour, liquid, leavening and other ingredients used. These affect the taste, colour, consistency, shape, and durability of the product in a virtually infinite variety of types. All these traits can be expressed linguistically, and captured in shorthand in names for the various types of bread.

Internationalization and migration mean that many of us are familiar with a range of local and foreign types of bread. When Scandinavian airline cabin staff come round the plane in the middle of a meal offering you 'more bread', their basket contains rolls and crispbread, neither of which I would refer to as 'bread'. I happen to know that the cabin staff have translated the Danish or Swedish 'mere brød' literally into English. 'Bread' is a generic term in Scandinavian languages for a wider range of bakery products than is the case in English. Admittedly no passengers are likely to starve because of the way English is being adjusted here, but the example underlines two points: different cultures and languages express reality differently; and one and the same language, 'English', is used in a variety of ways, by both native speakers and non-natives. International understanding comes at a price.

Jesus Christ's words 'Give us this day our daily bread'[11] were originally uttered in Hebrew, and first written down in Greek. Translations of the Bible into other languages reflect a variety of understandings of the Greek original, and probably familiarity with translations into Latin and other languages. In a twentieth-century British translation, the same sentence reads 'Give us the bread of life today'.[12] This is a more metaphorical reading, in which the bread necessary for physical survival is connected to spiritual survival, echoing Christ's words, at least in their rendering into English: 'man shall not live by bread alone'.[13]

1 January 2002, the EU commissioner for monetary affairs, Pedro Solbes, stressed the implications of a 'virtual' currency becoming a real one on this date: 'Citizens will hold a piece of Europe in their hands every day.'[14] Wim Duisenberg, the president of the European Central Bank, stated in like vein: 'It will, I believe, help to change the way in which we think about one another as Europeans. The euro is more than just a currency. It is a symbol of European integration in every sense of the word.'[15]

These two leaders are right in linking together a physical experience of something European with the currency's powerful symbolic value, and the fellowship of this experience being sensed by hundreds of millions of Europeans and non-Europeans, insiders and outsiders.

The countries that are currently being integrated into economic and political Europe were created in earlier centuries by powerful forces that succeeded in forging empires, nations, and states into viable units with which people could identify. These units have invariably been defined in terms of a number of *internal* features within a given territory, a cluster of markers of shared heritage, belief systems, and language of authority, once military and physical control had been established over a territory, and *external* features, characteristics attributed to others. To be a French national implies not being Swiss or Belgian, even if the French language is spoken as a mother tongue by nationals of all three countries.

Likewise being European involves internal and external identification, and particular features (common descent; specific traits of culture, identification, or social organization) may or may not be salient or relevant at any given point.[16] The geography and geology of New Zealand are definitely not European, but most of the present-day inhabitants other than Maoris and others from the South Pacific can trace their ethnic and linguistic ancestry back to Europe. The state and culture have been europeanized.

Perceptions of 'Europe' vary substantially from country to country. In countries on the geographical periphery of the European continent, such as Great Britain and Denmark, Europe is currently often referred to as though it is foreign territory. In the media, Europe often seems to refer to Them rather than Us, to foreigners, or a bunch of unaccountable bureaucrats. Such attitudes assume, falsely, that one's own nationals and government have no influence or involvement in the running of the EU. However, it is not surprising that there is confusion about Europe's borders and identity, since Europe is referred to in a range of competing and conflicting senses, depending on the context, and which characteristics are in focus. Many of the cultural values that can be considered to apply throughout present-day Europe draw on centuries of tradition and shared heritage among the peoples of Europe, or at least their dynastic rulers, scholars, ecclesiastics, artists, and traders. What exactly the key markers of European identity and 'Europeanness' are, though, is very unclear.[17] Europe is emphatically not synonymous with the European Union, which is a recent phenomenon.

In the media, Europe is often shorthand for the administrative and political decision-making bodies of the EU, the Commission and the Council. In other contexts, it refers to the member states. In still others, to the population of these states. When a newspaper article footnote explains that the author, John Brown, 'is a European civil servant',[18] what this presumably means is that he is employed by an (unidentified) EU institution. As the article in question happens to be critical of proposed EU legislation on terrorism, this interpretation is rather shaky and bold. Eurocrats are not permitted to air criticism of their employers in the media, and can be sacked for doing so. With EU institutions becoming more established, we shall probably see reference to European as opposed to national civil servants more often.

Some states that form part of geographical Europe, such as Switzerland and Norway, have no representation in the 'European' Parliament, a political body that initially had members from only six countries, and is now up to fifteen. By contrast, the Council of Europe has over 40 member states, including Turkey, which might be considered as being culturally different from the rest of Europe. Turkey can be seen as part of geographical Europe, but in earlier centuries it was indisputably beyond the European political and religious pale, an alien Islamic civilization that occupied the Balkans and Hungary for centuries, and threatened Vienna.

Turkey has been deemed ineligible for imminent membership of the EU because of human rights violations. Many other factors may also have influenced the EU, such as the standard of living in Turkey, labour migration, Islam, or the role of the military. Insisting on respect for human rights as a condition for EU membership is a prudent demand to make on a potential supranational partner, even if human rights are not intrinsically European but are by definition universal. Human rights tend to be invoked pragmatically and even hypocritically. In principle all the member states of the Council of Europe are required to respect basic human rights in their constitutions and practice, but Turkey has been a member for decades, as is the Russian Federation while violating human rights in Chechnya.

It is not uncommon for one's national or continental identity to become more salient when one travels, hence for Europeans to feel more 'European' when outside Europe. This experience is captured in the aphorism of Ralph Waldo Emerson, the American philosopher, 'we go to Europe to be Americanized'.[19] There may be unconscious factors surfacing, when Europe is contrasted with other cultures, or features that unite people across national borders may become clearer. For instance, Danes, Norwegians, and Swedes feel that they are culturally and nationally distinct within Scandinavia, but that they have more in common with each other than with other Europeans or with non-Europeans. Their own languages are also distinct, but can, with a certain amount of effort and exposure, become mutually intelligible. There is a lot of collaboration at all levels between these countries, when it is customary for people to speak their own language and understand the other two.[20] In recent years the trend has been towards English being used instead, for reasons that will be explored in Chapter 3.

We all have multiple identities. Fuzzy dividing-lines between national, cultural, and linguistic identity are wittily captured in the aphorism (variously attributed to George Bernard Shaw and Oscar Wilde) that the British and Americans are divided by a common language. When the Americans broke free from British rule, the desirability of an independent language policy was articulated by Noah Webster. He wrote in 1789:[21]

> A national language is a band of national union. Every engine should be employed to make the people of this country national; to call their attachments home to their own country; and to inspire them with the pride of national character . . . Let us then seize the present moment, and establish a national language as well as a national government.

Webster, who was eminent in many walks of life, saw the connection to high politics of a declaration of linguistic independence from British control. He understood the importance of language in national identity formation, and proceeded to produce the teaching tools that would facilitate this. Webster's *Blue-backed Speller* 'taught not only spelling but pronunciation, common sense, morals, and good citizenship'. His *American Dictionary of the English Language*, the product of forty years of labour, set new standards in the treatment of etymology (for which he drew on the dictionaries of twenty languages), the drafting of clear definitions, and coverage of scientific and technical as well as literary terms.[22]

The language policy evolved in the United States entailed privileging English vis-à-vis other languages. There was no question of linguistic power-sharing with indigenous North American languages, or with other immigrant languages. In North America in the eighteenth century, the French and British competed for power – military, political, and linguistic – and at one point there were more native speakers of German than of English.

The experience of English in the USA also shows that a European language can serve as a powerful instrument of state when transplanted elsewhere. The distribution of European languages globally, in particular of Dutch, English, French, Portuguese, and Spanish, shows that when people of European origin colonized large parts of the globe, they took their languages with them. Much of the world outside Europe has therefore been europeanized over several centuries. Through rather different processes of cultural change, many aspects of European culture have been americanized in the past century.

All these concepts and the traits they refer to are becoming increasingly blurred as a result of internationalization. The salience of any one marker of identity, cultural or linguistic, national or continental, will vary depending on the time and context. To put contemporary dynamic processes and developments into historical perspective, we need first to know something of when and how 'Europe' began to take shape.

A European language family?

Box 2.2   Languages of Europe

A. Indo-European

Albanian
Armenian
BALTIC: Latvian, Lithuanian
CELTIC: Breton, Irish, Scottish Gaelic, Welsh
GERMANIC: Danish, Dutch, English, Faroese, Frisian, German, Icelandic, Norwegian, Scots, Swedish

Greek
ROMANCE: Catalan, French, Galician, Italian, Occitan,
    Portuguese, Rhaeto-Romance/Ladin/Friulian, Romanian,
    Sardinian, Spanish (Castilian)
Romani
SLAVONIC: Belarusian, Bulgarian, Croat, Czech, Macedonian,
    Polish, Russian, Serbian, Slovene, Slovak, Sorbian, Ukrainian

B. Finno-Ugric

BALTIC-FINNIC: Estonian, Finnish, Ingrian, Karelian, Livonian,
    Veps, Votic
UGRIC: Hungarian, Ostjak, Vogul
Komi, Udmurt
Mordvinian, Mari
Saami

C. Other

Basque
Caucasian languages (circa 40)
Maltese
Sign languages (circa 30)
Turkish

Note:
• the primary source used for this classification is the
  Encyclopedia of the languages of Europe, ed. G. Price,
  Oxford: Blackwell, 1998
• extinct languages are excluded
• the languages of recent immigrants are excluded
• some languages listed as a single language are known to
  consist of several languages, e.g. Albanian (3), Saami (10)
• some languages have well-established variants within a
  single country, e.g. there are two standardized forms of
  Norwegian
• languages are distinct from dialects for political rather than
  linguistic reasons.

Most people are aware that there are families of related languages. Four EU official languages – French, Italian, Portuguese, and Spanish – are descendants of Latin, and belong to the Romance language family, though speakers of these languages are not mutually intelligible. The same applies to the languages in the Germanic family, of which Danish, Dutch, English, German, and Swedish are EU official languages. They share many features of grammar and word structure. Since all owe a considerable debt to Latin and Greek, the Germanic languages have some features of vocabulary in common with the Romance languages.

Multiple linguistic origins have contributed to English, which is a hybrid deriving from Celtic, Anglo-Saxon, Viking, and (Norman) French sources. This accounts for the diversity of English vocabulary. This can be seen as a source of richness and variety, but also represents a major hurdle for those learning the language. There is no trace of any languages spoken by the indigenous population before these invasions.

The Finnish language belongs to the Finno-Ugric family, and has grammar and word formation patterns quite unlike those of the other EU languages (with an elaborate system of cases which is considerably more complicated than case in Latin). Among the languages of applicant countries, Finnish has a fairly close relative in Estonian and a distant one in Hungarian.

Analysis of the distribution and characteristic properties of European languages, combined with the study of genetic variation (DNA analysis) and archaeology, has produced clear evidence that humans, *homo sapiens*, arrived in Europe roughly 40,000 years ago.[23] Humans evolved initially in Africa, and spread from there to Asia. Beginning approximately 10,000 years ago, agriculture and pastoralism developed in the Middle East, and spread slowly to Europe, from east to west, over a period lasting 4,000 years.

All schools in the French colonial empire taught that history began with 'nos ancêtres les gaulois' – 'our ancestors, the Gauls'. Substantial scholarship now proves that Africa is the cradle of humankind, leading one distinguished African scholar to suggest that: 'Nowadays it is the Europeans who should speak of "Our ancestors, the Africans".'[24]

The Basque language was spoken by hunter-gatherers in a wide area of what is now Spain and France, and is unrelated to all the languages that migration from Asia brought to Europe. It is therefore the oldest surviving European language, with its own distinctive structure.[25]

The genetic make-up of the population of Europe reveals that Europe is more homogeneous than other continents, this being due to a greater degree of population migration within Europe than elsewhere.[26]

The Romance and Germanic languages belong to the Indo-European language group, as do the Slavonic languages (see Box 2.2). They are therefore related to many languages spoken in Asia. This has been known since Europeans studying oriental languages in the eighteenth century noted the affinities between European languages and Sanskrit, Persian, Hindi, and Bengali. All these languages therefore have a shared ancestry. There is some controversy about whether the parent language can be placed geographically as having evolved in what is present-day Turkey, or further east,[27] but sophisticated statistical analysis of genetic, archaeological, and linguistic data is able to track down how long each group has lived in Europe, and approximately where their ancestors came from.

Thus most of the languages in the Finno–Ugric language family are still in central Asia. Of those present in Europe, the indigenous Saami languages of the far north (called Lapps by their colonizers) have been present in Finland for at least two millennia. Genetic evidence indicates that the Saami were gradually pushed farther north by speakers of Finnish, a Uralic language that was brought to Finland roughly 2000 years ago. Many centuries later, speakers of Scandinavian languages also repelled the Saami to the north in Sweden and Norway, and later attempted to eradicate their languages. Hungarian derives from nomadic Magyars leaving Asia in the ninth century AD, and successfully establishing themselves in part of central Europe. The Hungarian, Finnish, Estonian, and Saami languages are totally unrelated to the languages of their neighbours.

Indo-European languages are sometimes referred to as Indo–Aryan. The Aryans were a nomadic Asian group who took their language to Afghanistan, Iran, and India, where they formed the highest, or Brahman, priestly caste of Hindu societies. The term Aryan was misused as part of a racist political programme to base political hierarchies on biological myths. 'Extension of the name Aryan to include Europeans, and in particular Germans, supposed to be the original Indo-Europeans, is a fantasy that began in Germany and was especially dear to Nazi theorists. In Sanskrit, the old language of Indo-Iranians, *aryas* means noble, lord, ruler.'[28]

Geographically, the borders of Europe are unclear, particularly in the east, where no ocean or other physical feature marks a clear boundary. The Ural mountains and major rivers might qualify, but this is no absolute criterion, and reliance on it would suggest that the peoples and languages of the Caucasus should be included as European, which they are unlikely to be politically. Geological criteria lead to the

inclusion of Iceland, which linguistic and political criteria would reinforce, as Iceland was settled by Nordic people and still has strong
Nordic links.[29] Greenland, on the other hand, forms geologically and
linguistically part of North America, but belongs politically under the
Danish crown, though with a high degree of home rule. The acceptance of Malta, Cyprus, and Turkey as applicant member states of the
European Union indicates that political criteria are being applied rather
than strict geographical or cultural criteria.

These examples demonstrate that a range of possible criteria are in
force when demarcating what qualifies people as Europeans. To rely
on a linguistic criterion, membership of language families, in defining what is essentially European, would clearly not help, as all
European languages other than Basque are related to languages in
Asia. The contemporary distribution of languages in Europe reflects
the interplay over time of linguistic, geographic, cultural, and political criteria.

The classical inheritance

The label Europe itself, drawn from Greek mythology, was not widely
used before the fifteenth century, after which it progressively replaced
the term Christendom.[30] One of the key components of European
culture is Christianity. It has been a major spiritual and political force
for two millennia, but followed different routes, one radiating from
Rome, the other from Constantinople, both of which built on Greek
political, philosophical, and cultural traditions. The Roman empire
imposed, along with Christianity, a sophisticated military, social, and
legal system on many parts of Europe and North Africa.

In the medieval period, education was almost exclusively the responsibility of the Christian church. For centuries the primary language of
education, at schools and universities, in writing and speech, was Latin.
This inheritance is still visible in such designations as 'grammar school'
(which had nothing to do with the grammar of the mother tongue),
'Latin school' (the name for elementary education in much of northern Europe until the nineteenth century), 'Gymnasium' (still the term
for the upper secondary school in Germany and the Nordic countries),
and 'lycée' (a nineteenth-century French innovation with Greek con-
notations).

A strong emphasis on the Hellenic origins of European cultures
evolved from the late eighteenth century onwards, particularly in
Germany and Great Britain, 'in which contemplation of all aspects of

Greek and Roman life was supposed to have a beneficial educational and moral effect on the boys who were to be the rulers of Britain and the Empire'.[31] The vision of Greece that underpinned this type of education excluded the Semitic and African influences that contributed significantly to ancient Greece, this selective focus reflecting racist thought that sought to legitimate European global dominance and the assumed 'superiority' of Europeans.[32]

Study of the classical languages and cultures was conceived as a deliberate counterweight to the influence of the French Revolution, and was therefore essentially conservative. Bertrand Russell analysed the strengths and weaknesses of British education of this kind:[33]

> The aim was to train men for positions of authority and power, whether at home or in distant parts of the empire . . . The product was to be energetic, stoical, physically fit, possessed of certain unalterable beliefs, with high standards of rectitude, and convinced that it had an important mission in the world. To a surprising extent, these results were achieved. Intellect was sacrificed to them, because intellect might produce doubt. Sympathy was sacrificed, because it might interfere with governing 'inferior' races or classes. Kindliness was sacrificed for the sake of toughness; imagination, for the sake of firmness.

One suspects that many of the underlying values are still present in western European countries, and have been taken over in the United States, which ascribes to itself a God-given mission to lead the world. Note the strong continuities between the statements in Box 2.3.

Box 2.3   Continuities of Us and Them

English is . . . a strong, a harmonious, a noble language... Before another century has gone by it will, at the present rate of increase, be spoken by hundreds of millions . . . That language is rapidly becoming the great medium of civilization, the language of law and literature to the Hindoo, of commerce to the African, of religion to the scattered islands of the Pacific.

Edwin Guest, 1838[34]

European dominion naturally supports science and literature, together with the rights of humanity, and to prevent the destruction of a barbarous power would be an act of high treason against intellectual culture and humanity.

> *Barthold Niebuhr*, born 1776 in the German-Danish border region, when advocating European settlement in Asia, in a lecture in 1852[35]

Probably everyone would agree that an Englishman would be right in considering his way of looking at the world and at life better than that of the Maori or Hottentot, and no-one will object to England doing her best to impose her better and higher view on these savages . . . Can there be any doubt that the white man must, and will, impose his superior civilization on the coloured races?

> *Lord Grey*, Minister at the British Foreign Office, 1899[36]

The first conquest of Algeria was accomplished militarily and was completed in 1871 when Kabylia was disarmed. The second conquest has consisted of making the natives accept our administrative and judicial systems. The third conquest will be by the School: this should ensure the predominance of our language over the various local idioms, inculcate in the muslims our own idea of what France is and of its role in the world, and replace ignorance and fanatical prejudices by the simple but precise notions of European science.

> *Rambaud*, French Minister of Public Education, 1897[37]

I don't see why we need to stand by and watch a country go communist because of the irresponsibility of its own people.

> *Henry Kissinger*, Foreign Secretary of the USA, on intervening to replace President Allende's democratically established government in Chile by Pinochet's military dictatorship[38]

The principal conflicts of global politics will occur between nations and groups of different civilizations. The clash of civilizations will dominate global politics. The fault lines between civilizations will be the battle lines of the future.

> *Samuel P. Huntington*, in *Foreign Affairs*, Summer 1993

Study of the 'classical' languages, Latin and Greek, was firmly entrenched in education in much of Europe until the second half of the twentieth century.[39] Other curriculum areas, including study of the mother tongue and 'modern' foreign languages, gradually increased in importance. The dominance of literature in university departments of language is an innovation of the twentieth century, and reached Britain via the Indian empire, where study of the 'classics' of English literature was pioneered as a key instrument for promoting imperial values.[40] Notions of the purity or authenticity of modern European languages evolved when these were disseminated worldwide under colonialism, and as a result of wars between rival powers in Europe. Thus belief in the uniqueness of the German language evolved as a direct consequence of Napoleon conquering Germany.[41]

Christianity in Europe is characterized by competing variants of the faith, Catholic, Protestant, and Orthodox. These differences have served as mobilizing factors in warfare over centuries, and are still in evidence in Northern Ireland and in the Balkans, which has for several centuries also been the meeting-point between Christianity and Islam.

Many European cultural traditions and products, in art and architecture, in philosophy and societal institutions, in literature and journalism, are hybrids that blend local and cosmopolitan elements. The word 'cosmopolitan' entered English via French, and derives from a Greek word meaning 'citizen of the world'. Our cultural achievements may be flagged as national treasures, but most of them pre-date the nation-state and nationalism, and transcend national borders. For instance, music knows no boundaries in Europe, neither in religious worship, nor in the 'classical' music tradition that evolved from the sixteenth century onwards. The British regard Handel as a quintessentially British composer, but he was of German origin (called Händel), and built on Italian musical traditions.

The British king whom Handel wrote music for was of German lineage. Some earlier monarchs had been conquering Vikings and Normans, or were invited in from Scotland and the Netherlands. Royal families have typically married across national borders to strengthen dynastic bonds. They also adapted to changing times. Thus the Swedish royal family is in direct descent from one of Napoleon's generals, Bernadotte. The present queen of Sweden is of German origin. Sweden is a typical constitutional monarchy, in which the royal family is as powerful a patriotic and 'national' symbol as any. National identity, building on a selective interpretation of historical, religious, and linguistic markers of identity, is eminently fluid, and does not exclude cosmopolitan, global, or European elements.

Watersheds such as the Renaissance, European global expansion, and the industrial revolution can be seen as one side of a coin, on the reverse of which were the violence that went with Christian crusades against Islam, the persecution of the Jews and Roma (gypsies), the slave trade, and exploitative colonialism. Western supremacy was legitimated in terms of cultural difference, a hierarchical ordering that united some against others. Europeans were divided amongst themselves, but were united in opposition to the enemy at the gate – Islam, the Ottoman empire, the Orient, the Other. There was also a great deal that their cultures and histories shared in common across national divisions.

English, the new Latin?

The way Latin was adopted by a conquered people was insightfully analysed by Tacitus, whose uncle, Agricola, was charged with converting the British to Roman norms in the first century AD:[42]

> To induce a people, hitherto scattered, uncivilized and therefore prone to fight, to grow pleasurably inured to peace and ease, Agricola . . . trained the sons of the chiefs in the liberal arts and expressed a preference for British natural ability over the trained skills of the Gauls. The result was that in place of distaste for the Latin language came a passion to command it. In the same way, our national dress came into favour and the toga was everywhere to be seen. And so the Britons were gradually led on to the amenities that make vice agreeable – arcades, baths and sumptuous banquets. They spoke of such novelties as 'civilization' when really they were only a feature of enslavement.

In the mid-twentieth century this phenomenon came to be known as a 'colonized consciousness', a term popularized by Frantz Fanon, the Caribbean psychiatrist who worked in Algeria and was a key theorist of colonial liberation. The language of the conqueror has played a pivotal role in empires.

After the collapse of the Roman empire, the functions performed by Latin changed. Latin served for centuries in western Europe as a lingua franca in the sense of a written medium for religious and legal texts and many reference purposes. It was also the primary language of learning in educational institutions. Latin permitted communication beyond merely local needs, for which local languages were used. Latin was the caste language of the literate few, especially the clergy, who were responsible for education. It was the language used for scholarly writing in Europe, and was still in use long after local languages had become firmly established. Isaac Newton was a typical seventeenth-century scholar in that he wrote scientific works in both Latin and English.

In the Orthodox Christian churches of eastern Europe, a local language was used for the liturgy rather than Latin, this leading to the consolidation of Greek, Russian, and Serbian variants of the faith.

There is a tendency to compare the role of English in the modern world with that of Latin in earlier periods. There are some shared features:

- both languages offer an extensive range of written texts in many genres;
- both languages access key domains of knowledge and influence (religion, science, medicine, history, politics, law, . . .);
- both languages permit contact across national borders;
- both languages have been learned for several years in schools in many countries.

On the other hand there are also major differences:

- During and after the medieval period Latin was not connected to a particular political or economic system, other than feudalism and institutional religion, whereas English was central to the industrial capitalism that the British empire was the leading exponent of until 1914, and the neoliberal economic world order that the United States has spearheaded since then.
- Modern technology and communications mean that English serves a fundamentally different and much more diverse set of functions as compared with the more limited ones communicated in Latin.
- Latin was not a mother tongue for anyone after the collapse of the Roman empire, whereas English is. Communication between native speakers of English and those for whom English is a foreign or second language is asymmetrical, often to the disadvantage of the latter. This communicative inequality is obscured when English is referred to as a 'lingua franca', a concept that appears to assume communicative equality for all.

There is a more detailed presentation of the factors that are contributing to the consolidation of the power of English in Europe, and the
implications for European language policy, in Chapter 3. Here it is
merely relevant to note that those who refer to English as the Latin of
the modern world generally seem to ignore the differences between
Latin in history and English at present.

It is also important to stress that Latin and the emerging European
languages were not the only source or medium for information in the
medieval and early modern periods. During the European 'dark
ages', science and medicine learned from the more advanced culture
of the Arab world, which had spread across North Africa, Spain, and
Portugal. Some of Aristotle's writings reached western Europe in
translations by Arab scholars into Latin. European scholarly interest in
the ancient Egyptian world, and in Chinese and Indian civilization
was intense in the eighteenth and nineteenth centuries. It was only
towards the end of this period that European civilization was projected as deriving exclusively from the ancient Greeks and Romans,
and as owing nothing to Asian, Arab, or African influences. This
Eurocentric focus is simply untrue to the historical facts but sits
snugly with the rise of racist ideologies and European dominance
worldwide.[43]

Language and nationalism

In the nineteenth and twentieth centuries, the most powerful source
of group identity was the *nation*, a key constituent of which was a
national language. There have been two main variants of the notion of
a monolingual nation-state in Europe, the belief that a state can and
should impose a single language on the citizens who live within its
borders.[44]

There are states that are based on a *national romantic* vision (*jus sanguinis*, 'Blut und Boden', blood and soil, associated with such writers
as Herder and Fichte in Germany, and Grundtvig in Denmark), which
holds that those who speak the same language have a common culture
and should be united within one state. This form of nationalism was
generally accompanied by suppression of the languages of minorities
within the state's borders. Denmark, for instance, was a multilingual
empire until the mid-nineteenth century, since which it has been continuously proclaimed as being culturally and linguistically
homogeneous, which it has never been.[45]

Other states are inspired by the *republican* ideology that replaced monarchic rule in France in 1789, *jus soli*. The message of freedom, equality, and fraternity for everyone within a given political, territorial area, irrespective of the language of the home, was disseminated in a single language. At the time of the French Revolution, less than half of the population of France were in fact French-speaking. A key language policy document submitted to the National Convention on 6 June 1794 by the Abbé Grégoire laid out a strategy for imposing French and annihilating all other languages on French territory. It was entitled 'Sur la necessité et les moyens d'anéantir les patois et d'universaliser l'usage de la langue française', 'On the need and means for eliminating dialects and universalizing the use of the French language'. While the national romantic tradition is concerned with uniting one's ethnic fellows, the republican tradition is potentially universal, in that its values are held to be generally valid.

In both the national romantic and republican traditions, the language of the dominant group is given a privileged status. Speaking the same language is seen as a significant national task, particularly for the education system, even when states are invariably characterized by substantial linguistic variation, the inescapable presence of different languages and of different dialects of the same language. The nationalist task has often involved historical amnesia about the *de facto* linguistic variation that existed within what became the nation-state. In the United Kingdom, speakers of Irish, Welsh, Gaelic, and other minority languages were for centuries under major pressure to drop their languages.

Nationalist ideologies that draw on both the romantic and republican traditions are an essential cement in the construction and maintenance of nation-states and their legitimation. The notion of an 'imagined community' of one's fellows is central to national identity, solidarity with others whom one is not personally acquainted with but with whom one is assumed to share a common destiny.[46] Flags, anthems, royal or presidential families, institutions, education systems, churches, armies, sports teams, and a language, all serve such cohesive purposes. Our national identities rework the collective memory of historical events, mythical or real, and present-day symbols and imagery. As one of the pioneer theorists of nationalism, Ernest Renan, noted in 1882, 'nationalism is a daily referendum'.[47]

The national romantic imperative can have the centrifugal consequence of peaceful separation, as in the division of post-communist Czechoslovakia, or of violent fragmentation, as in the collapse of Yugoslavia (see Box 2.4). States defined in terms of cultural traits may be welcoming to a diaspora of kin who live beyond the borders of the 'mother country', and who may by virtue of their ethnic ancestry be entitled to citizenship. This applied to people of German origin in the Soviet Union, even to those who no longer spoke German.

Box 2.4   End of a federation and its language

One of the many factors that contributed to the civil wars in Yugoslavia was the misuse by political leaders of ethnolinguistic nationalism. Slovenia was the only part of Yugoslavia that managed a peaceful transition (there was one minor military confrontation) during the 1990s.[48]

Differences of language do not cause conflict.[49] In polarized situations, language differences can serve as a mobilizing factor, along with differences of religion, living standards, access to political and economic power, narratives of past history, and other factors contributing to ethnic and national identity.

Communist Yugoslavia acknowledged in the Constitution and in practice the linguistic diversity that existed within the state, and accorded territorially based language rights to many groups, rather than pretending that language differences did not exist or would melt away. However, the language of the federal state, Serbocroat, was by many not seen as being above ethnic interests and neutral. Throughout its existence, from 1919 to 1990, Serbocroat had also been known by Serbs as Serbian, and by Croats as Croatian or Croatoserbian. The differences between the languages are minor so far as grammar, vocabulary, and pronunciation are concerned. The Latin alphabet is used in Croatia, Cyrillic in Serbia.

Since 1990 both Serbian and Croatian have had an army and a state behind them, and hence qualify as distinct languages. Tribal loyalty proved stronger than Yugoslav federal nationalism, which was seen as having failed politically, economically, and culturally. Better political leadership might have achieved a totally different outcome, but the country was not run democratically, and civil society was weak.

There is an interesting moral in this for those who see English as a post-national or post-ethnic language. If a language that is used for international, lingua franca, or supranational purposes is seen as favouring one ethnic group through an inequitable distribution of economic benefits, this is likely to breed resentment. Will English in the EU develop so that it is independent of British or American control and norms, and if so, will there come a time when native speakers are not at an advantage? Or will there be resentment or worse?

Three examples will show the ways that conceptual, terminological differences are bound to impact differently on language policy at the supranational level. They must inevitably lead to language policy being thought of in different ways. This has serious consequences at the micro level (individuals from different backgrounds talking at cross-purposes) and at the macro level (different understandings of what a language is, and what it means for a state and the national interest). These complications are compounded by the fact that awareness of language issues is often not particularly high.

- The concept *dialect* entails low prestige in many countries, and high prestige in others. Dialects of Danish have low prestige, and little effort has gone into maintaining them. Conversely, since German is spoken in several countries, and Germany was a loose federation of smaller states until the nineteenth century, and is still a federal state with a decentralized education system, there are high-prestige dialects throughout the German-speaking world.[50] The term 'dialect' is therefore likely to be pejorative for some, but not for others.
- *Nation* and *national* are used in conflicting senses. Referring to English as the 'national' language in the United Kingdom obscures the fact that the Welsh, Scots, and Irish are nations within a kingdom in which they now have national parliaments. The relative fragility of Welsh and Gaelic, except in certain districts, does not make these languages less 'national' for their speakers. The attempt to revive these languages in recent decades,[51] and similar upgrading of regional languages in many countries, testifies to their importance for these communities, even if they have been citizens of a 'nation–state' that for generations chose to ignore linguistic

diversity. The 'United Nations' is a misnomer, as the body represents the governments of just over 200 states, in a world which boasts far more nations. Indigenous peoples refer to themselves as 'first nations'.

• In France, *French* is more than a national or official language. When going through the process of ratifying the Maastricht Treaty in 1992, the French Parliament passed a Constitutional Law that declares that the language of the republic is French. The republic is seen here as embodying the public will and its expression in all official functions, including education. The Law on the Use of the French Language of 1994, the Loi Toubon (see Box 2.5), aims at ensuring the perpetuation of the exclusive use of French in as many domains of life as possible in France.[52] It states: 'Langue de la République en vertu de la Constitution, la langue française est un élément fondamental de la personnalité et du patrimoine de la France' ('The Language of the Republic by virtue of the Constitution, the French language is a fundamental element of the character and patrimony of France'). Declaring that French is something special belongs in a tradition that has been official ideology for centuries – see Box 2.5.

Box 2.5   The French view of the national language

In a conference paper given in the USA in 1996, Yves Marek, who was counsellor to Jacques Toubon, Minister of Culture and Francophonie, at the time of the drafting in 1994 of the Loi Toubon, provides fascinating insight into French official thinking about language policy.[53] For him the concept 'the Language of the Republic' is above that of official language, and means the language used 'in all fields of Society, including in the private sector'. This belief has two implications internationally:

• When explaining the French government's refusal to recognize that linguistic minorities exist (a position that the government has modified slightly in recent years), he states: 'the declaration of 1789 cannot allow any collective right . . . the defenders of the Republic and of

> human rights are on the side of the central power. . . .
> There is no demand in France for the linguistic rights of
> so-called minorities . . . since we have no minorities we
> avoid the very idea of discrimination between so-called
> minorities'.

This seems to imply that each state is free to decide on all language policy matters, irrespective of minority or individual
wishes, and irrespective of obligations under international
human rights law. This statement is in conflict with the
General Comment of 6 April 1994 of the UN Human Rights
Committee on Article 27 of the International Covenant on
Civil and Political Rights, a clause that deals with minority
rights. This establishes that the existence of a minority does
not depend on a decision by the State but requires to be
established by objective criteria.[54]

* It is claimed that French principles apply at the EU level:
  '. . . our principles are confirmed at the level of the
  European Union.' Marek endorses the notion of 'the right
  of any citizen to claim national protection, in the name of
  human rights, of the official language. That is the solution
  of the European Union'. He claims that French is a
  minority language in need of protection so as to resist
  the 'most oppressive language, I mean English'.

This seems to imply an understanding of human rights according to which a single national language can be imposed within
a state, while at the supranational level it is an individual and
collective right to claim complete parity for languages so that
none dominates.

One cannot help wondering whether Marek's paper is in fact
an intellectual game or provocation, as his parting comment is
extraordinarily frank and revealing: 'in the field of linguistic
rights, like in other fields of human rights, there is no right but
only . . . politics'. This statement demonstrates all too clearly
the need for conceptual clarification in work on language
policy, and the difficulty of such work being handled dispas-
sionately and professionally at the supranational level.

It is possible that people from all fifteen EU member states are equally devoted to their languages, but it is likely that French has a longer, richer history of celebration of past glories, and a more elaborate ideology of linguistic superiority, than other languages (apart from languages that are regarded as literally being the word of God, as with Arabic). This ideology was successfully exported to other countries. Revolutionary languages, both the French of republicanism and the Russian of communism, came to be regarded as instruments of empire and conquest with a clear cultural mission. Language experts were part of this, as captured vividly in the title of Louis-Jean Calvet's book *Linguistique et colonialisme: petit traité de glottophagie* ('Linguistics and colonialism: a small treatise on linguistic cannibalism', 1974). The discourses rationalizing colonial linguistic hierarchies are extensively documented.[55]

Ideologies of linguistic supremacy

Throughout Europe from the seventeenth to the nineteenth centuries, French served as an elite link language. It was spoken at courts from Spain to Russia. It was unchallenged as the language of 'unity' of a continent plagued by dynastic rivalries, wars and domestic uprisings, and competition over territory, colonies, and markets. French was the sole language of international diplomacy until the end of the First World War, when the presence of the Americans at the conferences elaborating the peace treaties ensured that parity was given to English. As recently as 1971, the President of France, Georges Pompidou, declared in a BBC interview that 'French is the natural language of the peoples of Europe, English that of America'.[56] What he probably meant was that he was hoping that French would remain the dominant language of EU institutions, even after Denmark, Ireland, and the United Kingdom joined what was then the European Economic Community. But in claiming something special for French, Pompidou was echoing a familiar refrain.

It used to be customary to refer to French as the language of reason and civilization. The ideology of the intrinsic superiority of the language was first articulated at length by Antoine de Rivarol in 1778 in an essay on 'L'Universalité de la Langue Française', written for a competition set by the Academy of Berlin, where the court at the time was keen to emulate France. It is a wide-ranging treatise that claims that the sentence structure and grammar of French are more logical and natural than that of any other language, hence purer, clearer, and closer to the reality of thought. Rivarol's essay includes the famous sentence: '*Ce qui n'est pas clair n'est pas français; ce qui n'est pas clair est* encore anglais, italien, grec ou latin'[57] – '*Whatever is unclear is not French*; whatever is unclear is merely English, Italian, Greek or Latin' (italics in the original). His argument is that in all languages other than French, your thoughts run wild because of the convoluted sentence structure. Such beliefs lived on into the twentieth century. In 1918, the influential linguist Antoine Meillet wrote, in a chapter entitled 'On the use of the great languages of the civilized world', that French derives from Latin forms but reflects 'universal reason. . . . A good instrument for pure intelligence, for rational thought . . . There is no prose richer or more subtle than French prose, and there is no language with more precise, more nuanced, more supple prose than French prose.'[58]

This intermingling of aesthetic value judgements with objective description has been eschewed by later generations of linguists, but the tendency to idolize and glorify French, and rank it higher than other languages, can still be seen in political discourse, including that of government-funded bodies promoting French internationally. There is an echo of Rivarol's maxim in several policy papers produced by the French government in 1995, when campaigning for changes in language policy in EU institutions. The French made the point that the unclear English of non-native users of the language was an inferior instrument for international communication, a feeling that many interpreters and translators in Brussels would doubtless agree with.[59]

The French are, of course, not alone in singing the praises of their own tongue. Joshua Fishman has collected a sample of texts in scores of tongues that are 'in praise of the beloved language'.[60] Colonizing powers invariably glorified their own language and stigmatized local languages, this attitude being epitomized by Lord Macaulay, whose educational minute in India in 1835 set the tone for language policy throughout the British empire. It determined a focus on English rather than local languages, at a time when there was a considerable interest among British expatriate scholars in learning Indian languages. Indeed our understanding of the family of Indo-European languages is crucially indebted to these Orientalists. Macaulay wrote: 'I have never found one amongst them who could deny that a single shelf of a good European library was worth the whole native literature of India and Arabia.'[61] The colonial exercise was not merely about conquering territory and economies, which the wealth of nineteenth-century Europe is testimony to, but also about conquering minds. This is encapsulated in Macaulay's famous dictum, in the same policy document, on the purpose of British education for Indian leaders. It was to produce 'a class of persons, Indians in blood and colour, English in taste, in opinion, in morals and in intellect'.

It is little comfort to know that Macaulay himself was a reputable scholar (later famous as the author of a history of Britain), who was proficient in classical and modern languages. It is equally little comfort to know that key intellectuals from imperial Britain and France, Macaulay and the Abbé Grégoire, who were responsible for policies of linguistic marginalization and genocide, were active in movements for the abolition of slavery. The *mission civilisatrice* of the French, at home and abroad, was inconceivable in any language other than French. In the British empire, even if many local languages were used for initial literacy and missionary purposes, English was the vital language of power, a status that remains unchanged in almost all post-colonial countries.

Ideologies of linguistic superiority do not stand up well to scrutiny. Any language has the potential to serve any purpose, provided it has enough resources devoted to it. Any spoken language can be learned in infancy, and many children learn several simultaneously. The uses to which a language is put has nothing to do with the intrinsic nature or structure of the language.

However, the acquisition of basic literacy skills is intrinsically more difficult in some languages than others. Recent research in thirteen European countries has shown that native English-speaking children in Scotland took a year and a half longer to reach the same reading standard as many children on the continent.[62] Languages with fewer irregularities, and less complex clusters of consonants, like Finnish and Greek, are simply easier. The learning load is greater in English (most of all), Danish, French, and Portuguese.

Acquiring basic literacy in Danish or English (both Germanic languages) or in French and Portuguese (both Romance languages) is therefore demanding, even for those with these languages as a mother tongue, because of the mismatch between speech and writing, traits such as silent letters, and the same pronunciation serving several functions that are differentiated and made visible in writing.

The pre-eminence of French and English in key areas of international contact, which is due to colonialism, and the choice of these languages in many international organizations, should not obscure the fact that several languages have broad international currency. In eastern and central Europe, the Scandinavian countries, Finland, and the Baltic states, German has been a strong influence, through trading links dating back to the Hanseatic League. German was the language of the court in Denmark in the eighteenth century. An excessive use of French was satirized by the Danish playwright Ludwig Holberg (1684–1754), the first significant playwright to write in Danish, in the play *Jean de France*, which deals with the affectations of a young Dane who has returned from Paris with a French name, French manners, and a ludicrous amount of French vocabulary. This sort of 'civilization' was comic in a country in which Faroese, German, Greenlandic, Icelandic, Norwegian, and Swedish were all heard.

In Sweden in the mid-nineteenth century, translations of fiction into Swedish were made in approximately equal quantities from French, German, and English.[63] Translations cover a very wide range of types of writing, with the result that cultural innovation can be achieved when a new genre is adopted through processes of translation. By the 1920s the balance was tipping strongly towards English, though French still accounted for 16 per cent and German for 15 per cent. The figures for 1986–90 were 5 per cent French, 3 per cent German and 92 per cent for English.

International linguistic hierarchies invariably change over time. Several factors have constrained the influence of German as an international language. Germany was stripped of her colonies in Africa and Asia when defeated at the end of the First World War. The prestige of German was irreparably damaged by Nazism, which assigned a key expansionist role to German. Rudolf Hess predicted that English would become 'a minor Germanic dialect of no world importance' once the Nazis had established the thousand-year Reich.[64] It is a historical irony that the British Council, which successfully exports British culture and the English language worldwide, was established in 1934 as a direct consequence of the successful activity of Nazi Germany in promoting its language and culture abroad, particularly in the Middle East.[65]

From national to supranational identity

Citizens of the EU have a national identity connected to the member state that they come from. They may also have dual national identity, for example Scottish and British, or Sicilian and Italian. Some adopt the national identity of the state that they have migrated to. All also have, whether they know it or not, European citizenship. This was included in the Maastricht Treaty of 1992 without much clarification of what this might involve or how it related to national citizenship. The

Amsterdam Treaty of 1997 stipulated that citizenship of the Union 'shall complement and not replace national citizenship'. The construction of the European Union, and a supranational identity that supplements rather than replaces national identity, involves creating a common political culture, and building consensus on a wide range of issues.

While ethnic identity tends to be a defining feature of national identity, there is also an essential element of civic nationalism: 'Such a civic, as opposed to ethnic, conception of "the nation" reflects both the actual historical trajectory of the European nation-states and the fact that democratic citizenship establishes an abstract, legally mediated solidarity between strangers.'[66] This holds for states in the national romantic and the republican traditions. Solidarity at the supranational level is non-ethnic, but is a comparable 'solidarity between strangers' in European civil society. This is likely to evolve as a European-wide public space and political culture develop, assuming that the legitimacy of 'Europe' increases. This is a major task in the ongoing political and cultural unification of Europe. A rationale for achieving it, and for the catalytic role that a European constitution could play, has been elaborated by the eminent German philosopher Jürgen Habermas,[67] who stresses that 'the official multilingualism of EU institutions is necessary for the mutual recognition of the equal worth and integrity of all national cultures'.

The EU cannot draw on any powerful patriotic groundswell of emotion when fashioning European identity, even if a flag and an anthem are there, leaders and institutions. The elements that make up supranational identity are unclear. So too is whether this 'European' identity is multilingual, and what this might mean in practice.

The supranational identity of Europe is most clearly visible in the economic, political, and military spheres, but collaboration and consensus here would not be possible without underlying cultural affinities and shared assumptions. The creation of a new supranational entity involves an imaginative leap, but it is scarcely into the unknown. The lack of commitment of ordinary citizens to the European project is due both to the strength of feelings of local and national identity, and to uncertainty about where we are heading. The most important 'European' topic in 2002 in Britain was the euro, and whether the British should adopt it, whereas in Brussels and many capital cities, it was enlargement, and how up to a dozen additional countries could be accommodated. EU goals have perhaps always been vague and abstract, but it was clear in the formative post-1945 years that a primary goal was to avoid the mistakes of the past, and in particular war.

Throughout history there have been many wars in Europe, culminating in two devastating ones in the twentieth century, referred to as 'World Wars', and a third that lasted for over forty years, the 'Cold' war. It is estimated that roughly 70 million Europeans died through war, revolution, and famine between 1914 and 1945. These barbaric events, and the totalitarian and patriotic ideologies that permitted them, are difficult to reconcile with the faith in the idea of material, social, and cultural progress that followed the eighteenth-century Age of Enlightenment and global conquest.

Inhuman, intolerant ideologies are still present in our societies. There is a long tradition of thinkers who have been prepared to lend intellectual credence to them, as well as politicians who are able to exploit them. In the general introduction to a series of readers of such texts, George Steiner wrote in 1970: 'The theory of man as a rational animal, entitled to a wide exercise of political and economic decision, of man as a being equally endowed whatever his race, has been attacked at its religious, moral and philosophical roots' by right-wing thinkers.[68] If more democratic principles are tending to prevail, and the new political arrangements are achieving some success, we can concur with E. M. Forster: 'Two cheers for democracy: one because it admits variety and two because it admits criticism. Two cheers are quite enough: there is no occasion to give three. Only Love the Beloved Republic deserves that.'[69]

One of the motive forces behind bringing the economies of European states together was to establish forms of interdependence that would render military aggression impossible. This was to be achieved by settling territorial disputes between France and Germany and by ensuring that the re-industrialization process after the destruction of the 1939–45 war should address the needs and mutual suspicions of these countries and of the countries that the Nazis had occupied.[70] Investment from outside Europe was essential for this, and could only come from one source, namely the USA. The Marshall Plan was part of a strategy to position America as the pre-eminent force globally through the Bretton Woods agreements on trade, the World Bank and the International Monetary Fund, the United Nations, and NATO. It became clear soon after 1945 that Soviet aims were incompatible with those of their wartime allies. A successful economy in western Europe was seen as an essential bulwark against the communist bloc. Marshall aid was administered by the

Organisation for European Economic Cooperation, formed in 1948, and transformed in 1961 into a global body, the OECD, the Organisation for Economic Cooperation and Development. A massive propaganda campaign was conducted to persuade Europeans of the virtues of the US economic model.[71]

The formation of the first EU institutions involved a mixture of American and European motives. Some on both sides of the Atlantic in the 1940s had plans for a 'United States of Europe', an idea which visionaries like Victor Hugo had mooted a century earlier. The USA insisted, as a condition for Marshall aid, on the economies of European states being coordinated and integrated. American pressure was therefore decisive for the form of European collaboration that was put in place from the late 1940s. The European Coal and Steel Community came into being in 1952, with Jean Monnet at its head. This led by a tortuous route to agreement on the formation of a European Economic Community, which formally came into existence in 1958. The first sketch of a European Political Community, with an Executive Council, a Court of Justice, and a Parliament was produced in 1953. The gradual build-up of EU institutions and structures was the result of hard-nosed assessments about where the national interest lay, and how this would benefit from Europe-wide activities, rather than a more visionary faith in over-arching European values. The French have aspired to European leadership, and this could be achieved best by a strategic partnership with Germany, whose economic strength underpinned the EU, but which was to be rendered incapable of stepping out of democratic line.

The British were ambivalent about joining the EU because of their imperial links, and their belief that they have a special relationship with the USA. President De Gaulle blocked British entry in the 1960s because he saw Britain as a Trojan horse for American interests. Current participation in the secret Echelon espionage system and the 'war on terrorism' seems to confirm British willingness to do America's bidding, without this in any way indicating that the relationship is symmetrical. The British were the first to suggest, in the late 1990s, that the EU ought to have a military dimension, once it became clear that this was compatible with NATO rather than an alternative to it.

When the EU was on the political drawing-board in the 1950s, the principle of parity for the languages of the participating states was established. Thus the rules of procedure of the European Court of Justice of 7 March 1953 stipulate that the official languages of the court are French, German, Italian, and Dutch, the primary languages of the initial six member states. Listing the languages not alphabetically, but naming French first, suggests that French was assumed to have a greater role to play. The relative strength of French in EU affairs is attributable to its earlier use in international relations, to the location of EU institutions in cities in which French was widely used, Brussels, Luxembourg, and Strasbourg, and to speakers of French, along with the Germans, occupying the political high ground in shaping the new Europe.

When President Pompidou agreed to Britain 'joining Europe' in 1972, it is reported that one condition he insisted on was that the pre-eminence of French as the dominant language of EU institutions should remain unchallenged. British Prime Minister Edward Heath reportedly agreed that all British civil servants connected to the EU should be proficient in French. Pompidou's worries about the risk of the French language being eclipsed by English were, as is now obvious, fully justified.

The interlocking of national traditions and the national interest with the processes of interaction at the supranational level is manifestly complex. Functioning in several languages multiplies the degree of difficulty, which has major implications for how the European project is seen and implemented. Some analysts believe that after decades with the EU being concerned with economic issues, from agricultural subsidies to the common market and the euro, the biggest issue in the coming years is cultural rights.[72] In the light of the harmonization of policies on immigration and refugees, uncertainty about the influence of enlargement on the labour market (such as whether Polish labour will besiege Germany), and the polarization between the west and Islam since the terrorist attack on New York on 11 September 2001, there is no doubt that cultural matters have acquired more salience.

How supranational identity will evolve in response to changing cultural and linguistic identities is far from clear. Nationalism can be active or quiescent, and will tend to be activated at times of political struggle and otherwise remain implicit or banal.[73] Supranationalism is still in its infancy, but is likely to operate in similar ways. It will be flagged openly (elections, logos, policy initiatives, photo opportunities, etc.) and will need to draw on many of the quiescent shared features of our common European heritage. It will be an active process that needs continuous assertion and negotiation. Supranational identification will take many forms. It may be embraced by minority groups as a means of reducing their dependence on the state, i.e. more power in Brussels may mean less in London or Madrid. In these processes, it is likely that no single EU language can occupy the space that a national language played in each state in the nation-building phase of the eighteenth to twentieth centuries. It is arguable that English may acquire comparable over-arching functions, but at present the supranational European public sphere is not tied to a single language.[74]

Diversity and the common cultural heritage

Our cultural identities derive from a blend of the universal and the particular, the national and the local. This mix of shared and distinct aspects of a common European heritage is made explicit in the clauses on education and culture in the Maastricht Treaty of 1992. This commits the EU to

> fully respect the cultural and linguistic diversity of member states . . . The community will contribute to the flowering of the cultures of the member states, while respecting their national and regional diversity. At the same time it will bring the common cultural heritage to the fore. Action by the community will be aimed at encouraging cooperation between member states. If necessary, it will also support and supplement their action to improve knowledge of the history of the European peoples, conservation of cultural heritage of European significance, non-commercial cultural exchanges, and artistic and literary creation.

The underlying values and ideals that all EU member states are supposed to live up to were identified in a Declaration of European Identity of 1973 that recognized the variety of national cultures but identified common legal, political, and moral values.

Vaclav Havel, the Czech president, presented the idea of a *Charter of European Identity* to the European Parliament on 8 March 1994.[75] The values referred to are those of representative democracy, the rule of law, and civil society that aims at creating 'freedom, peace, human dignity, equality and social justice'. In fact these ideals are not specifically European, since they underlie the 'universal' human rights declarations elaborated under the auspices of the United Nations since 1945. In Europe they evolved gradually over centuries, as a result of changes in religion (Protestantism and the Reformation encouraged more individualism, and publication of the Bible in local languages made it more accessible), in philosophy (rationalism, a belief in progress, free thinkers challenging feudalism, absolutism, and theocracy), parliamentary systems (rights for citizens, greater representation in government), literature (fiction dealing with existential social issues), journalism, and changes in public and private life.

Political representation through universal suffrage is a common feature of member states, but the outcome of the popular vote depends on both whether people actually turn out to vote, and whether the parliamentary system has proportional representation or is 'first past the post'. The British General Election in 2001 saw the lowest turn-out since the introduction of universal suffrage. This suggests at the least a low level of political activity, and more probably reflects a sense of disillusionment with the political process. Tony Blair's New Labour party won another huge parliamentary majority, but in fact only a quarter of the electorate voted Labour.[76] In most other European countries a comparable election result would lead to a coalition government with two or more parties needing to negotiate policy continuously with other parties, and in general to be more accountable and sensitive to public opinion.

It also needs to be recalled that the free expression of public opinion was not permitted in states that were under fascist, military, or communist rule, and that this was the case in many European countries in the twentieth century. Even in democratic states, the freedom to influence public opinion through the media is far greater for central government, which increasingly concentrates on matters of presentation or spin doctoring the public, and for powerful corporate bodies, than for others.[77]

Another common element of our European political heritage is the constitutional principle of the separation of powers, those of the judicial, legislative, and administrative wings of governments. The way these powers intersect varies in each country, reflecting differing degrees of dependence on common law, Roman law, Napoleonic law, case law, written constitutions, certain types of court, and the unique traditions of national legal professions. The existence of a distinct 'legal culture' in each state does not mean that they do not also have a great deal in common.[78]

All EU states subscribe to the *rule of law*, which is, according to *The New Shorter Oxford English Dictionary* (1993): '(a) any valid legal proposition; (b) the doctrine that arbitrary exercise of power is controlled by subordinating (government, military, economic, etc.) power to well-defined and impartial principles of law.' Such principles are applied in nationally specific legal traditions. Concepts such as a fair trial, freedom of expression, and the right to a private life are understood in specific ways in different cultures.[79] Box 2.6 shows that the concept 'rule of law' is multi-faceted, and not a straightforward term with a narrow equivalent in all languages, even if many of the essential concepts derive from a common Latin base.

Box 2.6   The rule of law, and its multiple meanings

Translation equivalents in the EU database *Eurodicautom* (<www.europa.eu.int/eurodicautom>) for the English term *rule of law* into Danish and French.

French	Danish	Literal translation into English
règle de droit	retsregel	law rule, legal act
état de droit	retsstat	law state, a state governed by law
principes de droit	retsprincipper	principles of law
prééminence du droit primauté de droit	retsstatsforhold	primacy of law, matters pertaining to a state governed by law
principe de la légalité	legalitetsprincip, princip om lovmæssig forvaltning	the principle of legality, the principle of legally valid administration

The table demonstrates the range of possible meanings of the English term. Though the table reveals considerable diversity in the three languages, they all draw heavily on a shared Latin heritage (*rectus, regere, status, lex,* etc.):

Danish *ret, regel,* English **right**, **rule**, **regulate**, French 'règle';

Danish *stat*, English **state**, French 'état';
Danish *legalitet,* English **legality**, French 'légalité';
Danish *princip*, English **principle**, French 'principe';
Danish *lov* (as in *lovmæssig* above), English **law**.

This is treacherous semantic territory, even within the same language: for example, lawful activity is not the same as legal activity. The European Charter of Human Rights, Article 5(4), stipulates that the detention of someone suspected of a crime must be lawful. The best translation of this into Danish is *retmæssig*, since the reference is to legislation and case law; *lovlig* refers to legislation only. Legal translation is notoriously difficult. A Danish study, *Human rights in translation. Legal concepts in different languages*, by Marianne Garre (see note 79), demonstrates that in Denmark there is no policy to ensure that human rights instruments are translated consistently into Danish. Some instruments are not translated at all, which leads to conflict between English and Danish conceptual universes.

Contemporary western states are characterized by a strong degree of cultural hybridity, reflecting the diversity of origins of the people living in the country, both of groups of long standing and those of more recent labour migrants and refugees. We are now experiencing a potentially infinite range of influences from all over the world. But states cling to the myth of cultural and linguistic homogeneity, and are increasingly marketing themselves through cultural stereotypes that project a distinct brand, a lifestyle image such as Cool Britannia, and the glamour and hedonism of ads for airlines, cities, and global corporations, in many of which the national element is still strong. For the moment, Carlsberg 'is' still Danish, Nokia Finnish, and BMW German (the B stands for Bavarian). It is also possible that 'state branding is gradually supplanting nationalism. The brand state's use of its history, geography, and ethnic motifs to construct its own distinct image is a benign campaign that lacks the deep-rooted and often antagonistic sense of national identity and uniqueness that can accompany nationalism'.[80]

There are powerful forces behind the marketing of English as the contemporary language of European unity. Symptomatic of the wishful thinking of global English is the publicity marketing *The International Herald Tribune* (earlier *New York Herald Tribune*; the European edition is edited in Paris[81]). It describes itself as 'The world's daily newspaper. Since 1887 . . . The global village has a hometown newspaper . . . It's the newspaper the whole world reads.' Evidently the global village, another metaphor much used by the cheer-leaders of globalization, is monolingual – or at the very least, only one language matters.

The EU projects itself as a new political brand that connotes affluence and political collaboration. For the line-up of potential member states, the brand evidently connotes some kind of economic and political club that is worth joining. However, studies of attitudes to EU institutions in the existing member states reveal very patchy faith in the EU. A Eurobarometer survey conducted in the spring of 2000 revealed that whereas a majority of people in continental European states feel somewhat European, more than two-thirds of people in Britain feel exclusively British. A Eurobarometer survey conducted in the spring of 2001 revealed that only 41 per cent of EU citizens trust the EU and its institutions.[82] There is wide variation between national groups: 63 per cent of the Portuguese trust the EU, whereas only 25 per cent of the British do. British youngsters are also more ignorant about, and have lower expectations of, the European Union, than others of the same age in every other member state.[83] The divergent figures reflect a range of interpretations of 'Europe', past, present, and future, and uncertainty about how the momentous political, economic, and cultural changes that we are all involved in are reshaping our identities at the individual, group, and national levels.

If an EU supranational identity is ever to become a profound experience for Europeans, the shared values that this identification will draw on will have to go beyond economics and politics. They will take cultural and linguistic symbolic form in specific types of communication and imagery. How 'Europe' is being imagined, and in which languages this process is occurring, are therefore fundamental issues.

The issue of political legitimacy is a major problem at the European level, since the EU is seen as operating secretively, and in effect being run by a bureaucratic elite in a set of institutions in partnership with corporate world lobbies, and politicians. The inter-governmental conferences at the culmination of each six-month Presidency (Gothenburg and Laeken in 2001, Sevilla and Copenhagen in 2002) are currently concerned with the balance of power between EU institutions and national governments and parliaments, and with power-sharing with new member states. 'No amount of tinkering with the rules can resolve their increasing alienation from the European constituency that these arrangements are supposed to serve.'[84] Perhaps more attention to language policy might ensure better communication and make it more democratic?

Chapter 3

Global trends impacting on European language policy

Our language . . . stands pre-eminent among the languages of the West . . . Whoever knows that language has a ready access to all the vast intellectual wealth which all the wisest nations of the earth have created and hoarded in the course of ninety generations . . . It is likely to become the language of commerce throughout the seas of the East.

Thomas Babington Macaulay, 1835[1]

Within a generation from now English could be a world language – that is to say, a universal language in those countries in which it is not already the native or primary tongue.

British Cabinet Report, 1956[2]

71% of Europeans consider that everyone in the EU should be able to speak one European language in addition to their mother tongue. Almost the same proportion agree that this should be English. A large majority (63%) believes that it is necessary to protect their own languages more as the enlargement of the EU is envisaged. This view is shared by 90% of the people in Greece and Finland.

Eurobarometer Report 54, 15 February 2001[3]

A global mass-media créole founded on American English is a soul-destroying prospect. So is the continuation of inflamed regionalism and language hatreds.

George Steiner, 2001[4]

All language communities have the right to preserve their linguistic and cultural heritage.

Dalai Lama, 1998[5]

Multilingualism and the dominance of English

I would like to begin with a note on my linguistic biography, since I typify the multilingualism and mobility of labour that the EU seeks to promote. I grew up speaking only English, and now use three languages every day (English, Danish, and Swedish), and an additional two frequently (French and German), all of them for reading and in speech, and sometimes in writing. I studied French and German at school, and at university level. I have lived as an immigrant in Denmark for thirty years, after shorter periods in French-, German-, Serbian-, and Spanish-speaking countries. My university post is in a Department of English in Denmark, a country where higher education posts are awarded on the strength of applicants' qualifications, irrespective of mother tongue. Most of my colleagues are therefore Danes with impressive proficiency in English.

My children are trilingual from home, and learned a fourth language (Russian or French) to a reasonably high level in the upper secondary school, while specializing in the natural sciences. Their generation has had much more chance of foreign travel and studying abroad than did mine, and interacting with people from different linguistic backgrounds.

There is nothing exceptional about this multilingualism in many parts of the world, including continental Europe. The Chief Executive Officers of 200 top global corporations are multilingual, unless they come from the United States and the UK. The Swedes and Dutch average more than three languages, the French and Germans nearly three, as documented in a recent Harvard study.[6]

The City of London offers financial services in over 100 languages, but this has more to do with its capacity to attract foreigners to work in London than with the linguistic competence of British people. In Britain only 35 per cent of the population claim competence in a foreign language, whereas the figure in Sweden is 88 per cent.[7] The number of languages spoken in the home by children of school-going age in London is over 300.

Ariel Dorfman, the Chilean-American writer, in his wonderful book *Heading South, looking North: a bilingual journey* (Penguin, 1998), analyses his personal experience of bilingualism, language loss, and re-acquisition, in a vivid portrait of a turbulent life in the USA and Chile. The book is a *New York Times* Notable Book. When Dorfman, who holds a professorial chair at a prestigious US university, wrote a short

article in this newspaper entitled 'If only we could all speak two languages', he was at the receiving end of a torrent of denunciation and
hate mail. Evidently to suggest that Americans might benefit by being
bilingual (which, of course, is what millions of minority language
speakers have been throughout the history of the USA) can be seen as
un-American and can trigger a McCarthyite response.

The 11 September 2001 crisis revealed that the United States intelligence services did not have sufficient competence in Arabic or
Pashtun for monitoring activities of direct relevance to national security, even though there are loyal citizens of the USA with the
appropriate linguistic background.[8] This is one of the ironies, or
tragedies, of the way education is organized, when it concentrates
almost exclusively on learning English, irrespective of the mother
tongue background of pupils. Foreign languages are in fact learned successfully in formal education, even in Britain and the USA, in a variety
of ways, but by a minority of students.[9] There is abundant evidence
from experience worldwide that education can be organized so as to
make people competent in two or more languages, whether their
mother tongue is a minority language or the dominant national language, provided a number of conditions are met.[10]

If monolingualism is a curable disease,[11] it is one affecting many
people without their realizing it. The disease is particularly widespread
in 'big' states that have traditionally seen themselves as linguistically
self-sufficient. A significant development in western Europe in the
1990s has been that the member states of the EU have endorsed the
desirability of schoolchildren acquiring competence in at least two
foreign languages, an achievement that is quite common in 'small'
countries such as The Netherlands and the Nordic countries. The EU
now endorses the goal of multilingualism for all. It is perhaps taking its
cue from the minority language communities of Europe, which have
been the pioneers, according to the former Director of the European
Bureau for Lesser Used Languages, Dónall Ó Riagáin:[12]

> Although marginalized in many senses, the speakers of the
> European Union's minority and regional languages are the orig-
> inal proponents of the new Europe which all of us are now
> committed to build. Bilingual before the LINGUA programme
> was ever dreamt of, preaching tolerance and advocating unity in
> diversity before Schuman and Monnet were born, they are now
> building pan-European networks to promote cooperation and
> the sharing of information.

Multilingualism will only be achieved if the experience of grassroots and elite multilingualism worldwide is related to the global economic, political, and cultural trends that determine whether languages thrive or perish. This broader context will be approached by analysing the factors contributing to the increased use of English in Europe. They are listed provisionally in Table 1.

The table shows that there are many supply and demand factors that influence the advance of English. It also assumes that the fate of all languages is interconnected, since languages form part of interlocking constellations at the sub-national, national, and international levels, at each of which both structural and ideological factors contribute to the relative power of the relevant languages, and to hierarchies of languages.[13] *Structural* implies that material resources underpin the status of the languages or activities in question, hard cash, investment in buildings, companies, products, institutions, university departments, teacher training, time on the curriculum, and much else that generates a pattern of language learning and use. *Ideological* refers to attitudes to languages, beliefs about their value, utility, and merits, and how the consciousness industry uses languages, and shapes our understanding of languages and attitudes to them.

Table 1 Factors contributing to the increased use of English in Europe

A. Structural

1. English is an integral dimension of ongoing globalization processes in commerce, finance, politics, military affairs, science, education, and the media. The adoption of English as the key corporate, institutional, and scholarly language for such activities is symptomatic of this trend. The frequent use of English in networking, NGOs (Non-Governmental Organizations), subcultural youth groups, and the internet consolidates the language at the grassroots level.

2. The Americans and British have invested heavily in promoting their language globally since the mid-1950s.

3. Higher education in the USA, the UK, and Australia attracts increasing numbers of students from all over the world, including continental Europe, in part because the language of instruction is English.

4. There has been substantial investment in the teaching of English in the education systems of continental European countries.

5. Levels of foreign language competence vary widely, but there tend to be more people who are proficient in English in the demographically small countries.

6. In continental Europe there is an increasing tendency for universities to offer courses and degrees taught in English. This is a general trend, particularly at graduate level in the north of Europe, and in such fields as Business Studies. In some schools the trend is to teach a content subject through the medium of English.

7. There is a poor scholarly infrastructure at European universities and research institutes for the analysis of language policy, multilingualism, and language rights, reflecting a lack of investment in this field.

8. Responsibility for language policy in each country tends to be shared between ministries of foreign affairs, education, culture, research, and commerce. They each tend to have little expertise in language policy, and between them there is inadequate coordination, if any. In countries with a federal structure, responsibility is even more diffuse.

9. As English is used extensively by native and non-native speakers from different parts of the world, there is no simple correlation between English and the interests of a particular state. The connection of English to the dominant economic system and to global networking remains.

10. The mobility of labour, more extensive international links, and cross-cultural marriages reinforce a pattern of language shift towards dominant languages, particularly English.

B. Ideological

11. Major differences in the ideologies underpinning the formation of states, and in the role ascribed to language in these (*jus sanguinis*, Herder, e.g. Germany, versus *jus soli*, citizenship, e.g. France) mean that language issues are understood differently in different countries, this impeding a shared understanding of language policy issues.

12. Attitudes to multilingualism are affected by people's exposure to and use of foreign and minority languages. These affect people's awareness of linguistic diversity and language rights, and their motivation for learning additional languages.

13. Levels of awareness about language policy issues range widely between and within each EU country. They tend to be relatively high in, for instance, Finland and Greece, and low in Denmark and England.

14. There is a popular demand for English that is strongly connected to a language that is projected in advertising and the media as connoting success, influence, consumerism, and hedonism.

15. Ranking languages for their purported qualities or limitations, through processes of glorification and stigmatization, correlates with language hierarchies and their hegemonic rationalization.

These factors will be explored in this chapter in relation to four key domains, in each of which the role of language is central:

- commerce
- science
- culture
- education

whereas the political domain will be pursued in the following chapter, which deals with EU institutions and the interlocking of national politics with the supranational bodies. The domains are all interconnected, and additional domains, such as military activities (alliances, peace-keeping, the arms trade) or the media might have been given separate treatment, as these also reveal how globalization processes are strengthening English.

There are structural and ideological elements in society that maintain inequality between groups identified on the basis of 'race' (racism), gender (sexism), or language (linguicism).[14] Sexism and racism may be embedded in the forms of a language. We may or may not be aware that there is a problem of basic justice involved, and may or may not wish to engage in 'verbal hygiene'[15] (a preferable term to the much-abused one 'political correctness'). Minority language speakers are victims of linguicism if their languages have no place in the education system, or are stigmatized as being irrelevant in the modern world, and no resources are allocated to them. Another instance of linguicism is when speakers of a particular language are given preferential treatment over others for certain types of employment (on native speakers of English, see Chapter 5). In many international encounters, meetings, or conferences, there is a pecking order of languages, and little thought tends to be given to ensuring equality in communication. When a Eurobarometer Report (54, 15 February 2001) discovers that 90 per cent of the people in Greece and Finland believe that it is necessary to protect their own languages more when the enlargement of the EU takes place, this suggests a fear that europeanization threatens their languages, that these 'small' languages might fall prey to linguicism at the supranational level.

Both structure and ideology need to be changed if inequality is to be reduced, and ideally eliminated.

It is when serious injustice is experienced by speakers of different languages that language policy tends to acquire a high political profile. This may trigger a crisis of national identity. In states with a

multilingual composition, there is a tension between conflict and compromise, to use the title of a series of books analysing how
multilingualism has been handled in Belgium, Finland, and
Switzerland.[16] These are countries that do not fit into the monolingual
state model that has been the norm elsewhere in western Europe, as
discussed in Chapter 2. Great power politics saw fit to allow Belgium
and Finland to emerge from occupation and colonization. The new
state needed to share power between linguistically defined groups.
Belgium has seen conflict, territorial segregation, and a re-ordering of
economic and linguistic power, whereas in Finland, major guarantees
for the Swedish-speaking minority have ensured a more harmonious
evolution. Switzerland was geographically distinct, and developed a
decentralized power structure of cantons that could build unity across
divisions of religion, language, and political party. The experience of
both Finland and Switzerland shows that groups defined along ethnic
and linguistic lines can live equitably and harmoniously with each
other.

'Ethnic conflict' is a dangerous term if it is based on the premise that
ethnic groups cannot live together constructively within the same state.
Peaceful coexistence occurs in states that share political and economic
power equitably. The management of diversity in western societies
raises a series of issues, both analytical (in political science, law, minority rights, theories of integration, education) and practical (policies for
indigenous and immigrant groups, 'national' minorities in multilingual
states), that are being addressed in many contexts.[17] Language rights
figure prominently in many of these ongoing efforts.

Language policy lessons from outside
Europe

Language policy in Europe can draw on experience in the management of multilingualism elsewhere. In Canada, Australia, and South
Africa, there is a tension between the power of English and the rights
of speakers of other languages. This tension can ideally prove to be a
productive one that leads to compromise rather than conflict, to the
successful management of multilingualism rather than the neglect and
atrophy of some languages.

In *Canada*, resentment at the marginalization of French, at times
violent, led to a protracted process of redefining the balance of power
between speakers of English and French from the 1960s onwards.[18]
What evolved was a politically negotiated prescription for linguistic

power-sharing at the federal level, and a large measure of autonomy at the provincial level. This led to the establishment of a series of activities and institutions designed to strengthen French in Québec in all key domains of public life and commerce, i.e. structural change. In more recent years, some of the indigenous 'First Nations' have also achieved significant language rights and greater autonomy. The EU has much to learn from Canada, not least in relation to negotiating and managing the balance between language use at two levels, in Canada the federal level and the provinces, and in the EU the supranational level and the member states. In both contexts there are external pressures related to globalization. The North American Free Trade Agreement (NAFTA) was signed in the three dominant languages of the continent, English, French, and Spanish. As it is exclusively a trading agreement, there are no provisions for language policy, with the consequence that the laws of the linguistic market are allowed free rein. This is likely to strengthen English at the expense of other languages, and there is evidence that it is strengthening US corporate power.

In *Australia*, language policy became a national need when a series of factors converged during the 1980s: a realization that Australians needed to evolve a new sub-Asian national identity rather than continuing to see themselves as an exclusively English-speaking outpost of Britain; a recognition that the many Aboriginal and immigrant languages were cultural values that could and should be built on; and a realization that a diversity of language qualifications was needed for contact with the wider world and for exports to particular markets. The political will to engage in serious language policy was generated by a coming together of key constituencies in the political, commercial, and minority and indigenous rights worlds. The guiding parameters in formulating language policy were encapsulated in the four Es:

- Enrichment (cultural and intellectual),
- Economics (foreign trade and vocations),
- Equality (social justice and overcoming disadvantages), and
- External (Australia's role in the region and the world).[19]

In Europe these criteria might be adopted in synthesizing and extending some of the existing language policy work, with an additional E, Europeanization.

In post-apartheid *South Africa*, language policy has played a major role in the transformation to a more democratic society. Language policy in South Africa builds on a Language Plan of Action for Africa that was approved by African Heads of State in 1986, which encourages all states to have a clearly defined language policy, to ensure that all languages within the boundaries of member states are recognized and accepted as a source of mutual enrichment, and to work for a replacement of European colonial languages by African languages.[20] The goals of South African language policy are:[21]

1   to promote national unity;
2   to entrench democracy, which includes the protection of language rights;
3   to promote multilingualism;
4   to promote respect for and tolerance towards linguistic and cultural diversity;
5   to further the elaboration and modernization of the African languages;
6   to promote national economic development.

The fundamental assumptions on which language policy is based are that:

1   language policy is an integral part of general social policy;
2   language is a resource, not a problem;
3   language is a fundamental human right;
4   the state has to facilitate, coordinate, and initiate strategies geared to the promotion and protection of the language rights of the citizens of the country;
5   persuasion, encouragement, and incentives rather than coercion are the appropriate policy stances in the highly sensitive area of language practices and language usage;
6   no language is superior to any other;
7   language policy development and implementation take time.

What is significant in each of these contexts is that the principles that should guide language policy have been made explicit. Implementation has involved the allocation of structural resources, budgets, responsibilities in ministries or special agencies, and serious commitment to a wide range of activities in status, acquisition, and corpus planning. If European countries are to engage more actively in language policy, responsibility will have to be placed squarely in specific ministries and institutions, as well as at the supranational level, and the necessary expertise built up. What is also needed in the current European context is to identify the contours and constraints that result from globalization trends, and their impact on the continental mosaic of languages.

Trends in commerce

The conventional wisdom has been that you produce in your own language but sell in the language of the buyer. This is still largely true, and there is evidence that companies which are unable to operate in a given foreign language do not succeed in markets where this language is required.[22] On the other hand the traditional role of national borders and languages is changing as a result of the globalization of commercial operations, with different corporate functions scattered round the world, new technologies, and the concentration of corporate power into fewer, larger units in a neoliberal economic system primarily driven by the United States. Such global bodies as the OECD, the World Bank, the IMF, and the World Trade Organization[23] all serve to strengthen corporate power and the position of English. The fragility of the system is manifest from the gyrations of boom and recession, protectionism defying the rhetoric of a 'free' market, and from the resistance that the intensification of global inequalities generates.[24] It is also clear that the ways in which these underlying processes are worked through differ markedly in a variety of contexts, and that the gospel of reliance on market forces alone is thoroughly discredited.

Many of the far-reaching changes in the EU that were adopted in the treaties of the 1990s, economic and monetary union in particular, were prefigured in plans made by the European Round Table of Industrialists, and coordinated between corporations in the Transatlantic Business Dialogue.[25] Economic union has been the *sine qua non* of EU activities, which fits with the kind of Europe that the Marshall plan and the OECD have fostered. Unification of the EU market is now complete, and unification of the currency is in full swing. What then needs consideration is what forms of linguistic unification are occurring, and how these dovetail with political and cultural unification.

Earlier unification took place within each nation-state. A national market privileged French in France, Castilian Spanish in Spain, and so on. The commercial exchanges within a national territory took place within a unified linguistic market, though the marginalized languages in the territory often succeeded in surviving despite these pressures.

What we are currently experiencing is unification of a global market, with English as one among several vibrant international languages, among them Arabic, Chinese, Hindi, and Japanese, though clearly none of these has the same status in globalization as English. Spanish now has more mother tongue speakers than English, but they are geographically concentrated in the Americas and the Iberian peninsula, and Spanish is not nearly as widely learned or used as a foreign language as is English. French has not been able to remain in the same league as English, but it still has more users of the language as a first or second language than ever before. There is massive promotion of the language internationally. *The Economist* of 20 December 2001 quotes a figure of $1 billion a year on various schemes to promote French culture and language. The Direction Générale de la Coopération Internationale et du Développement had a budget in 2000 of 11 billion francs.[26] The Agence intergouvernementale de la Francophonie brings together 47 states and governments as members, and an additional eight states as observers. However, there is not the slightest doubt about which language is most in use in the global finance and trade organizations, in the United Nations and its various bodies, in NATO, and in the global media, with Hollywood, CNN, Newscorp (Murdoch), and the BBC hugely influential.

On the other hand, labelling English as the world's lingua franca, or as 'the' language of the internet, is wishful thinking. Many languages are used as lingua francas, and many languages are used on the internet, including demographically small ones. The status of English may well be challenged in the future.[27]

The trend in leading transnational corporations, whether in pharmaceuticals in Switzerland, telecommunications in France, or cars in Germany, is to shift to English as the in-house corporate language. A Danish survey of company plans early in 2001 reported that one third of major Danish companies reckon on a shift to English within ten years.[28]

It is more than likely that the transition to a greater use of English will be a protracted one, and for many employees an uncomfortable one, and that many functions will continue to be performed in the local language. A statement by DaimlerChrysler top management in Germany on 26 April 1999 explains that English is the joint working language at the managerial level in Germany ('Englisch ist die gemeinsame Arbeitssprache des Managements'). Competence in English will be increasingly required at this level. The company provides incentives, interpretation, and language training to strengthen the implementation of English, and hopes the transition will be undertaken in a spirit of 'tolerance and pragmatism'. It is intriguing that the word 'management' is used in a German text alongside well-established German equivalents (*Leitung, Führung*). It is indicative of the prestige attached to English in the modern world, its association with innovation and a specific type of professionalism.

Loan words are of course being adopted in all European languages, as welcome arrivals in some languages (including German, popular with many but not all German speakers), as an intrusion in need of modification (e.g. Norwegian) or resistance (e.g. Icelandic) in others. Borrowing often triggers a readjustment of the relevant semantic space, sometimes displacing and sometimes replacing local words.

This company policy document also makes it clear that linguistic shift occurs only in one direction. There is no suggestion that Chrysler employees should be learning German, though anyone going to work in Germany would find it imperative to acquire German (except for the armed services of occupying powers, France, Russia, UK, USA). The absence of reciprocity also applies when the Atlantic is crossed in the other direction. A German transnational company operating subsidiaries in the USA is likely to function exclusively in English in its operations there. Siemens has reduced the number of Germans working in their operations in the USA, because they found that Germans in North America were at a disadvantage vis-à-vis native speakers.

In entertainment, popular culture, 'lifestyle', and consumerism, americanization and McDonaldization are massively influential. Hollywood products are ubiquitous on television screens, either dubbed or in the original language, on both private and public service channels. The EU/USA deficit in the audiovisual sector in 2002 was estimated at $7 billion. According to figures from the European Audiovisual Observatory, US film in 1998 took over 90 per cent of the Dutch and German box office, over 80 per cent in the UK, and rather less elsewhere in Europe.[29] The picture is not uniform: for instance, Danish filmmakers have enjoyed considerable success in recent years, nationally and internationally. In 2001, 30 per cent of the cinema box office take in Denmark went to local films. This is a sign of considerable cultural vitality, particularly when one recalls that the market is small (5.3 million people), and only twenty feature films are made each year. Danish producers state that EU funding, via the Media+ programme, has played a significant role in strengthening the Danish film industry (US films have on average a budget that is four times larger than European ones) and its acceptance by distributors in other EU countries.[30]

On television channels throughout Europe there was a marked shift in the 1990s from predominantly European content, either domestic or imported from other European countries, to US dominance. The popular music market (accounting for between 90 and 95 per cent of albums sold) is American-British dominated. Young people are therefore vastly more influenced by Anglo-American culture than their parents, resulting in more familiarity with US values than with those of neighbouring European countries. In the Swedish referendum on joining the EU in 1994, the youngest voters were the only age-group that was negative to the EU. 'Europe is not a meaningful concept of current youth culture.'[31]

The flow of cultural products from Europe to North America is a tiny trickle. The market share of films from the EU is 2–3 per cent.

Advertising plays a key role in creating consumer habits, manufacturing desire and consent. In the United States, more money is spent on advertising than on the entire education system. Figures for the expansion of advertising revenue reveal constant growth, even at times of economic slowdown. 'Spending on global advertising increased sevenfold between 1950 and 1996, and grew one third faster than the world economy', with the result that advertising is now so all-embracing that 'all aspects of our lives are now at the service of the selling machine . . . There are now five world-class super-groups incorporating dozens of once independent agencies', one in London (WPP), two in New York (Omnicom and Interpublic), and two in Paris (Havas Advertising and Publicis), 'each making between 33% and 66% of its revenues outside the home market'.[32] According to a top executive in the trade journal *Advertising Age*: 'Most clients today demand that their agencies offer global reach and seamlessly integrated communications capabilities.'[33]

The globalization of media conglomerates entails dissemination of an ideology of consumerism and materialism, with no attention to the ecological consequences of this consumption. What we are experiencing is not so much the Knowledge Society, one of the mantras of the EU, as a Global Billboard Society.[34]

Public relations are a subdivision of the advertising world. According to the US Bureau of Labor Statistics, there were 118,280 PR workers in the USA alone in 2001. Their mission is to help clients 'manage issues by influencing – in the right combination – public attitude, public perceptions, public behaviour and public policy'.[35]

American goals have been explicit and consistent since the Second World War:[36]

It was the triumphant American state that fashioned the present 'global economy' at Bretton Woods in 1944, so that its military and corporate arms would have unlimited access to minerals, oil, markets and cheap labour. In 1948, the State Department's senior imperial planner, George Kennan, wrote: 'We have 50 per cent of the world's wealth, but only 6.3 per cent of its population. In this situation, our real job in the coming period is to devise a pattern of relationships which permit us to maintain this position of disparity. To do so, we have to dispense with all sentimentality . . . we should cease thinking about human rights, the raising of living standards and democratisation.' The World Bank and the International Monetary Fund were invented to implement this strategy.

English is an integral dimension of the globalization project. Rudolf Troike, Director of the Center for Applied Linguistics in Washington, DC, established with Ford Foundation funding, stated in 1977 that the process of establishing global US hegemony was 'greatly abetted by the expenditure of large amounts of government and private foundation funds in the period 1950–1970, perhaps the most ever spent in history in support of the propagation of a language'.[37]

The British empire laid the foundation for the globalization of English. In the 1950s, when decolonization was inevitable, considerable effort went into ensuring that English would remain the cement binding colonial economies and cultures to British interests, which were themselves already subordinate to American ones. British and American policy for the global spread of English was coordinated in the pioneer phase of creating the academic infrastructure, institutions, and professionalism that would ensure that native speaker expertise was considered relevant worldwide.[38] The product was English as a Second Language, a teaching tradition that has varied slightly on each side of the Atlantic but shared a common goal, as formulated in the British Council *Annual Report*, 1960–61, p. 16: 'Teaching the world English may appear not unlike an extension of the task which America faced in establishing English as a common national language among its own immigrant population.'

In the USA, English was supposed to replace the mother tongues of immigrant and indigenous peoples. This is known as subtractive language learning. Globally, this was not an explicit goal, but English was often introduced from the start of formal education, and there are now elites in Africa (Afro-Saxons is the term used by the distinguished

Kenyan, Ali Mazrui) and India who speak exclusively English. It is not uncommon for Indian grandparents who do not speak English to have no language in common with their grandchildren. The young, upwardly mobile, internationally oriented generation of Indians and Africans have more in common with 'global' culture than with the mass of inhabitants of India and Africa.

Globalization was seen by the eminent French sociologist Pierre Bourdieu as:[39]

> . . . a pseudo-concept that is both descriptive and prescriptive, which has replaced 'modernization', that was long used in the social sciences in the USA as a euphemistic way of imposing a naively ethnocentric evolutionary model by means of which different societies were classified according to their distance from the economically most advanced society, i.e. American society.
>
> . . . the word (and the model it expresses) incarnates the most accomplished form of *the imperialism of the universal*, which consists of one society universalizing its own particularity covertly as a universal model (like French society did for a long time, as the presumed incarnation of the Rights of Man and the inheritance of the French Revolution, which was seen, particularly in the Marxist tradition, as the model for all possible revolutions).

Globalization is understood by Condoleezza Rice, President George W. Bush's foreign affairs adviser, in precisely this sense: 'The rest of the world is best served by the USA pursuing its own interests because American values are universal.'[40] The Clinton government concentrated on consolidating economic hegemony through regional and global trading agreements. The Bush administration is expanding the military so as to ensure global economic and political dominance in the long term.[41] Successive US governments have rejected the option of cooperative multilateral frameworks for the management of the new post-Cold-war world, preferring 'unipolarity by pursuing a policy of primacy'.[42] The policy options elaborated in the Pentagon in the early 1990s are being implemented in the Bush government in the 'war on terrorism' of the early 2000s.

The corporate world is hand in glove with government in the USA, and increasingly so in the UK. The Blair government stands for the corporate take-over of many functions that have hitherto been the concern of the state. George Monbiot's book *Captive state: The corporate takeover of Britain* (Macmillan, 2000) documents the many ways in which corporate power determines national and local government policy in countless fields, including agriculture, energy, the environment, urban planning, the health system, university research, and general education.

The pattern is familiar from the USA, where, for instance, schooling is 'a commodity, widely traded on the stock market, and worth around $650bn'.[43] Corporations are now the main providers of educational materials in North American schools: 'oil and chemical companies have been particularly generous in providing materials to explain nature to young people . . . a generation of American youngsters is trained to regard nature in a way that coincides with corporate objectives'.[44] According to the US Consumers' Union, nearly 80 per cent of the sponsored teaching packs distributed to American schools by some of the biggest corporations 'contain biased or incomplete information, promoting a viewpoint that favours consumption of the sponsor's product or service'.[45] The usual culprits include Procter and Gamble, Kelloggs, and the Mobil Corporation.

According to the European Round Table of Industrialists, 'The provision of education is a market opportunity and should be treated as such'; British schools now have educational material provided by Cadbury's, British Nuclear Fuels, McDonald's et al.[46] Moreover, the running of schools is increasingly in the hands of corporations. The London Borough of Lambeth's Education Action Zone is run not by the local authority but by Shell. Likewise, British Aerospace, ICI, Tesco et al. are all deeply involved in school management, as are such pillars of the special relationship between Britain and the USA as Kelloggs and McDonald's.[47]

At universities the same pattern is evolving. Corporations increasingly influence research and teaching agendas, which may compromise the independence of universities. Two independent researchers have examined the influence of oil companies on British universities.[48] They identified nearly 1000 research projects being conducted for oil and gas firms, some faculties as largely dependent on industrial money, and five times as much money being spent on research into oil and gas as on renewable energy – in other words, an inverse relationship between research needs and research funds. There are many university posts baptized with a corporate name. Some are more personal, such as the Rupert Murdoch Chair of Language and Communication at Oxford University. Vice-Chancellors are company directors; government funding, policy, and monitoring bodies are dominated by business executives.[49] Public service television and radio is under intense commercial pressure. We are now in a position where the *public* interest is guaranteed by the *private* sector, whose primary commitment is to their shareholders, whether their business is oil, entertainment, or education.

The English language itself is a significant product, which is, according to the British Council, second in importance to the British economy after North Sea oil. The British Council's homepage refers to the 'English language industry' of language schools, publishers, universities, and ancillary services.[50]

The 'Blair Initiative', announced on 18 June 1999, aims at increasing Britain's share of the global market in foreign students substantially. The massive expansion of British, American, and Australian universities into distance education, initially in such fields as accounting and business administration, is a related development. Universities must produce the post-colonial, post-national global citizens who are competent to work in English for transnational corporations, finance houses, and international bureaucracies. In 2001, the number of foreign students in the UK was 220,000, of whom 132,000 were Europeans; 563,000 foreigners attend language schools in Britain each year, one of the British Council's functions being to service this industry and promote quality.[51] The income generated in education and language services is estimated at 13 billion euros.[52]

The trend of using English as the teaching medium at continental universities can be seen in almost all scientific areas.[53] It often applies only to single courses, and occasionally to a whole degree, the aim being to attract foreign students. The trend towards an entire degree being taught in English is most visible in business schools. English is being introduced currently alongside the local language, Danish, Dutch, or French, but a shift to English only is possible.[54] In Norway, a draft new higher education law has omitted the sentence that was present in the old law, 'The language of instruction at Norwegian universities and higher education institutions is usually Norwegian', for undisclosed reasons.[55] What the implications are for local languages is unclear. The corporate world is well aware of the need for multilingualism, while entrenching the position of English in-house. Uncertainty about the implications of these trends confirms the need for more coordinated and explicit language policy formation.

The export of English is market-driven, as it always has been. In November 2000 the then British minister for Education and Employment, David Blunkett, echoed official statements of the previous fifty years when stating: 'It makes good economic sense to use English fluency as a platform to underpin our economic competitiveness and to promote our culture overseas.'[56]

The interlocking of education, English, and corporate interest applies globally as well as locally. In post-communist states, business and education have been up for international grabs. The British Council network, the English Language Teaching Contacts Scheme (ELTeCS), provides support for teachers of English through the export of British know-how and ELT products. The British Petroleum corporation (now merged as BP Amoco) is funding a 'Science across Europe' scheme which is being marketed in tandem with the British Council in the education systems of many countries (12 by June 2001) in central, eastern, and south-eastern Europe. The webpage is funded by the pharmaceutical giant SmithKlineGlaxo.[57]

The Shell corporation is funding a project to upgrade 'English language education specialists' in Bulgaria, which is expanding into an English across the curriculum scheme, particularly in the natural sciences.

All this may be professionally stimulating for those concerned, people who often teach in frugal conditions, and I would not wish to suggest that such activities are valueless – quite the opposite. It is perfectly logical that there is a popular demand for a language that can be seen to open doors. But such schemes are obviously not ideologically innocent. The motivation of neither the oil and pharmaceutical industries nor the ELT business is purely altruistic. If 'the business of America is business', as President Calvin Coolidge put it in 1925, manifestly English for business is business for English. And part of the business of americanization is englishization.

The Transatlantic Business Dialogue, which brings together American and European corporations, dovetails with the G8 and related heads of state networks, confirming the meshing of state and corporate structure. There are plans for a single market incorporating Europe and North America, a Transatlantic Economic Partnership, which will develop 'a worldwide network of bilateral agreements with identical conformity procedures', these developments being summed up by Monbiot:[58]

> Before long . . . only a minority of nations will lie outside a single, legally harmonized global market, and they will swiftly find themselves obliged to join. By the time a new world trade agreement has been negotiated, it will be irrelevant, for the

WTO's job will already have been done. Nowhere on earth will robust laws protecting the environment or human rights be allowed to survive. Elected representatives will, if these plans for a new world order succeed, be reduced to the agents of a global government: built, coordinated and run by corporate chief executives.

If this trend continues, with the commercial world setting the pace, and with the encroachment of English into countless spheres of public and private life, it is arguable that all European languages other than English may be on a fast track towards second-class status.

One might think that this is inconceivable in the case of languages that have served all purposes in a state for centuries, such as Dutch or German, when the state continues to operate in this language, and when the EU is in principle committed to maintaining the vitality and equality of the eleven official languages. However, it is probable that the only EU country where the issues have been analysed thoroughly by the government, so as to document current trends and anticipate their impact, is Sweden.[59]

The status quo may soon be shattered by a challenge from transnational corporations that would like the EU to implement an English-only policy. A recent doctoral study in international law, summarized in an American law journal, analyses the regulations governing language use at the supranational EU level. It concludes that French language protection measures (the Loi Toubon) represent national protectionism that is in conflict with EU law, the Maastricht Treaty, and the principles of a common market with the free movement of goods, services, labour, and capital.[60] The author boldly recommends that adopting a single language would serve 'to unify, rather than divide, Member States'. Corporate lawyers may therefore soon choose to challenge national language legislation on precisely these grounds. Language protectionist measures could be seen as trade barriers that interfere with the workings of the market. Marketing solely in English, except where there are safety issues involved, could be the next logical step in unifying the market.

Whether this interpretation would hold, if a case were taken to the European Court of Justice, is an open question. Some case law (see the examples quoted in Chapter 5), and the Charter of Rights agreed on in Nice in 2000 (though this is not yet legally binding), would argue against it. The court has shown a tendency to be autonomous and create law through its decisions, just as national courts do. The legal issue is complicated by uncertainty about the relationship between EU treaties, World Trade Organization principles, and existing case law from the European Court of Justice.

It is also unthinkable that the governments of EU member states are reckoning on writing off their languages in this way. They are currently committed to national languages, and to a system of functioning multilingualism in EU institutions. Whether the present arrangements can withstand the pressures of globalization remains to be seen, and will depend not only on what the future of languages is in commerce but in many other domains. One essential domain to consider is science.

Trends in science

There has been lively communication between scientists across Europe since the seventeenth century. They saw themselves as searching for universal truths, irrespective of mother tongue and national origin. They therefore tended to be multilingual. A reading competence in several languages was also expected of scientists in North America until well into the twentieth century.[61] This has progressively changed, as science has become more institutionalized, and English has become the globally dominant language of science. The question then is whether the pre-eminence of English in the scientific world is occurring at the expense of other languages of scholarship, existing or potential, and whether a single privileged language, along with the paradigms associated with it, represents a threat to other ways of thinking and their expression. This is a major issue for the contemporary scientific world, one that native speakers of English have quite probably not given much thought to. English may be functioning as a scientific Tyrannosaurus Rex.[62] If scholarship is constrained within a single language, there is a risk of knowledge being monopolized and creativity stifled, according to French scholars, who challenge the notion that there should be a single scientific lingua franca.[63]

A century ago, German was the dominant language of the natural sciences and medicine. The present-day obligation to publish or perish in English is such that some scholars in Germany and Austria are concerned about the marginalization of their language, and the unfairness of a system that permits some to function in their mother tongue, whereas others have to use a foreign language. If work is published only in German, it runs the risk of being ignored by the international scholarly community, which increasingly functions exclusively in English, uses approaches favoured in the Anglo-American world, and is serviced by 'international' journals whose editors tend to be nationals of the USA and the UK.

Scholars in Scandinavia have also expressed concern that a hierarchical division of labour between English and Scandinavian languages is evolving. In 2001 the Nordic Council of Ministers commissioned surveys of whether each Nordic language is suffering attrition because of English taking over territory that was occupied earlier by the national language. For each language a survey was conducted of whether 'domain loss' was occurring, i.e. a study of whether the national language is losing out to English in the key domains of school and education, science, business, civil administration and the EU, culture, and consumer affairs and private life.

The studies were produced to a tight schedule, but provide documentation of trends that have been little studied earlier. The provisional results show that the more recently consolidated Nordic languages, Faroese, Greenlandic, and Saami, are extending their range, and are recovering from their earlier exclusion from many domains. The well-established languages, Danish, Finnish, Norwegian, and Swedish, are definitely vulnerable in the domain of scientific publications. This is especially the case in the natural sciences, medicine, and technology, where nearly all scholarly articles and books are written in English.[64] There is concern that scholars working in English are unable to communicate their professional expertise in the mother tongue, and that the language itself is atrophying in particular areas, rather than continuing to develop and adjust. Action is needed to remedy this state of affairs, because any information for the general public in a democratic society has to be made available in a local language.

No-one is suggesting that scholars should drop English, or that English should not be used in networks dealing with highly specialized topics that are studied by only a few scholars worldwide. However, the pressures to publish 'internationally' rather than locally are intense, and are seen as applicable to all scholars. This can lead to a neglect of local or national topics. It can also lead to a false sense of priorities when posts are filled, if writing for an 'international' journal is assumed to imply better quality than in a national one. In Norway, a system of performance pay for university staff was introduced in the 1990s, as a result of which there is a cash bonus for each scientific publication. A book written in an 'international language', which almost invariably means English, triggers a bonus of 15,000 crowns, whereas one in Norwegian gets a mere 7000. An article in English in a refereed journal is rewarded by a bonus of 7000 crowns, one in Norwegian 1000.[65]

This is grossly unfair to scholars in the social sciences and humanities, whose concerns are often necessarily anchored in local languages and cultures.

The exclusive focus on writing in English, reinforced in the demographically small European countries by the use of textbooks from the English-speaking world, also has the effect of reducing the use of French, German, and other scholarly languages. The status of many of the scientific languages of Europe is explored in a substantial collection of papers, *The dominance of English as a language of science. Effects on other languages and language communities*, edited by Ulrich Ammon.[66] Some of the main cross-cutting themes include the following:

* The use of English in research publications and in university teaching is expanding almost everywhere. In some subjects, typically the natural sciences, technology, and medicine, it is the norm except in French- and Russian-speaking areas. A linguistic division of labour, with English for specialist scholarship and the local language for popularization, is by some seen as a problem (e.g. in Spain and Sweden), by others as no problem at all (in Belgium and German-speaking Switzerland), or as a matter for the reader to decide (by the contributor from Hungary).

* Attitudes to the dominance of English vary considerably. Some assume that a single global language of science is all to the good, others bewail the marginalization of other languages of science, and the cultural, political, and economic knock-on effects. The use of German and French internationally is diminishing. Russian is likely to suffer the same fate, as Russian scholars become more competent in English.

* Legislation to counteract the invasion of English (as in France) can facilitate a symbiosis between the local language and English as scientific languages, but few governments appear to have explicit language maintenance policies other than traditional national ones that predate globalization (e.g. Austria, Germany).

* Proficiency in English has improved radically in some countries (Hungary, Finland, Russia), but possibly not in others (Austria, Belgium, France, Germany). These differences may correlate with the degree of use of English as a medium of education, or at least the extensive use of textbooks, in some cases beginning at undergraduate level, some not until doctoral level.

* The advance of English involves opening up to freedom of information (Russia, Hungary), and has led to a greater acceptance of

americanization (France), but there is no simple correlation between English as an international language of science and English as a national language.

- The status of English as the benchmarking medium for scientific activity leads to the writing of scholars in other languages being ignored. Thus two Americans, Charles Ferguson and Joshua Fishman, are often credited with being pioneers in establishing the study of diglossia and the sociology of language, but there were significant predecessors on precisely these topics who wrote in French, whose writings are ignored.[67]

It is worth singling out the study of Finland, by Harald Haarman and Eugene Holman, since it reports on productive multilingualism in operation. OECD statistics show that Finland has devoted a higher proportion of gross national product to research and development work than all other EU countries except Sweden.[68] Finland has a history of scholarly multilingualism and openness to intercultural contact, one likely result of the country having been colonized for 650 years. Finland now contributes to global technical standards and innovation, especially in telecommunications, and is a pioneer network society. Finnish schoolchildren perform outstandingly well in OECD comparisons of competence in reading, mathematics, and the natural sciences. Education is provided through the medium of the mother tongue from start to finish of formal education, with foreign languages taught by well-qualified, bilingual teachers. Finland's educational and economic success story builds on a healthy balance between several local languages (e.g. doctoral dissertations are written in Finnish or Swedish, and Vuokko Hirvonen has written the first in an indigenous language, Saami). Major use is made of English domestically and externally (doctoral dissertations are predominantly in English in some fields, primarily in Finnish in others, a few are in French or German). One conclusion, for which Manuel Castells is cited, is that 'technological modernization in Finland is evolving within the framework of high standards of living, whereas in the USA, modernization is intensifying at the cost of the quality of life'. The article permits optimistic generalizations about how a demographically small country can strike a balance between the maintenance of strong local cultural and linguistic values, and being an active participant in, and contributor to, globalization.

Efforts are being made to persuade national governments and the EU to take a more active role in ensuring the bilingualism or multilingualism of scholars. Scholars from German-speaking countries are advocating a number of measures that would contribute to a more equitable scholarly world (see Appendix 5).[69] This could be achieved through:

- funding for multilingual abstracting services and journals,
- programmes of multilingual teaching,
- the translation of academic publications,
- basing the evaluation of academic achievements not by giving preference to publications in an international lingua franca but by rewarding multilingualism,
- promoting multilingual discourse communities, for instance by ensuring that participants at a conference or seminar can understand more than one language,
- the provision of training programmes for young academics that facilitate these goals.

There is in fact already a good deal of coordination at the European level. European education systems vary a great deal in their structure and funding,[70] but are all strongly influenced by the OECD, which has long been evaluating education, advocating a Europe-wide system of higher education, a focus on education for the economy (the production of human capital), and an increased use of English.[71]

The European Science Foundation has been fostering collaboration and coordination throughout Europe for more than two decades. It describes itself as

a catalyst for the development of science by bringing together leading scientists and funding agencies to debate, plan and implement pan-European scientific and science policy initiatives.

ESF is the association of 67 major national funding agencies devoted to scientific research in 24 countries. It represents all scientific disciplines: physical and engineering sciences, life and environmental sciences, medical sciences, humanities and social sciences. The Foundation assists its Member Organisations in two ways: by bringing scientists together in its scientific programmes, EUROCORES, forward looks, networks and European research conferences, to work on topics of common concern; and through the joint study of issues of strategic importance in European science policy.[72]

Among recent policy issues explored by the ESF are ethical dimensions of medical research, the use of Genetically Modified Organisms, especially in foods, and principles of good scientific practice. These are unquestionably of universal relevance, touching on the principle of research as the independent search for knowledge, and the role of the state or of private corporations in funding research.

The longer-term goals of unifying science throughout Europe are being formulated in a series of policy documents initiated by the EU Commission, which proposes, by means of the Sixth Framework Programme for Research (2002–2006), to establish a 'European Research Area'. This builds on the Bologna Declaration of European Ministers of Education, 19 June 1999. This was signed by representatives of all EU member states, Norway and Switzerland, and ten states that are applying for membership of the EU (Bulgaria, Czech Republic, Estonia, Hungary, Latvia, Lithuania, Malta, Romania, Slovenia, Slovakia). It commits these states to establishing a 'more complete and far-reaching Europe, in particular building upon and strengthening its intellectual, cultural, social, and scientific and technological dimensions'. It refers to a 'Europe of Knowledge', a 'European area of higher education'. It seeks to intensify cooperation in university teaching and research so as to ensure that Europe is at the forefront of scientific developments and can attract foreign students, who predominantly choose the USA. A number of practical measures relating to degree structure, mobility, and quality assurance are recommended, all of which are expected to be undertaken with 'full respect of the diversity of cultures, languages, national education systems and of University autonomy'.

The follow-up meeting, the Prague Summit of European Education Ministers in 2001, also pledges a commitment to a 'European Higher Education Area'. The means to achieve this involve seed money from the ESF and the EU to create large transcontinental research institutions and programmes. It is particularly in technology and the natural and computer sciences that this is seen as being necessary. By contrast, one of the first three programmes established by the ESF to launch EUROCOREs (ESF Collaborative Research Programmes) is on the origin of languages.[73]

A joint statement by the ESF, All European Academies (ALLEA), and the European University Association, sent to the European Council of Research Ministers on 26 June 2001,[74] while endorsing the overall goals of the new Framework Programme, stresses the importance of building on innovative research environments of whatever size, and reiterates the importance of fully integrating the Humanities and Social Sciences in the new Framework Programme. The European Research Area takes shape in the context of European cultures and societies, and the contribution of these disciplines is needed in other areas to fully understand multi-culturalism and multi-lingualism in Europe. They are needed to address cultural identity, diversity and integration in Europe and the challenges, concerns and fears aroused by scientific and technological developments.

Hubert Markl, the President of the Max Planck Society, which currently operates 79 research institutes, foresees the establishment of a 'European Intellectual Area', which should embrace all countries that see themselves as European.[75] He sees the need not merely to formulate research needs in terms of how international funding might facilitate what would have been done nationally in any case, but in broader, global terms. He wishes to build on the cultural diversity that has brought Europeans together over centuries. Funds for attachment to a foreign research centre for periods of longer than a single year are likely to create better conditions for learning the language of the local culture rather than muddling along in English, and all European cultures have much to offer, not only the 'big' countries.

These views, like the statement of the senior university personnel and the ESF, seem to indicate that there is concern that the 'one size fits all' model for higher education in Europe, with a uniform BA, MA, and PhD structure (the goal of the Bologna process), combined with funds mainly being available for collaboration in the natural sciences and technology, runs the risk of turning into 'one culture fits all' or even 'one language fits all'. This would involve sacrificing Europe's cultural heritage and the dynamic ongoing processes of adjustment to the changes, positive and negative, brought by globalization. It would bring about a European Higher Education and Research Area confined to the natural sciences and technology, and operational only in English.

Sounding warning bells about the loss of cultural values may sound like cultural romanticism, but the wish to create conditions in which all languages can thrive has nothing to do with chauvinist nationalism. It is a question of building on the substantial resources embedded in the diverse cultures of Europe, and the blessings of Babel, so as to counteract linguistic and cultural homogenization. English itself does not represent a threat to the other scientific languages of Europe. The primary language policy issue is whether other languages are also being effectively nurtured and promoted (as in the case of Finland and the wishes of German speakers), so that there is a culturally sound balance between an increased use of English and thriving local languages.

Trends in culture

Concern about domain loss is in essence a worry about cultural vitality. Replacing the national language by a foreign language also has to do with social justice. Danes are bombarded with ads in the cinema and on commercial television in which only English is used, although a substantial proportion of the population, particularly among those over the age of fifty, has no competence in English.[76] This shows one of the dangers of *laissez faire* at the national level.

A second consequence of the absence of an explicit policy, as in the Danish case, is that a vast amount of Hollywood entertainment is screened on television, both public service and private, and a smaller amount from Britain, but no effort is made to ensure that there is a regular flow of films from elsewhere in Europe. Satellite TV enlarges the range of what is accessible, to those with a dish or cable TV, but this too follows the law of the market rather than reflecting a national policy. On Danish national TV, films are shown with the original soundtrack. This has two consequences. First, Danes are exposed to a large amount of English spoken in an immense range of ways, and this facilitates the learning of English. Second, reading sub-titles in Danish is the most widely practised literacy activity in the country. The combination of English sound and Danish visual text makes for a powerful bilingual experience. Its importance needs to be related to the fact that functional illiteracy (inability to use the written language) is widespread among adults even in 'advanced' societies like Denmark.[77]

What is happening in Denmark is typical of cultural globalization, through which a diverse cultural landscape is being subjected to the commercial and consumerist pressures of large, privately owned media corporations. Television viewing with bilingual input (spoken English, written Danish) is a form of linguistic hybridization.

This can also be seen on the internet sites of SAS, Scandinavian Airlines Systems. A vast amount of information is provided in English, and only a limited amount in Danish, Norwegian and Swedish (each on the respective national websites).[78] One might feel that Nordic citizens should be able to access all information in their own language from an airline that has the governments of Denmark, Norway, and Sweden as significant shareholders in the company, which was established to serve national and Nordic interests. Website policy involves a compromise: English is used for the global market, and for local customers who are proficient in English. Local languages are used for particular local marketing campaigns. For some services, including booking by internet, proficiency in English is in fact required, which discriminates against some Scandinavians. Policy reflects a balance between using limited resources for providing and updating the website, and sensitivity to customer feedback on the quality of the services. In the internal affairs of the company, the three Scandinavian languages are widely used, in speech and in writing, and English occasionally. Many international activities require this. The brand slogan 'It's Scandinavian' (what the advertisers call the strapline), on CNN or in the *Financial Times,* has to be in English. Within Scandinavia, 'It's Scandinavian' means using both English and Scandinavian languages.[79]

Domain loss is symptomatic of cultural change and innovation. The internet is possibly the most significant innovation in the use of the written language since the invention of print. Its use has expanded massively for both large and small languages. By early 2000 there were discussion groups in over 100 languages on the net.[80] It is far more economical to publish in several languages on the internet than in print. The net facilitates networking in languages that do not have the advantage of a large commercial market. This technology means that the dissemination of information is no longer a zero-sum game, either language X or language Y. Large numbers of Europeans can access newspapers and information in many languages rather than in just one, and engage in interaction in virtually any language of their choice.

On the other hand development of the necessary software for language technology, for information retrieval, for machine translation or translation support, search instruments in databases, and dictionaries, requires major investment. The EU has invested in language technology for its own services, initially following a principle that an equal amount should go to each language.[81] However, this principle no longer holds, and market forces mean that investment in language technology has primarily been made in the 'large' languages, which therefore benefit from better facilities and software. The Nordic countries are therefore coordinating efforts in research and development in this field in order to ensure that the Nordic languages remain at the forefront of information technology.[82] Language technology is a *sine qua non* in modern administration, private and public, and therefore a key factor in the vitality of languages.

While a lot of the uptake of English occurs as a result of top-down pressures in professional life, education, and the workplace, sub-cultural use of English in such fields as popular music, dance, sport, or computers reflects bottom-up processes of identification with particular activities, and shared interests that have their own momentum, though they may be connected to consumerism that is corporate-driven.[83] Part of the explanation for the strength of the popularity of English is this synergy between top-down and bottom-up processes. The promotion of other languages can only rarely tap into these psychological needs and wishes (listed in Table 1 under the category of ideological factors accounting for the expansion of English).

German has not since 1945 been able to draw on a comparable appeal, even though Germany has for centuries had a major influence throughout Europe, and is a hugely important market for exports from its neighbours in The Netherlands and Denmark. For many small and medium-size companies, German is in fact more important than English. Large companies in each country generally have subsidiaries in the other. It would therefore make sense for the learning of German to be a major national priority in neighbouring countries. One would expect that understanding of the culture of the German-speaking peoples would be well established at all levels of education. To communicate appropriately involves much more than the trivial chat that characterizes many 'communicative' teaching methods, and in which 'Pupils order meals they are not going to eat, plan journeys they are not going to make and hear about people they are never going to meet'.[84] Making intelligent sense of a newspaper in Berlin presupposes far more than routine formulae for restricted commercial or social ends. Doing good business presupposes sensitive insight into a different way of acting and speaking. What is therefore needed as a learning goal is a *lingua cultura* rather than a crude *lingua franca*.[85]

Most foreign language teaching in Europe aims at situating the learning of a language within its cultural contexts, so that one learns Italian in order to understand Italian culture, and how people think and behave in Italy, and in this way aims also at becoming reflective about one's own culture. But in Denmark, although German is available as a subject in schools from roughly age 13 onwards, it is seldom learned for many years, or to very high levels of competence. Recruitment of students specializing in the language in higher education is very low. In fact in Denmark, and possibly in several EU countries, recruitment is low for all languages other than English.

Many factors account for the limited appeal of German in Denmark:[86]

- media coverage of Germany totally fails to reflect its political importance, the richness of the cultural life of the society, and its tourist attractions, projecting little other than a stereotypical world of political scandal, racist violence, and secret police archives under communism;

- Danish attitudes are ambivalent, as Danes lived under German occupation during the Second World War, but Germans are very welcome as tourists, and the history of the war that younger Danes have been brought up on has tended to focus on a myth of heroic resistance, whereas the reality was much muddier, with a fair measure of collaboration;

- although German has been learned as a foreign language for 1200 years,[87] and has been an important language in Denmark historically, and is still spoken in the bilingual border region, it is perceived as being a difficult language because of its grammatical structure – whereas in fact Danish and German are so close typologically (word roots, pronunciation, many features of grammar) that there is a smaller learning task than for most languages;

- the German government since 1945 has been concerned to establish its democratic credentials and refrain from any promotion of the German language that could recall Nazi ideology, which attributed almost mystical properties to the language.

The promotion of culture and language abroad has long been an instrument of the cultural diplomacy of nation-states, beginning with the establishment of the Alliance Française in 1883 with a mandate to maintain the international influence of France by promoting its language. The para-statal organizations entrusted with this work, in which language teaching plays a central role, are named after august nationals of international fame (Goethe, Cervantes, Dante) or more nationalistically (the British Council). Their activities aim at creating goodwill, by providing a stimulating injection into the cultural life and education systems that they assist, and are directly or indirectly connected to influence and commerce. In former colonies, the French and British have much more influence on the host country, particularly in educational language policy, although it is now primarily the World Bank that is responsible for shaping education to conform to a globalization agenda.[88]

Government-funded cultural promotional activity is in the realm of 'high culture', as is the EU activity programme 'Culture 2000' (covering the period 2000–2004), which relates to history, cultural heritage, artistic and literary creation, European Capitals of Culture, and numerous cultural topics. The action does not refer to languages, though clearly the assumption is that local languages are used.[89] This action, in programmes named KALEIDOSCOPE, ARIANE, and RAPHAEL, also aims at 'strengthening the feeling of belonging to the European Union, while respecting the diversity of national and regional traditions and cultures'. Policy has been strongly influenced by efforts by the French government to direct EU funds into strengthening European cultural industries, whereas their partners have been more reluctant to intervene in the workings of the market.

The right of the Commission to negotiate on behalf of the EU on all aspects of the common commercial policy explicitly covers trade in services and the commercial aspects of intellectual property rights, which are becoming increasingly important in world trade. There are complicated EU rules that dictate whether unanimity between the member states is required, or qualified majority voting, which is becoming the norm in most fields. But on the insistence of France, which is determined to shield its national and cultural heritage as far as possible from the forces of globalization, a change was introduced in the Nice Treaty of 2000. 'Article 133(6) now provides that a whole set of agreements, namely those relating to trade in cultural and audio-visual services, educational services, and social and human health services, can only be negotiated jointly by the European Commission and the Member States acting by common consent ("mixed agreement"). They also require unanimity in the Council.'[90]

The task of bringing European cultures together is also the mission of the European Cultural Foundation, which is based in Amsterdam, and receives funds from the Dutch lottery. Its goal is 'to promote cultural and educational activities and research of a multinational nature and European character . . . committed to the importance of the cultural dimension within the process of a wider European integration . . . a sense of belonging for all its people'.[91] In 1998 it brought academics, Members of the European Parliament, and people working in the translation and interpretation services of the EU together for a conference on language policies in the EU. The gathering was convened on the explicit understanding that a set of working parties would be established to devise strategies for language policy in several key domains of civil and political life. At the conference itself, it transpired that this goal was too politically sensitive, and nothing emerged apart from a conference report.[92] The timing was perhaps unfortunate. The conference was held shortly before elections to the European Parliament, at a point when the Commission headed by Jacques Santer was about to resign because of widespread evidence of corruption and incompetence. The upshot is that language policy continues along familiar but often obscure lines.

It is difficult to assess how much impact EU culture policies that are restricted to high culture will have, but they are modest in scale. Likewise, the budget for the European Year of Languages, 6 million euros, was minuscule as compared to funds for regional development or agriculture. Many of the ongoing cultural changes in Europe are due to americanization at all levels of culture. Europe is experiencing cultural homogenization through countless processes in the media, advertising, patterns of consumption, and trends in commerce, science, education, and defence. Governments have difficulty in influencing these, which is why action at the supranational EU level is potentially important.

The forces behind globalization and americanization are challenging all national cultures and languages. Simultaneously, these languages are yielding to pressure to grant more rights to minority languages. Despite the vast pressures that minority languages have been subjected to by states that sought to monopolize linguistic power, whether republican France, fascist Spain, monarchic Britain, military Greece, or communist Estonia, minority languages have survived. They are increasingly recognized as being entitled to use in all key domains, without this representing a threat to the nation-state. This is the spirit in which the Council of Europe's Charter for Regional or Minority Languages operates. It had been signed and ratified by enough member states for it to come into effect in 1998. Several European states that have been reluctant to concede that there are linguistic minorities within their borders, France and Greece in particular, are bowing to international pressure for greater language rights. The Charter is a good example of international collaboration resulting in a higher profile for language policy issues.

The European Parliament has passed a series of resolutions in favour of the maintenance of linguistic diversity. On 13 December 2001 it adopted a Resolution on Regional and European Lesser-Used Languages.[93] The resolution considers that the EU has a duty to support the member and applicant countries in developing their cultures and protecting linguistic diversity within their borders. It allocated one million euros for safeguarding regional and lesser-used languages, dialects and cultures. Even this token sum is worth being grateful for.

Trends in education

Trends in globalization in the field of education that impact on language policy in Europe are connected to trends in commerce, science, and culture. Considering education as a market opportunity is probably not a widespread conviction in Europe except in the upper strata of the corporate world. State education systems have been a key national domain, central to the formation of nations and the consolidation of national languages.

The internationalization of education that the EU strengthens in a range of actions (named to evoke towering European figures such as ERASMUS, LEONARDO DA VINCI, and SOCRATES, or, more functionally, LINGUA[94]) does not change the status quo in national education systems, except for ensuring a small measure of diversity in student intake, and often an increased use of English. EU actions provide funding for the mobility of students (and to a lesser extent staff and researchers), so that they can experience a second culture and language first-hand. The EU's efforts can also be seen as contributing to europeanization in the sense of a strengthening of European identity, both at the level of personal cultural experience and in relation to a supranational institution, the EU Commission, that is in a position to dispense largesse. That they do so in a fashion that is experienced as bureaucratic, frustrating, and time-wasting is another story.

The numbers involved are impressive, except when seen in relation to the total number of students in secondary or higher education. From 1994/5 to 1999/2000, the number of French university students benefiting from a SOCRATES/ERASMUS exchange increased from 10,000 to nearly 17,000. There was a comparable increase for Germany and Spain, whereas the figure for British students fell from 12,000 to 10,000, a symptom of British students not seeing the same need as continental European students to diversify their linguistic and cultural competence.[95]

Attracting foreign students in higher education has long been a goal of countries with a language that is widely learned as a foreign language, particularly English, French, and German, a process that began during the time of colonial empires. The pressure to make money out of this operation is a symptom of modern universities being expected to operate in an increasingly entrepreneurial fashion, and become more self-funding. This trend, already well established in North America, involves a new identity for the academic: 'A professor's ability to attract private investment is now often more important than academic qualifications or teaching ability.'[96] Hefty personal bonuses for qualities of this kind are now awarded at some Danish universities.

English is privileged in the competitive market for foreign students mainly because the language is so widely learned as a foreign language. Its outdistancing of French and German started in the 1950s and has accelerated since. This strengthening of English as an international language reflects the 'American century' but is also, paradoxically, a result of major investment by France, Germany and the rest of continental Europe in the teaching of English. It is also paradoxical when americanization is seen as a threat to local cultural and linguistic values, a position that has been most strongly articulated by the French, though less energetically in recent years.

There are commercial pressures that derive from membership of the World Trade Organization. One goal of the WTO, according to the US government, is to 'liberalize trade in educational services (higher and adult education, and training services), . . . to contribute to the global spread of the modern "knowledge" economy . . . and eliminate obstacles that make it difficult for foreign suppliers to market their services'.[97] Similar representations to the WTO have been made by Australia and New Zealand,[98] also countries that offer English-medium instruction. The three countries carefully avoid giving the impression that providers of 'international' educational services will barge in on national basic education, though this is now the norm for private educational services in North America. In the case of Canada, a direct consequence of NAFTA and WTO rules is that US corporations now have more influence over professional teaching standards than does the Canadian government, to the point where the corporate agenda, driven by an economic rationale, is essentially attacking the 'history, culture, and values' of Canada.[99]

Exams administered from Great Britain, in English and with British content, are held worldwide. The University of Cambridge Local Examinations Syndicate is the second largest examination organization, after Educational Testing Services of Princeton, New Jersey. In 1996 it organized exams in 154 countries.[100]

There is therefore already a substantial global 'trade in educational services', by means of which the role of the English language is strengthened at all levels of education. The logic of the market, promoted by the OECD and serviced by the WTO, means that continental Europe is likely to be increasingly at the receiving end of this US corporate thrust, beginning with higher, adult, and further education. The activities of the EU, in either facilitating or resisting this trend, are therefore of vital importance.

In EU policy papers, the promotion of the 'knowledge economy', the 'learning society', and educational flexibility for changing economic needs figures prominently, in particular in the 1995 White Paper on Education and Training, *Teaching and learning: towards the learning society*.[101] One goal of this was to bring school and the business sector together, so as to ensure that education can equip the European economy to compete successfully with the USA, Japan, and China. Other proposals, for vocational education, contact between member states, and strengthening of the learning of each other's languages, are designed to strengthen feelings of being European, and 'in this way Europe will prove that it is not only a free trade area, but an organised political entity, and a way of coming successfully to terms with, rather than being subject to, internationalization'.[102] Europeanization is seen here as a local variant of globalization.

The section on 'Proficiency in three community languages'[103] cites a set of valid cognitive and intercultural reasons for learning foreign languages, and states boldly: 'Multilingualism is part and parcel of both European identity/citizenship and the learning society.' Both claims are normative, in the same sense as globalization is. Multilingualism and the learning society are projects and future goals rather than anything that has ever existed in Europe. The White Paper is in fact clearly attempting to create or 'imagine' Europe. The cultures in focus are essentially those of partner EU countries and those that European languages give access to internationally, particularly the USA.

Foreign languages are studied for a variety of educational, cultural, and practical purposes. The foreign languages chosen to replace Latin on school timetables were primarily languages of major international influence. English Departments in Germany tend to be called 'Institut für Anglistik und Amerikanistik', a clear signal that the English language is studied in relation to the UK and the USA. English as it is used in many parts of the world is now firmly established as part of the identity of the subject 'English', to the point where there are books and journals concerned with the English languages.[104]

An important factor accounting for the relative success of English teaching in several parts of Europe is the fact that there is so much exposure to English outside school. English is becoming progressively less 'foreign' in continental Europe, in that the language is not only learned for use abroad or literary purposes. English has several internal functions in such countries:

- it is an obligatory or central school subject;
- competence in English is a requirement for continuing into higher and further education. In the demographically small European countries, textbooks in English are widely used in higher education in virtually all subjects;
- proficiency in English is required for many types of employment;
- there is considerable exposure to English in the media, pop culture, public and private life.

In such countries, there are good grounds for referring to English as a *second* language rather than a foreign language.[105] This is increasingly done in The Netherlands and Scandinavia.

One of the potential purposes of foreign language learning is to lead to people being more tolerant of other cultures (or at least of some of them), less ethnocentric, and less prejudiced. Among the hopes formulated by the European Parliament, on 17 July 2000, when declaring the year 2001 as the European Year of Languages, is the conviction: 'It is important to learn languages, as they can lead to an increased awareness of cultural diversity, and can contribute to the eradication of xenophobia, racism, anti-semitism and intolerance.' There is, alas, no guarantee that conventional foreign language teaching reduces prejudice. If attitudes to foreign languages in society at large are not supportive, and if the languages are not seen as enhancing career prospects, the necessary motivation may not be present.

An alternative to the learning of specific languages is the subject 'Language awareness' (French: *l'éveil aux langues*), which has been advocated for several decades, and has recently been effectively instituted in Switzerland and France. The idea is to develop language skills, and knowledge about languages, in relation to a whole range of languages and cultures, for instance those present in a linguistically diverse local community. Experience of this kind should trigger positive attitudes to other languages and cultures, promote competence in the mother tongue and the analysis of communication, and some familiarity with the structure of other languages, and ultimately democratic, well-informed, and critical citizens. Initial experience in 50 schools in France, with normal rather than specially selected classes, indicates that language awareness produces good results, particularly on the attitudinal side.[106]

In Britain the misplaced belief that English can open all doors worldwide is leading to a failure to equip British citizens to function in a multilingual world. Among the findings of the Nuffield Languages

Enquiry of 2000, a major consultation exercise involving business, academics, and educational planners, is that:[107]

> English is not enough. We are fortunate to speak a global language but, in a smart and competitive world, exclusive reliance on English leaves the UK vulnerable and dependent on the linguistic competence and the goodwill of others . . . Young people from the UK are at a growing disadvantage in the recruitment market . . . The UK needs competence in many languages – not just French – but the education system is not geared to achieve this . . . The government has no coherent approach to languages.

In continental Europe, education systems are strongly geared towards learning English, along with substantially less investment in the learning of other foreign languages. It is difficult to generalize about trends, or levels of achievement, since the picture varies substantially from country to country, and there are multiple goals for foreign language teaching (see the categories used in Table 2, 'Social goals and language correlates', pages 102–103). There is a good deal of educational innovation, for instance several types of bilingual education.[108] Box 3.1 covers specific EU support activities. The Council of Europe has been instrumental in coordinating and disseminating a great deal of 'best practice' in foreign language learning from all over Europe. Like the EU, it also campaigns for diversification in the languages learned, and attempts to encourage the learning of less widely learned languages. It has also produced an impressive set of instruments that can assist governments and educational planners, such as the *Common European framework of reference for languages: Learning, teaching, assessment*,[109] the *European language portfolio*, and a guide for the development of language education policies in Europe.[110]

Box 3.1   EU support for foreign language learning

Commission funding, administered by the Directorate-General for Education and Culture, supports a number of actions:[111]
- innovative learning that merits a 'European quality label',
- early foreign language learning,
- content-based language learning, involving the integration of a subject such as geography or a science with a foreign language,[112]

- links, information-sharing,
- in-service and pre-service training,
- activities as part of the European Year of Languages, 2001.

These are drops in the ocean of foreign language learning in Europe, but tally with the goal of qualifying EU citizens for a mobile labour market, a wish to promote and disseminate best practice, and a hope that more intercultural understanding and europeanization will result.

The Language Policy Unit of this Directorate-General has commissioned research projects aimed at
- assessing an early start in foreign language learning,
- mapping out the training of foreign language teachers in several EU countries,
- charting the experience of the teaching of other subjects through the medium of a foreign language,
- the impact of the use of new information technologies and the internet on the teaching of foreign languages, and the role of teachers of a foreign language.[113]

One of the trends that the EU seeks to promote is *early foreign language learning*. This has been recommended in political circles for many years, even though there is a considerable body of evidence that indicates that a focus on the age factor alone will not produce success. The EU commissioned a study in 1997 of 'Foreign languages in primary and pre-school education: Context and outcomes. A review of recent research within the EU', conducted by scholars from five countries.[114] The recommendations relate to funding and infrastructure, parental involvement, continuity through the various levels of schooling, adequate time, teacher training, sensitivity to learners with different degrees of success, appropriate pedagogy for each age group, measures to ensure learning a diversity of languages, research to evaluate outcomes and relate these to contextual factors and pedagogy and means of arousing interest in languages, and guarantees that the minimal conditions for success are in place before innovation is attempted.

There are neurological aspects of language learning which suggest strongly that acquisition of perfect pronunciation of a foreign language, indistinguishable from that of native speakers, cannot be achieved after puberty. It is also an educational fact that if the number of hours devoted to learning a foreign language remains unchanged, but the total is merely spread over a larger number of years, there may well be no overall improvement in language competence from an early start. Foreign language learning is affected by overall cognitive and educational development, and therefore needs to be integrated into a policy that addresses linguistic competence *in toto*. It was therefore reassuring that the French Minister of Education, Jack Lang, when announcing that foreign languages would be taught throughout primary education by the year 2005, stated that 'Foreign languages will contribute in specific ways to learning the national language and literacy'.[115]

One EU-funded body that is attempting to contribute to the strengthening of language learning in Europe is the European Language Council.[116] It has stimulated liaison between a large number of universities, and contributed to projects in the areas of language testing,[117] interpreter training, and clarification of how universities might foster multilingualism in their own activities. However, it mainly depends on the efforts of individuals over and above their normal professional obligations, which is a cumbersome way of marshalling expertise. Such networking is not necessarily driven by the professionalism of well-established associations and research communities. Whether it will have any impact on institutions or language policy in general remains to be seen.

Two general conclusions can be drawn. These various schemes show the fragility of links and efforts at the supranational level. The amount of funding available is minute in comparison with what is invested nationally in schools and higher education infrastructure. There may well be a strong case for reform of foreign language teaching in many countries, but focus on a single factor, such as age or school exchanges, pales into insignificance when compared with fundamentals such as teacher competence and established national traditions.

If the massive investment in the teaching of English is to be
counterbalanced by real success in the learning of other languages, national education systems need to devise more
rigorous plans for ensuring a diversification of the languages
learned. Bodies such as the European Language Council, that
are in principle committed to multilingualism, function virtually
exclusively in English. This suggests that the europeanization
of education is comparable to the globalization of science.
Market forces, unless robustly counteracted, will subordinate
foreign language education to corporate-driven globalization,
and merely consolidate English.

Sample Eurotexts on language policy

In 1995, language policy was considered at the highest level in the
political hierarchy of the EU. A set of European Council conclusions
on 'Linguistic diversity and multilingualism in the EU' were approved
on 12 June 1995 by Ministers of Foreign Affairs, and five
Commissioners, including the President, Jacques Santer (see Appendix
1). The text endorses linguistic diversity in a very wide range of
Commission activities and EU actions. It also appears to commit
governments to implementing a set of language policies nationally,
and not only in the education system.

In 2001, policy for the fifteen member states of the EU was formulated in a Resolution of the Council of the European Union on 'the
promotion of linguistic diversity and language learning in the framework of the implementation of the objectives of the European Year of
Languages 2001' (draft of 23 November 2001, for approval by
Ministers of Education). The text has been reproduced as Appendix 2,
as it is a typical sample of EU official discourse. It consists of a set of
statements:

- a lengthy preamble recapitulating fourteen numbered earlier policy
  statements,
- a set of underlying principles representing a rationale for language
  learning,
- the administrative framework clarifying the EU's involvement,
- reference to the resolutions of the Council and Parliament establishing the European Year of Languages 2001,

- eight points for action to strengthen a wide range of language learning activities,
- three tasks for the Commission, relating to the implementation of the Resolution, use of a diversity of languages in its relations with third and candidate countries, and drafting follow-up actions by early 2003.

Table 2, 'Social goals and language correlates', presents the specific proposals that member states are 'invited' to implement, classified according to goals for the individual and the wider society. The inspiration for the table is a more comprehensive plan undertaken in Australia, Joseph Lo Bianco's *National Policy on Languages*, written for the Australian Commonwealth Department of Education, 1987 (page 63). In Table 2:

- the items printed in *italic script* are proposals included in the 2001 Resolution, the remainder are from the Australian plan;
- the 'Social goals' listed are a combination of Lo Bianco's categories and terms used in EU work to promote foreign language learning, immigrant language learning, and europeanization;
- the categories in all three columns merge into each other, and are not mutually exclusive.

A cynical view might be that the 1995 and 2001 texts are just so much pious hot air, Eurobabble that only diplomats and lawyers read, and that politicians and bureaucrats are not held accountable for. It is impossible to know what constituencies, national agendas, or pressure groups have influenced their production and precise formulation. The terms 'multilingualism' and 'diversity' are themselves open to several interpretations, and could refer to the individual, the nation, or supra-national affairs.

One is tempted to wonder whether concern at the advance of English on the part of speakers of French accounts for these texts being produced during French and Belgian presidencies. Point 13 in the 1995 text (Appendix 1), however, flatly contradicts a French proposal to restrict the number of working languages in EU institutions, which other countries refused to go along with.

The Resolution (Appendix 2) is mainly concerned with the teaching of EU official languages, but also refers to the languages of 'non-native speakers', a term that can refer either to regional minorities (e.g. speakers of German in Belgium) or to immigrants. The

Table 2 Social goals and language correlates

	Social goal	Approximate language correlate
Individual goals	Equality of opportunity for all individuals and social groups	Adequate first language teaching for all *Adequate second language teaching for minorities* Eradication of adult illiteracy
Societal goals	Equitable social integration	Equality of access to services Sign language services
	Intercultural tolerance, combating prejudice and racism	Language awareness programmes
	Cultural and intellectual growth	*Widespread teaching of foreign languages of cultural importance*
	Openness to foreign cultures	*An early start to foreign language learning* Support for the teaching of immigrant languages
	More effective foreign language teaching	*Innovation in teaching methods, also through teacher training* *Stay in the foreign country during study of the language*
	Educational progression	Foreign language education in an integrated scheme throughout primary and secondary education
National goals	Enhanced economic opportunities	Teaching of languages of economic importance
	Vocational training	*Teaching of languages for mobility and employability*
	Regional cohesion	*Teaching of regional and neighbouring languages*
	National cohesion	*Ensuring competence in the national language, while respecting the language and culture of origin of non-native speakers*
	Diversity	*Teaching a wide range of languages*

Table 2 cont.

	Social goal	Approximate language correlate
Europeanization goals	European coherence	*Exchange of experience in quality assurance and testing between countries* *Implementing the Common European Framework of Reference for language learning* *Cooperation with language centres and institutions in other member states*
	Cooperation and mobility	*Teaching two foreign languages*
	National and European security	Teaching of languages of geopolitical importance Promotion of EU languages and cultures externally

reference to 'languages and cultures of their country of origin' is clearly to immigrants.

It is very difficult to find out whether any of these proposals have been followed up in a systematic way, for instance with budgets, explicit policies, and monitoring designed to preserve linguistic diversity across Europe. Such Council documents are not legally binding. The texts clearly reflect a range of ongoing commitments and compromises. Many governments are in no position to live up to the recommendations. It is more than doubtful whether the necessary infrastructure exists in Ministries (of Education, Culture, Foreign Affairs, Commerce) to ensure implementation. The Commission has no mandate to do so, except through educational actions that are of limited scope.

As globalization and europeanization appear to be to the advantage of speakers of English, at least in the short term, the British and Irish may go along with a rhetoric of linguistic diversity but be convinced that English will ultimately be accorded a special status. In the field of education, as in commerce, science, and culture, the interlocking of europeanization with americanization and englishization reflects the unresolved, fluid tensions between the national interest and national languages, between the supranational 'general interest' and supranational languages, and between the expansion of English and the diversification of language learning.

One of the paradoxes is the question of whether there can be a clear dividing-line between policy issues that are a national concern, to be determined in each country following the principle of *subsidiarity*, or a legitimate supranational issue. Many language policy issues involve decision-making at the local or individual level, but the notion that this means that 'languages' are a matter for the state and not for Brussels would be a delusion, and obscure the reality of how languages operate in many domains in the contemporary world. Before we can feel that we are on firmer ground in addressing language policy issues, we need to know how languages operate in EU institutions in Brussels, Luxembourg, and Strasbourg. This is the topic of Chapter 4.

Chapter 4

Languages in EU institutions

Translators are bridges between peoples.

Victor Hugo

While the upcoming economic and political union is brought up in every field of endeavour, languages remain the great unspoken truth in the construction of Europe.

Marc Abélès, 1999[1]

Europe as . . . the continent of liberty, solidarity and above all, diversity, meaning respect for others' languages, cultures and traditions.

Laeken Declaration, European Council, 2001

The translators . . . with so many languages in use, their job is complex enough without having to convert monolingual muddle into multilingual muddle, and the problem can only worsen as more countries accede.

Martin Cutts, 2001[2]

Study of the EU system

Communication is what makes the EU possible. It relies on interaction between people, and on written documents that report on and regulate behaviour. Operating in eleven languages is therefore central to the functioning of EU institutions and their interaction with the general public and with the representatives of member states.

Language policy is central to the question of how well the EU operates. It is a wide-ranging and complex question, because of the vast number of spoken and written activities involved, the language practices of a set of distinct institutions, by people from many countries with specific cultural traditions and expectations. Matters are made more complicated by enlargement entailing the addition of more states, peoples, and languages. Moreover, analysis of languages in EU institutions is difficult because of the many factors that impact on language policy, as shown in earlier chapters, and because much more is at stake than languages themselves.

Assessments of how well or badly the EU functions are therefore inevitably based on selective experience. Assessing how well multilingualism and the EU language services function can be based on:

* personal experience, as an insider or outsider,
* analysis of the rules and principles that are supposed to determine language use, and consultative documents on how the language services might be improved,
* research studies of the use made of languages in the translation and interpretation services, and of discourse during the elaboration and finalization of documents,
* research and consultancy studies of attitudes to the language services, and whether there is a need for change in them,
* research studies of informal communication in EU institutions,
* analysis of complaints about discrimination in the language services, and how these have been handled,
* the evidence of what multilingualism costs, and the dovetailing of financial costs with principles of efficiency, equality in communication between speakers of different languages, and pragmatic constraints,
* participation at conferences considering European language policy,
* consultations with those who operate and use the language services (both language specialists and others), Members of the European Parliament, civil servants, and members of the general public.

All of these have contributed to my awareness of the present situation, but to explore all these avenues exhaustively would require far more resources and time. There is an awe-inspiring wealth of evidence. Large numbers of people are involved: the language services of the EU employ over 1600 people full-time, producing 1.2 million pages per annum, and interpretation is provided for over 50 meetings per day (see Box 4.1, pp. 112–15, for basic facts and figures). The webpages of the EU institutions have good documentation about how insiders see things.

Assessments vary from the extremely positive to the dissatisfied or worried. Although many specific aspects of the multilingualism of the

EU have been investigated in small-scale research projects, and although the language services are constantly concerned with improving efficiency, the conclusion of one study of all the documents dealing with language policy in the archives of the Council over a 46-year period is that at no point has there been 'an in-depth rational analysis of the practical problems, the underlying causes, let alone solutions to overcome them'.[3]

The first book-length monograph analysing the system of languages in EU institutions and EU language policies was written by Normand Labrie, who is not from Europe but Canada, a country with a strong tradition of explicit language policy formation, legislation, and implementation.[4] A recent study by Virginie Mamadouh, from France, and working in The Netherlands, which builds on several studies in the intervening period, concludes:[5]

> The linguistic arrangement of the European Union is a highly
> political issue that has been carefully avoided by politicians both
> at the national and the supranational level . . . doing nothing is
> still taking a position. The maintenance of the current linguistic
> regime sustains institutional multilingualism formally but favours
> *de facto* linguistic homogenisation with the increasing use of inter-
> national English in informal situations.

This position is at one end of a continuum, at the other end of which is the Directorate-General of the Translation Service, whose representatives are confident that multilingualism is being served well in the EU. They also believe that the service will rise to the challenge of coping with additional languages, when enlargement takes place, as effectively as in earlier enlargements: 'for us it is not a political issue, just an organisational challenge'.[6] The same confidence is felt in the interpretation service, which is preparing for a significant increase in the number of EU languages.

On the other hand, the Consultative Document of the Commission 'A strategy for the Translation Service for 2002 and beyond' (of 15 December 2001) admits that language policy issues tend to be ducked:

> The language question is extremely sensitive in most, if not all,
> of the current member and applicant states. There has, therefore,
> been hitherto a reluctance at the political level to discuss it except
> in the most general terms. One consequence of this has been that
> the task of providing multilingual backup for the Union's treaty

obligations and other activities is often treated as a solely administrative function, rather than an essential element of the political
process.

In other words, language policy is politically explosive, and if, as a
result, languages are regarded as mere practical tools of communication,
the fundamental way in which languages create and shape the way we
see and understand the world is ignored. This realization, from a service which is close to the heartbeat of the European political process,
has direct affinities with the way contemporary linguistic research
understands the relationship between language use and social structure
(particularly in the specialization known as critical discourse analysis[7]).
Language is not simply a reflection of reality, it is a conceptual filter
through which we constitute reality and see the world.

The standardization of national languages was inextricably involved
in the consolidation of nation-states through the creation of 'a unified
linguistic market, dominated by the official language'.[8] What we are
currently experiencing is the beginnings of a unification of a European
linguistic market. Many traits of the national market are still in place,
and the contours of the supranational market are visible. To analyse
these contours, we shall consider how languages are actually handled in
EU institutions, and some examples of the complexity of rendering the
'same' message in different languages. The probable impact of enlarg-
ing the linguistic market by taking in new languages will be considered,
as this is already a major planning concern of the translation and interpretation services. Looking into the interlocking of economics and
language, and principles of equality, will be delayed until Chapter 5,
when criteria for guiding equitable language policies will be explored.

We need to identify briefly what the various EU institutions are, and
what they do. The activities are summed up in the White Paper on
European Governance, published in July 2001, in a passage presenting
'The community method':[9]

> The Community method guarantees both the diversity and
> effectiveness of the Union. It ensures the fair treatment of all
> Member States from the largest to the smallest. It provides a
> means to arbitrate between different interests by passing them
> through two successive filters: the general interest[10] at the level of
> the Commission: and democratic representation, European and
> national, at the level of the Council and the European
> Parliament, together the Union's legislature.

— The *European Commission* alone makes legislative and policy proposals. Its independence strengthens its ability to execute policy, act as the guardian of the Treaty and represent the Community in international negotiations.
— Legislative and budgetary acts are adopted by the *Council of Ministers* (representing Member States) and the *European Parliament* (representing citizens). The use of qualified majority voting in the Council is an essential element in ensuring the effectiveness of this method. Execution of policy is entrusted to the Commission and national authorities.
— The *European Court of Justice* guarantees respect for the rule of law.

What would need adding is that the *European Council* meets four times a year, and brings together the fifteen heads of state and government and the Commission President. This is the supreme decision-making body, but it does not have the detailed legally prescribed functions of the other parts of the EU system.

Appendix 3 lists the 27 member and potential member states, giving their population size and the number of seats in the European Parliament envisaged in the Nice Declaration on the Enlargement of the European Union, along with the weighting of votes in the Council of Ministers. The weighting reflects the relative power of the voices of the different member states, and is important because of the increasing number of subjects that can be decided on by majority vote rather than requiring unanimity.

Use of the same word, 'Council', for two important EU bodies unfortunately makes it difficult for the outsider to navigate in EU waters (and the Council of Europe is not an EU institution), not least because the Council of Ministers is often referred to in official papers as *The Council of the European Union*, and abbreviated to *Council* (as it is in the Governance text quoted above). In addition, 'Council' has a shifting identity, as it may consist of Ministers of Agriculture in one room, Ministers of Energy in another, and so on. It also changes character every six months, since Council meetings are the responsibility of the member state acting as 'President' of the EU, in collaboration with the Commission (which also has a 'President', the most recent ones being Jacques Delors, Jacques Santer, and Romano Prodi). The Council of Ministers has less visibility in the media than the Commissioners. Decision-making is the prerogative of the Council ('legislative and budgetary acts' in the text quoted above), albeit on the initiative of the Commission. One of the frequent criticisms of both bodies is that they operate in secret and are therefore outside public scrutiny. More visibility for the Council would probably improve public perceptions of the EU, as this is where member states work together on a basis of parity.

One reason for pardonable ignorance about EU institutions is that they have changed rapidly since 1992. The relationship between individual member states and the supranational EU entity is constantly being renegotiated and extended, as integration intensifies. 'Europe' in the EU sense is a building site, to use the image popularized by Joschka Fischer, the German Foreign Minister. The institutional architecture is being constructed around the 'twin pillars' of Political Union and Economic and Monetary Union. Fischer is one of the European leaders who has sought to trigger debate about where the union is heading in the longer term, and what type of partnership edifice it is that Europeans are constructing.[11] The building site image is appropriate, since new pillars and additional floors are cumulatively added, when new fields and forms of collaboration are agreed on, for instance a military wing in the late 1990s. No-one can be certain where the current focus on institutional reform, a bill of rights, and enlargement is leading, or whether what we are erecting and constitutionalizing is some form of United States of Europe.[12] One of the intrinsic problems in this exercise is that a focus on law and procedures is unlikely to tap into the emotional bond that people feel with the national state or to create equivalent identification at the supranational level. What happens in Brussels and Strasbourg is remote from the lives of ordinary citizens, many of whom are sceptical about the entire exercise. Greater legitimacy and popularity for the EU project will only be achieved if the languages that are the crucial medium for negotiating and achieving supranational agreements and policy are seen to be functioning efficiently, equitably, and in democratically accountable ways.

The language services of the EU

The current tension between national and supranational languages, between monolingualism and multilingualism, personal and institutional, can be summarized as follows.

Individuals from a member state, senior politicians, civil servants, and experts, are provided with translation and interpretation so that they can continue to function *monolingually*. The EU system is the monolingual nation-state upgraded to the supranational level. The interactional processes and textual products, on the other hand, through interpretation and translation, combine individual monolingualism with the *interactive multilingualism* of the conduct of EU affairs in eleven languages.

Employees of EU institutions are unlike national representatives in that they do not serve a government but undertake duties for a supranational institution. Their employment requires them to be functional in more than one language. They are therefore *personally multilingual* (using this term as shorthand for proficiency in two or more languages) and contribute to the maintenance of *institutional interactive multilingualism*. The rare exceptions to this rule are highly placed individuals who are monolingual in either French or English.

It is the personal multilingualism of EU employees in two or more languages that permits the interaction of EU citizens on EU business. Citizens may be able to operate directly in more than one language, but the language regime does not expect this of them. The EU translators and interpreters are the people described aptly in the Translation Service's presentational brochure as forming 'A multilingual community at work', whereas outsiders can in principle remain monolingual. The widespread bilingualism of minority language speakers, such as the Welsh, the Basques, and the Finland Swedes, is one that plays no role in EU institutions, and only a very minor one in EU actions.

The family of languages upgraded to the EU institutional level is a select one, but all eleven official languages are functioning internationally in the sense of being used in the external affairs of nation-states. They are being used in ways that extend their repertoires, since the EU involves new types of international collaboration and textual production. The concept *international language* was first used to refer to planned languages, of which there are many, but only Esperanto has managed to become well established (see Chapter 5). The tendency to refer only to the 'big' languages such as English, Arabic, or Russian as international ignores the fact that every single EU official language has been used outside its national heartland, and that membership of the EU consolidates this trend.

EU institutional support for multilingualism applies only to those languages that happen to be official. Estonian and Latvian, each with a little over one million speakers, will soon qualify; Catalan, with more speakers than Danish and Finnish, still won't. Choice of which languages are upgraded to the supranational level as EU official languages is grounded in the principle that states have a single dominant national

language, except in atypical cases with two (Finland) or three
(Belgium). The Irish language is symbolically acknowledged as a treaty
language, but otherwise the Irish operate in English. Other minority
languages (e.g. the Finnish Constitution recognizes three Saami languages, Romani, and Finnish Sign language) have no rights in EU
institutions.

The 'family of Europe', a frequent image in the media, complete
with 'founding fathers' like Monnet and Schuman, speak different
languages rather than being multilingual. From the purely linguistic
angle, the language family of Europe is divided along clearly demar-
cated lines (that were identified in Chapter 2). The family gathered
around the European table in Brussels and Strasbourg has many linguistic members missing, since the only ones who are welcome are
those who became head of the family back home. Enlargement is
bringing in new members to the EU 'family'. The Laeken Declaration
of 2001 proclaims that: 'At long last, Europe is on its way to becoming one big family', a cliché from which only the word 'happy' is
missing, and which seems to have forgotten that families experience
more or less loving relationships – is the Franco–German duo heading
for divorce, or will there be a rapprochement, since their economies
are wedded to the euro?[13]

Box 4.1   Facts and figures about EU translation and interpretation

Languages. Services are provided for Danish, Dutch, English,
French, Finnish, German, Greek, Italian, Portuguese, Spanish,
Swedish. These are the official and working languages of EU
institutions (see Box 4.3). Services for additional languages
are provided *ad hoc.*

Services. The European Commission, Parliament, and Court of
Justice each have their own language services. There are separate services for translation (the written word) and
interpretation (speech). A 16-page brochure 'Translation and
interpreting', published in 2001 in the eleven languages,
describes how these services work, and lists relevant websites.[14]

The *Translation* Service is a Directorate-General of the Commission, based in both Brussels and Luxembourg, employing (in 2001) 1300 specialist staff, 1219 as translators, and 81 linguists in research and development, management, training etc., plus 524 support staff, receiving 700 translation requests per day, and producing more than 1.2 million pages per year. Some 20 per cent of the work is done by freelance translators. The numbers of translators range from 157 for German and 144 for French to 90 for Swedish and 87 for Finnish.

The Joint *Interpreting* and Conference Service ('joint' meaning it services several EU institutions, though not the European Parliament) employs nearly 500 interpreters full-time, and draws on over 1400 freelance interpreters.[15] Every working day, some 750 interpreters are on duty.

Qualifications. Translators and interpreters are initially qualified in two foreign languages, but often learn additional EU languages during their employment, and can translate or interpret from a wider range of languages. The average for interpreters is nearly four languages.

Specialization. Interpreters do not specialize in particular topic areas, whereas translators are grouped into sections for
* legal, economic, and financial affairs, competition and information,
* agriculture, fisheries, regional policy, and cohesion,
* external relations, customs union, development, enlargement, and humanitarian aid,
* research, telecommunications, energy, industry, environment, and transport,
* social affairs, human resources, and consumer policy,
* statistics, internal market, enterprise policy, information market, and innovation.

Technology. Major use is made of information technology to streamline work on translation processes through the multiterm termbank, the Celex database of legal instruments, translation retrieval, and other in-house databases. The Eurodicautom glossary can be accessed by the general public.[16]

Automatic translation is available through the SYSTRAN system, that can generate a rough translation between eighteen pairs of languages, from five source languages into eight target languages. Demand for this, for purposes of browsing, and fast translation, is increasing.

Cost. One person in eight at the Commission works for its language services.

Translation and interpretation at the Commission cost 0.3% of the total EU budget in 1999. The total cost of the Translation Service of the Commission in 2001 was 220 million euros.

The annual cost of the interpretation system for eleven languages in the European Parliament is 274 million euros.

Translation and interpretation at all the European institutions cost 0.8% of the total EU budget. This corresponds to two euros per year for each European citizen.[17]

The average cost of 175.5 euros per page of translated text also includes the cost of related activities in building up termbanks and databases.

Enlargement. Technical assistance is being provided to applicant countries to promote work on the translation of EU legislation, checking the legal accuracy of translations, and training. Roughly 200 translators are needed for each language,[18] as well as interpreters and legal revisers. EU translators are encouraged to learn the languages of applicant states, and are entitled to spend four hours a week of office time doing so. There is also a three-year training programme for interpreters to add an applicant state language, including three months of residence.

Pairs of languages. Following the principle of a text, written or spoken, in any of the languages of the EU being translated or interpreted into all the other EU languages, the number of pairs of languages involved is:

Dutch, French, German, Italian	4 × 3	12
these 4, plus Greek, Portuguese, Spanish	7 × 6	42
these 7, plus Danish, English	9 × 8	72
these 9, plus Finnish, Swedish	11 × 10	110
these 11, plus 10 enlargement countries	21 × 20	420

There is a lucid presentation of the roles of the various EU institutions, and how the translation services operate in them, in a book written by three translators from the Commission.[19] This is a valuable presentation of many aspects of the work, as seen by insiders, and includes interviews with people in different branches of the EU system, including users of the translation services.

The work of the Joint Interpreting and Conference Service for the various parts of the EU is in the following proportions (figures for 2000; the Parliament and the Court of Justice draw on their own staff):

- 49.7%   Council of Ministers,
- 39.8%   European Commission,
- 6.6%   Economic and Social Committee,
- 2.1%   Committee of the Regions,

and much smaller figures for the European Bank of Investment, European Schools, European Foundation for the Improvement of Living and Working Conditions, European Centre for the Development of Vocational Training, European Agency for the Evaluation of Medicinal Products, European Environment Agency, Office for Harmonisation in the Internal Market (trade marks and designs), European Training Foundation, European Monitoring Centre for Drugs and Drug Abuse, European Agency for Safety and Health at Work, Community Plant Variety Office, European University Institute, EUROPOL, European Agency for Reconstruction, etc.[20]

The profession of conference interpreter was born when the League of Nations nominated French and English as its working languages in

1919.[21] Other languages could be used provided that interpretation into French and English was provided. Interpretation had to be done consecutively, one voice at a time, until technology, first used at the Nuremburg trials, made possible simultaneous interpretation, through a system of microphones, headphones, and interpreters in cabins.

It is impressive to see interpretation into as many as eleven languages in action. The weekly press conference that the EU Commission gives is a brisk affair, with brief statements by EU officials in perhaps three languages (English and French – and Italian, if Romano Prodi is participating). Journalists can then ask questions in any of the eleven languages, and all those present can follow proceedings directly or through interpretation into the language of their choice. For EU meetings for which full interpretation is provided, for example a Council meeting with delegations from each of the fifteen member states, separate booths for the interpreters for each language are needed. The interpreters will, like the delegates, have in front of them all the various documents that are being considered at the meeting. Receiving these in advance permits interpreters to familiarize themselves with any necessary technical vocabulary. At a conference on enlargement, interpretation was provided into and from 22 languages. Probably the only other forum where interpreters are provided in an equally large number of languages is international Sign Languages conferences.

Box 4.2   Interpretation types

Consecutive interpretation involves an interpreter rendering what someone has said in a second language, one person speaking at a time, and with no technological support. Mostly used informally.

Simultaneous interpretation, with interpreters in booths, using microphones and headphones, can take the following forms:

Speech in one language is *directly interpreted* into other languages, generally into the mother tongue of the interpreters, for instance the ten other EU languages. This takes place almost instantaneously while the speaker continues uninfluenced by the work of interpreters. There is total *symmetry* when the same conditions apply to all eleven languages.

Asymmetrical interpretation involves direct interpretation from several languages into a restricted number of languages. This allows participants to speak their own language, and assumes that they can understand a foreign language when there is no interpretation into their language.

Retour interpretation involves the interpreter working from and into two languages, e.g. a Finn working from English into Finnish and vice versa. This system is also called *bi-active* interpretation.

Pivot interpretation involves two steps: interpretation from several languages into a single pivot language (in one booth) and from the pivot language into other languages (in a separate booth), e.g. Finnish into English and from that into Greek. Typically each active language is covered by two interpreters. This is relay interpretation.

Remote interpretation involves interpreters who are located outside the conference room.

The EU institutions are likely to make much more extensive use of pivot/relay interpretation after enlargement, also for the existing official languages, provided savings can be made and quality maintained. This is recommended in the Podestà report for the European Parliament on preparations for enlargement (draft, 27 June 2001), and in 'Conference interpreting and enlargement. A strategy for the Joint Interpreting and Conference Service in the lead up to 2004, communicated to the Commission by Vice-President Kinnock', 10 December 2001.

The concepts *official* and *working* language derive from their use in the League of Nations, and later the United Nations. The UN started by granting Chinese, English, French, Russian, and Spanish the status of official languages (Arabic was added after the oil crisis of 1973), but with English and French as working languages. Since then the distinction has been made redundant by the same rights applying in principle to all six languages, and by the *de facto* dominance of English. Representatives of French- and Spanish-speaking states have protested about this inequality.[22] The UN's mandate is very limited, so that the term 'official' primarily relates to which languages can be used in UN business. 'Official' texts commit member states only if they have ratified them, which gives, for instance, a human rights covenant legal force under international law.

The principle of official languages having equal status established 'the fiction that a text written in "language" can be rendered into any number of "languages" and that the resultant renderings are entirely equal as to meaning'.[23] The same principle of textual equivalence applies in the EU to its eleven languages, with in theory the 'same' semantic content being expressed in each. Anyone familiar with translation processes, and products knows that squaring the circle of conceptual, cultural and linguistic difference is a utopian ideal that is remote from how different realities operate. In Box 2.1 the very concrete, everyday example of bread was given, in Box 2.6 the rule of law. The challenge of producing textual equality increases with more abstract concepts that may have a common semantic core but are generally understood in culturally specific ways.

The Treaties in 1957 establishing the European Economic Community and the European Atomic Energy Community (Euratom) were drawn up in the four languages of the founding states, and confirmed the principle of 'all four texts being equally authentic'. The status of languages in the EU derives from Regulation 1 of 15 April 1958 (see Box 4.3). The Regulation applies the principle laid down in Article 217 of the EC Treaty (Article 290 in the consolidated version) to the effect that 'The rules governing the languages of the institutions of the Community shall . . . be determined by the Council, acting unanimously'.

Regulation 1 gives the same rights as both official and working languages to all EU languages, the four of the six founding states, and additional ones for new members, up to the present eleven. Regulation 1, referred to bombastically on the website as 'The European Union's language charter', stipulates which languages are to be used in the conduct of EU business, and in incoming and outgoing documents, i.e. texts addressed to and dispatched from the EU.[24] The principle of equality is paramount for legal acts agreed on in Brussels (Eurolaw, directives etc.), which have the force of law in member states, overriding national law.

Between 60 per cent and 80 per cent of legislation in national parliaments involves implementing legal acts that have been approved at the supranational level. Producing these texts involves a protracted string of consultation and drafting processes, in EU institutions and member states, during which the principle of the eleven languages

Box 4.3   The European Union's language charter

Council Regulation No 1, determining the languages to be used by the European Economic Community (as amended)

THE COUNCIL OF THE EUROPEAN ECONOMIC COMMUNITY,

Having regard to Article 217 of the Treaty which provides that the rules governing the languages of the institutions of the Community shall, without prejudice to the provisions contained in the rules of procedure of the Court of Justice, be determined by the Council, acting unanimously;

Whereas each of the 11 languages in which the Treaty is drafted is recognised as an official language in one or more of the Member States of the Community,

HAS ADOPTED THIS REGULATION:

Article 1
The official languages and the working languages of the institutions of the Community shall be Danish, Dutch, English, Finnish, French, German, Greek, Italian, Portuguese, Spanish and Swedish.

Article 2
Documents which a Member State or a person subject to the jurisdiction of a Member State sends to institutions of the Community may be drafted in any one of the official languages selected by the sender. The reply shall be drafted in the same language.

Article 3
Documents which an institution of the Community sends to a Member State or to a person subject to the jurisdiction of a Member State shall be drafted in the language of such State.

Article 4
Regulations and other documents of general application shall be drafted in the 11 official languages.

Article 5
The Official Journal of the European Communities shall be published in the 11 official languages.

Article 6
The institutions of the Community may stipulate in their rules of procedure which of the languages are to be used in specific cases.

Article 7
The languages to be used in the proceedings of the Court of Justice shall be laid down in its rules of procedure.

Article 8
If a Member State has more than one official language, the language to be used shall, at the request of such State, be governed by the general rules of its law.

This regulation shall be binding in its entirety and directly applicable in all Member States.

Treaty of Amsterdam

Article 2, point 11.
11. In Article 8d [of the EC Treaty], the following paragraph shall be added:
'Every citizen of the Union may write to any of the institutions or bodies referred to in this article or in Article 4 in one of the languages mentioned in Article 248 and have an answer in the same language.'

having the same rights should be in force, though in practice they may not always be. It is unnecessary and impractical for all documents in the EU to be translated into every language, particularly those that are not ultimately going to take legal effect in member states. Constraints of time (tight deadlines) and expense (finite budgets, and pressure to increase productivity) also influence whether translations are available. Heads of department in the translation services have the right to challenge whether translation of a given document is in fact needed. It is not really necessary to translate 450 pages on asparagus production into Swedish and Finnish, when the north European climate does not permit the growing of this crop.[25] By contrast, the extensive regulations covering the transportation of dangerous goods should be available in all languages before they take effect, if lorry-drivers and their employers are to understand and follow them.

The issue of whether draft texts are sent out to member states in French or English only, or in all languages, raises the important question of whether civil servants and experts in each country have to be able to work with complex texts in a foreign language, invariably either French or English or both. There is research evidence from Sweden that indicates that this is a serious problem: approximately 61 per cent of the reading time of Swedish civil servants is spent on texts in Swedish, 28 per cent English, 6 per cent French, and 5 per cent German; 29 per cent of their written output is in English.[26] In theory such people ought to have the right to work in their own languages. The situation is similar in the European Parliament, where the complaint is often heard that texts are only available in French or English, and also that there are too many errors in the translations. It is a different matter for people employed permanently in Brussels or Luxembourg, who can be expected to function multilingually.

In fact in the internal operations of the EU, French was until quite recently unchallenged as the language in use in most day-to-day operations, without this preference being given a blessing legally or a special label. English is now also very widely used orally and in writing. When English and French are used for such purposes, they are sometimes referred to as *procedural* languages. The website refers to 'two or three *vehicular* languages' and to 'de facto *drafting* languages'.[27] Other terms, for example *in-house* or *administrative* language, are also used. On occasion these privileged languages are called the 'working languages' of the EU, falsely implying that other languages are not working languages.

Any formalized restriction of this sort would be in violation of Regulation 1, but reference is frequently made to a small number of working languages, both in scholarly studies and in the media, for instance when a leader in the *Financial Times*, on 3 December 2001, dealing with reform of the EU, suggests: 'The EU must agree on two or three working languages.' The joint letter by Fischer and Védrine, dispatched from Paris and Berlin on 2 July 2001 and reported on in Chapter 1, refers to a proposed restriction of Commission activity to 'a single one of the three working languages of the community institutions'.[28] This seems to assume that there are only three working languages. Prodi's reply refers several times to official languages and multilingualism, and confirms an unremitting commitment to these, both in external dealings and in communication between the various EU institutions (presumably primarily a reference to contact between the Commission and the Council of Ministers). These principles are, according to Prodi, 'essential in order that the construction of Europe will be a reality that takes the cultural and linguistic diversity of the continent fully into consideration'.[29] Prodi's reply deftly avoids reference to in-house procedures, and whether there are *de facto* two, three, or eleven 'working languages'.

In an empirical study in the early 1990s, Members of the European Parliament (MEPs) and Eurocrats were asked for their views on the need for new regulations restricting the number of working languages.[30] While MEPs were largely against change, a large proportion of bureaucrats stated that they would welcome it. It was mainly speakers of the 'small' languages like Danish and Portuguese (which is globally far from 'small') who did not want change, presumably because of the risk of their language being marginalized even further than is already the case.

The study also shows a large proportion wishing German to be used as a language with top priority and status, rather than a system with only English, or only French and English, as working languages, even though German is not widely used at present. A later study also revealed a marked preference for a bilingual (French and English) or a trilingual (English, French, and German) system rather than a monolingual one.[31]

There is also a wide range of views on whether new member states should necessarily have the same language rights as member states do under the present scheme of things. Again, the pattern is that fewer bureaucrats than MEPs seem to believe incoming languages/states should have the same rights. Perhaps not too much weight should be accorded to these findings, even though they are meticulous studies, since the proportion of informants who bothered to return the questionnaires was disappointingly low (for instance 48 MEPs from eleven countries), some of the questions were open to several interpretations, and presumably 'working language' can be understood in more than one way.

Restricting the number of working languages might appear to simplify matters, but not for those who would be discriminated against by such a rule, for instance representatives of member states who would have to operate in a foreign language. Formally reducing the number of working languages could not be done without changing the EU's 'language charter', and no government is likely to agree voluntarily to have its rights restricted in this way. By contrast, using primarily English and French as procedural languages in the internal affairs of the Commission can be seen as a pragmatic, operational matter. It obliges most Eurocrats to work in a foreign language, which some are bound to experience as being culturally and linguistically stultifying.

It is also not likely to make for efficiency, as a comment by someone who is 'arguably the most important civil servant' in the Commission[32] makes clear: 'the main problem facing translators is the poor quality of many original documents, which are often written by non–native speakers'.[33]

If agreement were to be reached on a restricted set of procedural languages, a good case could be made for, say, German and Italian – the largest Germanic language, and a Romance language that is phonetically and grammatically relatively simple, and both languages of major cultural significance. In fact the proposal has been made (according to anecdotal evidence[34]) that English, French, and German should be made the sole working languages, on one condition, namely that no–one is allowed to speak their mother tongue. If such proposals were to be taken seriously, it might do wonders for increasing awareness about how difficult it is to communicate effectively, precisely, and persuasively in a foreign language. The French and British press might have a field day. But as implementation would mean turning the present system upside down, it is unlikely to win much support.

The Legal Service of the European Parliament was asked for an opinion on the Parliament's language regime in August 2001, and produced a definitive statement of the law in a Legal Opinion.[35] This traces in detail the relevant, binding sources of law in treaties, various acts of secondary law (including Regulation 1), and the obligation to respect a general principle of non–discrimination. It draws the conclusion that the Parliament cannot of its own accord determine its own language regime, since the language regime of all Community institutions derives from a Council act, adopted unanimously. It follows that to make rules that specify that only certain of the official languages can be designated as working languages would be in breach of Community law. There is also case law that suggests that the European Court of Justice wishes to be vigilant in ensuring that people are not discriminated against on grounds of language in any EU activities (but see the cases on discrimination discussed in Chapter 5).

What this means is that any change in language rights in any one EU institution can only be undertaken by a unanimous decision at the highest possible level, the Council of Ministers. It is also difficult to envisage any change that would not be in conflict with the many proclamations of respect for diversity and a principle of non-discrimination. Legally the position is clear. Introducing an English–only system by the back door, the fear that triggered Fischer and Védrine's letter to Prodi in August 2001, ought to be impossible, and introducing it by the front door unthinkable.

Applicant states will therefore be entitled to the same rights as member states, and cannot be pressurized into having their language rights restricted when they become full members. Perhaps, though, things are not so straightforward. During the process of negotiating for membership, a narrow language policy is being imposed. In effect, English has been made the key language. Thus the Multi-annual Financing Agreement (Special Accession Programme for Agriculture and Rural Development) between the Commission and Poland stipulates that the agreement is drawn up in English and Polish, and only the English version is 'authentic', i.e. to be given legal weight in the event of a disagreement. Likewise in negotiations with all the other applicant countries, for instance the Czech Republic:[36]

1   Any communication between the Commission and the Czech Republic related to this Agreement shall be in English.
2   The Czech Republic shall ensure that for the Commission examination referred to Article 3(1) of Section A of the Annex, relevant national legislation, written procedures manuals, guidelines, standard control check–lists, relevant administrative notices, standard documents and forms shall be available in English, the Czech Republic shall provide texts in English expeditiously following a request from the Commission.

Presumably interpretation into and from the language of the applicant state is provided at high-level meetings, but otherwise the provisions cited here effectively oblige representatives of both the Commission and applicant states to function in English, even if there might be people on both sides who feel more comfortable operating in French or German, in speech or in writing – let alone in Czech and Polish, following a principle of reciprocity. A second consequence of all the documents arriving in Prague, Warsaw, Tallinn etc. in English is that monitoring and influencing the negotiation process, for instance on key matters such as agricultural subsidies, or the movement of labour, is filtered through English, making it more difficult for civil society, NGOs, and civil servants to participate.

Restricting the language of negotiations with applicant states to English is in clear contravention of the 'Council conclusions' of 12 June 1995, approved by Ministers of Foreign Affairs (see Appendix 1), and the recommendations of the Resolution of the Council of the European Union on 'the promotion of linguistic diversity and language learning in the framework of the implementation of the objectives of the European Year of Languages 2001', 23 November 2001 (Appendix 2). Both these policy statements stipulate a multilingual approach to external contacts. The Commission considers that it has the right to do as it pleases, and opt for English only.

In theory, all this changes at the point when an applicant state becomes a full member, and Regulation 1 comes into force for the additional language. It is important therefore to see what specific rights follow from Regulation 1, and whether they are always observed. The Swedish evidence, two detailed empirical studies of language use in EU institutions,[37] and much anecdotal data suggest that this is by no means always the case. One weakness of Regulation 1 is that it does not define what 'working language' actually means, or when there may be a departure from the principle of all languages being used. There is also a lack of conceptual clarity in the use of the word 'draft', at least when the Regulation is seen with other statements about language policy. 'Draft' occurs in the English version of Regulation 1 in the preamble and in Articles 2, 3, and 4 ('documents shall/may be drafted in . . .'). What is being referred to in each case is the final product, and not a provisional text. The rules refer to the language a text has been, or has to be, written in. This is clear in Regulation 1 in other languages (*rédiger* in French, *affatte* in Danish), the French text pre-dating the English one by fifteen years. The English text seems to be using 'draft' in the sense of 'legal drafting', drawing up a legal text. In many dictionaries of English, 'draft' does not figure as a verb in this sense. It is defined as exclusively meaning to produce a provisional document. This is also how the Translation Service website uses the word when referring to

English and French as 'the de facto drafting languages of the Commission'. But this is not what the Regulation is about. The use of 'draft' in English in the Regulation could therefore well be misunderstood by users of English as a foreign language, and even by native speakers without familiarity with legal language.

This example shows that the 'same' text in different languages may well in fact be different. There are even major differences in the French, English, and Spanish versions of the Charter of the UN, Article 33 on conflict resolution, which make fundamentally different use of modal verbs (those expressing probability and possibility). These differences send conflicting signals to users of the text in the various languages, which muddles and muddies the obligations of the Security Council.[38] The example also suggests that the plethora of labels for EU languages, with key words like 'working' and 'draft' being used in inconsistent ways, does not promote clear thinking about language rights. It seems to confirm that much language policy is based on custom and is not explicit. If there is a hierarchy which distinctly favours one or two languages, and the ways of thinking and acting associated with them, then there is a problem.

The problem used to be French. One of the translators informed me with a twinkle in his eye that the English used in EU documents was 'thinly disguised French'. There is a grain of truth in this, as French was the prevalent in-house language in the formative years of the EU, when the administrative procedures were run by graduates of the elite 'grandes écoles' and the École Nationale d'Administration, who had been trained as public administrators in a top–down, centralized system with a mystique of 'la fonction publique'. Insiders report that until 1973 'linguistic coherence was quite strong, with the French way of thinking and drafting predominating. That was a time when Germany was an economic giant but a political dwarf'.[39] This pattern continued throughout the 1970s.[40] There are many symptoms of this French dominance:

- In the years prior to the establishment of the EEC in 1958, the French made vigorous efforts to have French established as the sole official language of the embryo European organizations, but were forced under German and Flemish pressure to concede the principle of the equality of EU languages.[41]
- French administrative culture is visible in such concepts as the 'acquis communautaire', the 60,000 pages of legislation and case law that an applicant state must translate and adopt nationally prior

to joining the EU. Even if there are translation equivalents in other languages, the French term seems to be the main point of reference.[42]

- On the European Court of Justice website, the types of case that can be brought are specified in all language versions, but the French terms are given alongside their equivalents in other languages, implying that they are incomprehensible otherwise, since the terms originated in French legal culture. French does have a special status in the Court.

- When Finland was preparing for EU membership in the early 1990s, and undertaking the task of translating 150,000 pages of EU directives (half of which concerned agriculture), texts were initially translated from English, but a switch to French originals was made because the English source texts presented problems of 'reliability and interpretation'.[43]

- The Resolution on linguistic diversity referred to at the end of Chapter 3, and reproduced as Appendix 2, follows a distinctly French bureaucratic style.

- The obligation of translators to maintain the same sentence structure in all languages is a straightjacket that can assist uniformity, and comparability between languages, but is in conflict with traditions of clear writing in other legal cultures. If French has been the main point of reference for other language versions, it is French legal language, with its distinctive rhetorical structure and syntax, that has been transferred. Translators working permanently at an EU institution are likely to adopt such norms subconsciously over time, however much they take care to remain in touch with the language of the home country, and to translate optimally into it.

There have been studies of the quality of the Danish used in translations from other languages, mainly to assess whether EU Danish is excessively influenced by French legal and bureaucratic language. Different scholars draw different conclusions on the basis of the existing evidence.[44] There is an obvious need for quality control in both the production of such texts and their readability by the general public.

Spoken interaction in EU institutions is not based on stable, unchangeable stereotypes of how certain nationals behave ('the French/Germans/ . . . always . . .') but rather on intercultural relationships that evolve in processes that negotiate cultural identity and produce a new composite institutional identity: 'The Euro-civil servants demonstrate a rare capacity to speak another language than the mother tongue, understand the cultural trends that explain the strange behaviour or reaction of somebody, present themselves in order to be understood by their fellows . . . work is multilingual, teams pluri-national, the European spirit and interest are the one aim of everybody.'[45] This is the conclusion of a French anthropologist, Marc Abélès (evidently from a monolingual background – for many Europeans there is nothing 'rare' about operating in a second or third language) who has analysed patterns of interaction in EU institutions. He is convinced that communication among nationals from the fifteen countries functions relatively well in the modified French and English of 'euro-speak, franglais or frenglish'. He sees the EU political project as involving a synthesis of French centralization, German decentraliza-tion, and British deregulation, all geared towards a goal of formulating a 'European common good', the European 'general interest'.

Efforts have been made in the Commission for some years to per-suade employees of the Commission to write more clearly and more succinctly.[46] They build on efforts in many EU countries to bring legal and administrative language closer to citizens. The British gov-ernment started a campaign in December 2001 to make the EU's principles available in simple, direct language, and to eliminate Eurobabble.[47] The Swedish government has worked for decades to improve communication between government and the citizen, and has a unit in the Ministry of Justice specializing in Clear Language.[48] It liaises closely with those working with Swedish texts in the EU. This kind of link is extremely important, for consciousness-raising, for coordinating terminology development, and for synchronizing efforts at the national and supranational levels.

The brochure *How to write clearly* is a product of the Translation Service's Fight the Fog campaign,[49] where FOG is an acronym but 'the meaning is not fixed. There are several possibilities:

FOG = frequency of gobbledegook
FOG = farrago of Gallicisms
FOG = full of garbage.'[50]

The thrust of this work is to make text writers aware of ways of making their language more direct and straightforward: KISS – Keep It Short and Simple. If texts are shorter, this saves translation time. There is also a saving if the language is improved before translation is under-taken. This may be necessary if a non-native speaker has drafted it, but native speakers are not immune to the diseases of verbosity and obscurity. Some texts are deliberately unclear because of a political compromise, but this should not apply to Commission documents.[51]

The booklet *Clarifying Eurolaw*[52] provides a detailed example of how an EU directive can be rewritten in much clearer, simpler language, while still conforming to the principles of good law. It was written by Martin Cutts of the Plain Language Commission, which has a long tradition of advising private and public concerns in Britain on how their written texts can be made simpler and reader-friendly. It is one of the instruments that the Translation Service of the Commission is using as part of its Fight the Fog campaign, and a lengthy process of getting documents written in more lucid, precise ways. Here is an example of the 'tortured syntax' that the booklet seeks to debunk, and replace in direct comprehensible form:

> Whereas, in view of the size and mobility of the toy market and the diversity of the products concerned, the scope of this Directive should be determined on the basis of a sufficiently broad definition of 'toys'; whereas, nevertheless, it should be made clear that some products are not to be regarded as toys for the purpose of this Directive either because they are in fact not intended for children or because they call for special supervision or special conditions of use; . . .

The commentary is: 'The underlying idea is very simple: "A broad definition of 'toy' is needed because . . ." And it could say exactly that.'[53]

The Fischer/Védrine incident of 2001 was followed up by a 'Memorandum from the President to the Commission in agreement with Mr Kinnock' on 'Simplification and rationalisation of the language process in Commission procedures' (Kinnock is named because he is the Vice-President of the Commission with responsibility for reform). This stresses adherence to the principles of Regulation 1, and that efficiency and quality can benefit if working procedures are more clearly defined (better interaction between the various Directorates-General and the Translation Service), and if documents sent to the Translation Service are maximally short and polished. The brief Memorandum dovetails with a planning document 'A strategy for the Translation Service: perspectives for 2002 and beyond', which covers staffing levels, benchmarking, technology, training, and so on, and is guided by a wish to ensure that the vast number of activities are determined by 'real needs'.[54]

Multilingualism and linguistic hierarchies in EU institutions

Multilingualism appears to have become an EU mantra, but the concept is used in various senses and can obscure the extent to which EU multilingualism can serve to confirm monolingualism:

*   'Equal status for the official languages, or multilingualism, goes to the heart of what Europe is all about.'[55]
*   'The EU wants to preserve, defend and foster language diversity . . . The best way to bring people together is to respect their differences rather than to coerce them into unity. This is the sign of real respect for multilingualism in the EU.'[56]

Both statements must be understood as referring to *institutional* multilingualism of the kind that language services facilitate. These serve to 'foster language diversity' by enabling member states to continue to function monolingually. By contrast, *individual* multilingualism is referred to when the Directorate-General for Education and Culture claims that nearly half the citizens of EU states are 'multilingual', on the strength of surveys of foreign language learning (see Box 1.1). One doubts whether most of these citizens would describe themselves as multilingual.

Multilingualism is used in yet another sense in the introductory section of a policy paper on preparing for the future of the European Commission and the Translation Service:[57]

> Like the other institutions of the European Union the Commission is facing a number of major challenges in the immediate future. These include internal Reform, and the consequent improvement of working methods and procedures, the forthcoming enlargement, and the consequences of a new approach to governance.
>
> In all these areas it is essential that the political message to the citizens of Europe is presented in a clear and convincing manner, which in turn requires recognition of the need to give full play to the use of the national languages. Multilingualism is a democratic right of the peoples of Europe that needs to be preserved, as has again been confirmed by the EU Treaty.

The right in question seems to refer to the right of each European 'people' to their own language (a right to monolingualism?), which converts in the EU into the right to be informed in the relevant official language. This right presupposes institutional multilingualism via interpretation and translation (though the Treaty itself is not concerned with the internal workings of EU institutions). However, the thrust of the sentence might be to hammer home the point that the equality of EU languages, including additional ones as a result of enlargement, has to be maintained in EU institutions. The statement could be hinting at a need to counteract inequality and linguistic hierarchies within the EU. Perhaps the language services, made up of committed multilinguals, see themselves as the guardians of linguistic diversity, keen to counterbalance the massive pressures advancing English, and, to adapt a phrase first used by Neville Alexander of South Africa about Afrikaans as a dominant language under apartheid, to 'reduce English to equality'.

The pecking order of languages in the internal affairs of the Commission can be seen from the figures for documents submitted to the translation service for action. Until about 1970, German and French were accepted as the languages that most draft documents were written in, in approximately equal quantities, with the rights of Dutch and Italian seldom being exercised.[58] Since then there has been tacit German acceptance of a hierarchy with French at the summit, and English gradually climbing up to the top, and partially toppling French. The German government has occasionally complained about lack of use of German.[59]

The figures for documents needing translation clearly delineate the reordering of the linguistic hierarchy:

    1970   French 60%, German 40%;
    1989   French 49%, German 9%, English 30%, and a figure no
            higher than 3% for any of the remaining languages;
    1997   French 40%, English 45%;[60]
    2000   French 33%, English 55%.

According to the Translation Service's presentational brochure:[61]

The service received 1,224,755 pages for translation in 2000, of which 55% were drafted in English, 33% in French, 4% in German and 8% in the other 8 Community languages. The preponderance of English and French is explained by the fact that these are the de facto drafting languages of the Commission. Output is much more evenly distributed across the EU's official languages, pointing up the Translation Service's central role in the Commission's communications with the European Institutions, national administrations and EU citizens.

The figures for output from the Translation Service show a distribution with French and German as the largest, 13 per cent each, 11 per cent for English, 9 per cent Italian and Spanish, 8 per cent Dutch, Greek, and Portuguese, and 7 per cent Danish, Swedish, and Finnish. For meetings of the Commissioners themselves, all texts have to be available in English, French, and German.[62]

These figures cover a wide range of types of text translated: 'speeches and speaking notes, briefings and press releases, international agreements, policy statements, answers to written and oral parliamentary questions, technical studies, financial reports, minutes, internal administrative matters and staff information . . .'[63] Some 61 per cent of the work involves documents that are to be published (e.g. policy papers) and texts with legislative or administrative effect (laws and directives, regulations for EU programmes of activity, official documents for other EU institutions), which are known as 'legal acts'.[64]

When translators are working on a document, they can consult the person responsible for the original, and any improvement or clarification of the text can be accessed electronically by any translator. The final text is vetted by specialist legal translators, whose task is to ensure that the texts in the eleven languages have the same meaning in the sense of being maximally equivalent. In theory there is no text in one language that the others are translations of, even if most texts originate in either French or English. This principle reflects a complicated production process with no single author and the reality of many contributing to the words finally agreed on.

When French and English are used as procedural languages, all other languages pass via these rather than texts being translated directly from, say, Greek to Dutch. This is parallel to the system of relay languages in interpretation, when there is a two-step process from language X into a pivot language (see Box 4.2), and from this into Languages Y and Z.

When the groundwork is conducted in a single language, or perhaps two, with native and non–native speakers interacting, there is no equality of communication rights. Many documents are processed through an incredibly complex procedure of consultation and co–decision-making between the Council, Commission, and Parliament in a succession of phases. Members of the European Parliament from Scandinavia (and doubtless many others) are convinced that this gives native speakers of French and English an edge when it comes to setting agendas, for instance when chairing committees. The chair of a working party can decisively influence the final result, such as production of a policy paper, a linguistic advantage being converted into words that influence policy. How this works is demonstrated in a research study of the processes leading to a policy document prepared for the European Council meeting in Luxembourg in 1997 on a new 'European economy' and the management of unemployment. The text was decisively influenced in the direction of an uncritical endorsement of globalization through the role of the francophone chair, a skilled performer in the domain of 'bureaucratic–expertocratic politics'.[65]

The hierarchy of languages in the internal operations of EU institutions appears to be: (1) English; (2) French; (3) German; (4) the rest. For enlargement, and basing predictions on how the addition of Finnish and Swedish was successfully managed in an earlier enlargement, the expectation is that 75 per cent of texts from additional languages will be translated into English, 15 per cent into French, and 10 per cent into the remaining languages.[66] This prediction confirms the increasing pre-eminence of English.

Even though the rhetorical endorsement of 'complete' multilingualism and equality is not lived up to in the in-house affairs of the EU, and in some of its dealings with member states, the language services of the EU are in fact granting equal rights to speakers of all eleven languages in several significant ways:

- In *interpretation,* by providing facilities that permit everyone to hear and speak their own language (in 50+ meetings per day), even when the 'classic' model of interpretation from one language into the interpreter's mother tongue has been modified over time (relay interpretation, two-way: see Box 4.2). This is an important instance of what was referred to in Chapter 1 as *status planning,* through ensuring equal rights for speakers of all eleven languages in supranational use, and their actual use in supranational negotiations, including the treaties and declarations that result from them.

- *Translation and interpretation* ensure that documents are issued in all eleven languages, that the terminology and software necessary for each language are developed, and that all the languages are in a position to contribute to and draw on electronic databases, and in general to respond to the challenges of change in countless administrative, technical, and juridical fields. This is significant evidence of *corpus planning* and *status planning.*

- *Recruitment and training programmes* contribute to ensuring that qualified staff from each country are equipped to take up employment in the supranational institutions. It is estimated that applicant countries need about 200 translators per language to staff all EU institutions,[67] and approximately 80 full-time interpreters.[68] This activity represents a combination of *status planning* and *acquisition planning*, and is laudable since it is being done for all languages, irrespective of their demographic and economic base. A small market makes it difficult for people working with these languages to obtain research and development funding.[69]

There is therefore a considerable amount of language planning taking place in the EU institutions themselves, even if it is never called this. Through the resources of personnel and budget that are allocated to these functions, each language is strengthened as a valid instrument of national policy. In the countless fields of activity that are legislated for supranationally (the economy, agriculture, the environment, etc.), these languages do not run the risk of being phased out or downgraded to second-class languages. This may serve to counteract the increasing pervasiveness of English in commerce, science, and popular culture.

These EU activities are under pressure from globalization trends and the ongoing thrust of English within EU institutions. They also dovetail with language planning or its neglect in each member state. The government of Sweden is convinced of the need for a major language policy effort to strengthen Swedish. EU activities are not regarded as sufficient by the governments of Belgium, France, and Luxembourg, which are attempting to strengthen the position of French in EU institutions in the enlargement process in several programmes:[70]

- French language training for diplomats and civil servants from applicant states, and for EU civil servants;
- training in French for interpreters and translators from applicant states, and training in the languages of applicant states for francophone interpreters and translators employed in EU institutions;
- the promotion, in the domains of information technology and communication, of the use of French as a working language in EU institutions.

This activity, coordinated by the international 'Francophonie' organizations, and packaged in a rhetorical endorsement of multilingualism, is an attempt to resist market forces. Those who identify with French are worried about French losing out to the forces propelling English forward. Among people working in an EU institution, there are in fact probably speakers of each of the official languages other than English who are worried about inadequate use of their language in the internal affairs of the EU.[71] They feel that more use of Italian, Spanish, and other languages that are low in the EU hierarchy would enrich the EU and improve efficiency.

In the case of Danish, a concern expressed by EU interpreters is that Danes who attend meetings in Brussels, as politicians, civil servants, or experts, sometimes choose to speak English rather than Danish. This has two consequences. Generally Danes are not nearly as competent in English or French as they would be in Danish, even if they are superficially fluent. There are countless anecdotes about Danes saying something that they did not intend, such as when apologizing for needing to leave a meeting because they had 'flies to catch'. The Danish word for flight is 'fly', pronounced rather like the English 'flew'. Secondly, if a 'small' language is not seen to be used constantly, it is difficult to justify providing interpretation, and interpreters for other languages are more likely to learn an additional language that is certain to be used and require interpretation (e.g. to opt for Polish or Swedish rather than Danish). The Danish government ought to have a policy for what its representatives do when they function in Brussels, so as to maintain the position of Danish. They should also have a plan for ensuring that competent interpreters are trained regularly so as to meet the needs of the coming years. None of this takes place at present. Matters are left to chance.

Complaints about the functioning of the system are heard about all EU institutions. Evidence is sporadic rather than systematic, and needs to be counterbalanced by the simple fact that most work goes through without comment. There are internal control procedures that aim at ensuring quality. All translation work undertaken freelance is graded on a 10-point quality scale; the quality of interpretation is reviewed after each day. The Joint Interpreting and Conference Service commissioned an external survey of all aspects of its work on two days in January 2001, resulting in extensive reporting by users of the system and by interpreters.[72] The quality of interpretation is rated very highly, particularly when full interpretation in all eleven languages is provided, but 25 per cent of informants complained that they were unable to speak their own language, and 28 per cent were unable to listen to interpretation into their own language (in both cases, figures were higher in the Commission and lower in the Council). Delegates would like coverage of more languages, and less use of relay interpretation (for instance all interpretation from Greek and Finnish into Danish passes via a pivot language). Interpreters, on the other hand, are convinced that relay interpretation functions so well that listeners are often unaware that this system is in use.

Other typical complaints mostly relate to:

- documents not being available on time, a situation that is likely to be aggravated by enlargement and greater use being made of translation in two steps, using an intermediary pivot language;
- documents being over-long and unclear, which the 'Fight the Fog' campaign and the tightening up of internal procedures is designed to remedy, or at least alleviate;
- documents that ought to be in all languages only being available in French and/or English;
- errors or inadequacies in translations;
- EU website coverage being in a select few languages.

These symptoms of frustration need to be linked up to underlying causal factors:

- the absence of explicit policies for when less than total multilingual coverage, in speech and writing, is provided;[73]
- conceptual confusion when 'working' language is used in competing senses;
- a one-sided focus on costs that tends not to be counterbalanced by awareness of the importance of the language services for ensuring multilingual access to EU documents and communication;
- the implications of the way English is becoming the dominant language of draft texts and of negotiations for applicant states, and is constantly being marketed as Europe's lingua franca.

Many factors contribute to the preferential status of English as the in-house language. EU institutional practices dovetail with the way globalization results in English being used in many non-EU fora, particularly in the corporate world, science, the media, and foreign relations. In EU institutions, despite a rhetoric of equality and multilingualism, there has been a consensus on a hierarchy of in-house languages, the hegemonic language being French earlier, and now English in precarious tandem with French. This hierarchy is rationalized as being due to pragmatic constraints (time, 'efficiency') but is underpinned by a belief in the greater appropriacy of these languages (the purported superiority of French, or the role of the French in building up the EU, English now being thought of as a universal open sesame). These beliefs are premised on the assumption that linguistic hierarchies are normal and natural. They derive from a deep-rooted acceptance of the dominance of a single language within a nation–state, and of a few privileged international languages. The imprecision of key concepts such as multilingualism hinders clear thinking about the language policies in place. The investment of resources into English learning in continental education systems also means that more people are able to function in English. These structural and ideological factors (listed in Table 1 in Chapter 3) all contribute to an acceptance of the inevitability of English expanding. The result is fundamental inequality between speakers of English – those privileged are native speakers and fluent users of English as a foreign language – and the rest.

Ideas for change are mooted, for instance the suggestion that a single working language would be a solution to many of the language 'problems' of the EU. This was one of the radical proposals considered in 2001 by the Podestà committee on reform of the European Parliament in the light of enlargement. The idea was rejected as being wrong in principle, and as generating only modest savings.

The Eurobarometer Report (54, 15 February 2001) presumably also considered a single common language a possibility, otherwise it would scarcely have asked informants to react to statements of the following kind:

- 'Everyone in the EU should be able to speak English': 69.4% agreed, 22.5% were against, 8.1% don't know;
- 'The enlargement of the EU to include new member countries means that we will all have to start speaking a common language': 38 per cent agreed, 46.8% against, 15.2% don't know.

Responses to the statement 'Enlargement means that we have to protect our own language more/better' ranged as follows:

YES   Finns 90%, Greeks 90%, Luxembourgeois 78%, Spaniards 74%;

NO   Swedes 43%, Danes 33%, Austrians 32%.

These divergent symptoms of linguistic nationalism can be interpreted in several ways, but suggest that some groups are really concerned about the status of their languages.

Alternative solutions, such as much greater use of asymmetrical interpretation (i.e. interpretation being provided only into certain languages), would need to be explored, and strategies for assessing various scenarios elaborated. Some academic studies have attempted to identify the variables that can influence the establishment of optimal languages regimes,[74] and concede that there are no easy solutions. More specific proposals for investigation and follow-up will be made in Chapter 6.

If too little language policy is taking place nationally, it is not surprising that language policy at the supranational level is also a low priority. The considerable budget covering the translation and interpretation services (see figures in Box 4.1) is essentially a matter of facilitating activities that take place within EU institutions, and communications with governments and citizens, though there are spin-offs for national languages through the language planning undertaken. The EU budget for other activities in the fields of culture and language is modest. Few if any resources have gone into working out an overarching vision of what European multilingualism might consist of in the future, and what types of individual, institutional, and societal multilingualism are desirable. There is as yet no clarification of whether European linguistic identity is monolingual or multilingual. National identity used to be exclusive, whereas presumably a European linguistic identity is inclusive in the sense of the individual adding forms of supranational or international linguistic identity to the initial national one. This is comparable to what occurs in additive bilingual education, when the child learns a new language but not at the expense of the mother tongue. However amorphous or complex European identity may be, languages are the means by which new forms of political and cultural identity are taking shape.

In many international contexts, a *laissez faire* language policy is akin to a game of linguistic poker in which speakers of English, whether as a first or second/foreign language, increasingly hold all the good cards. Any major change of supranational language policy would need to be based on a great deal of preparatory groundwork. None of the EU institutions has commissioned studies to assess, for instance, how changed procedures or principles for language use could involve adjusting the existing language rights within a new framework based on explicit criteria for equitable communication. None have elaborated best and worst case scenarios for managing multilingualism in EU institutions, other than planning for the present arrangements to be adjusted to cope with enlargement. We need a vision of how supranational policies could reflect the complexity of the new supranational structure, scenarios that would be something different from national monolingualism plus interpretation and translation.

Chapter 5

Towards equitable communication

We came into the world like brother and brother:
And now let's go hand in hand, not one before another.
William Shakespeare, The Comedy of Errors, *V. i. 426, 1588*

Remember that the sole means of achieving peace is to abolish for ever the main cause of wars, the survival since the most distant pre-civilization world of antiquity of the domination by one people of other peoples.
Ludwik Lejzer Zamenhof, founder of Esperanto, 1915[1]

Words are, of course, the most powerful drug used by mankind.
Rudyard Kipling, 1923[2]

'When *I* use a word,' Humpty Dumpty said, in rather a scornful tone, 'it means just what I choose it to mean – neither more nor less.' 'The question is,' said Alice, 'whether you *can* make words mean so many different things.' 'The question is,' said Humpty Dumpty, 'which is to be master – that's all.'
Lewis Carroll, Through the looking-glass, *1872*

The ideal of formulating linguistic human rights is indeed a magnificent undertaking and also long overdue.
Nelson Mandela, 1998[3]

. . . clear, simple and precise drafting of Community legislative acts is essential if they are to be transparent and readily understandable by the public and economic operators.
The Interinstitutional agreement on common guidelines for the quality of drafting of Community legislation, 1999

There is a story of a newly appointed female minister in the Danish government who had to go to Brussels and chair a meeting soon after she took up office. She started the meeting by apologizing, in English, for not being fully in command of things because she was just at the beginning of her period. She evidently did not know that for native speakers of English this would mean she was menstruating. According to some versions of this story, which is supposed to be authentic, she said she was having her first period, which says something about how such humorous tales get embroidered.

What is not comic is that someone using English as a foreign language should be expected to know such subtleties in English. According to reputable dictionaries, the word 'period' has a dozen or so core meanings in English. The language policy issue at stake here is whether it is reasonable to expect that someone speaking a foreign language should use the language in exactly the same way as a native speaker. Anyone who functions regularly in a foreign language knows how extremely challenging it is to express oneself with the same degree of complexity, persuasiveness, and correctness as in one's mother tongue. We also know that being funny in a foreign language is extraordinarily difficult, and perhaps more likely to occur unintentionally. We all have our periods . . . of feeling less than fully competent.

The fundamental question for EU institutional language policy is how to ensure that all participants have equal communication rights. If the French and British can always use their mother tongues, how can one ensure that others have equivalent rights?

It is likely that monolinguals from Britain and the United States may not see that there is a problem when others are obliged to function in English. There is also a good deal of mythology about how tolerant English speakers are supposed to be, and how intolerant French speakers are reputed to be, of the way foreigners speak 'their' language. Another myth is that English is an easy language to learn and use. In fact it is in many ways a treacherous language, because of the complexities of structure and usage (reflecting its hybrid origins, and subtle variation in how near synonyms are used), and because there is massive variation in the ways English is spoken by people from different parts of the world, and even from different parts of the United Kingdom. It does not have a 'standard' pronunciation. 'BBC English', which phoneticians call 'Received Pronunciation', the model that foreigners are supposed to aim at, is spoken by only a small proportion of the population, and countless types of English can be heard on the BBC nowadays.

The reality of English as a prestigious language is tellingly captured by a South African who holds a key position in building up a more diverse, democratic post-apartheid society:[4]

It is amazing to observe the ease with which people who can't speak English, or speak it with a non-standard accent are often dismissed as unintelligent by white South African English-speakers, who more often than not have made no attempt themselves to master an African language.

This is comparable to the way it is assumed in many international contexts that you have to speak English in order to be taken seriously, as in the example from Bosnia quoted in Chapter 1. These examples demonstrate the points made in the quotes that begin this chapter: words are powerful drugs (Kipling), word meaning is essentially a matter of which participant 'is to be master' (Lewis Carroll), equality is an ideal that needs to be worked for and made explicit (Shakespeare), so as to avoid domination by one group of others (Zamenhof), and communicative efficiency is facilitated when language is optimally straightforward and transparent (guidelines for Community legislation).

Communication is more complicated when more than one language is involved. Those of us who have gone through the demanding process of learning a second language well, and use one regularly, are likely to be in a better position to understand the predicament of users of English or French as a foreign language. There is a clear need, at a time of intensifying europeanization, and when an increased use of English is impacting on other languages, to clarify principles of equity in communication, and to identify criteria that can guide language policy in the new multilingual Europe that is emerging.

We shall approach consideration of such issues by looking at:

- the goals and assumptions of language policy, and factors that influence this,
- the economics of language, and similarities between money and language as means of communication,
- language rights as human rights,
- language rights in the EU, as determined in cases at the European Court of Justice,
- alternative language policy paradigms: a Diffusion of English paradigm, and an Ecology of Languages paradigm,

- norms for English, now that it is used so widely by non-native speakers, and whether some form of English as a lingua franca can replace the traditional concern with English as a British or North American language,
- Esperanto as a means of creating more democratic communication among speakers of different languages.

Consideration of this broad range of topics will highlight some of the many variables that language policy measures need to take into account. More concrete recommendations for follow-up and implementation will be the subject of the following chapter.

Goals and assumptions of language policy

We can approach a clarification of the goals of language policy by seeing how far European countries follow comparable principles to those elaborated in South Africa, summarized in Chapter 3, reproduced in *italics* below, and the four parameters that guide Australia's language policy, in **bold** type below.

Language policy serves:

- *to promote national unity*: this is taken for granted in member states (though by no means unproblematical in Belgium, the Basque country, Northern Ireland,[5] and in several applicant countries), in addition to which there is an EU goal of unity at the supranational level;
- *to entrench democracy, which includes the protection of language rights*, **equality**: much EU rhetoric endorses democracy and respect for diversity, but language rights tend to be left implicit, and are generally given a low profile, rather than being actively fostered, which is also the case in many member states;
- *to promote multilingualism*, **external**: this is a goal both in some of the internal operations of EU institutions, and in actions to internationalize education and strengthen foreign language learning and student mobility;
- *to promote respect for and tolerance towards linguistic and cultural diversity*, **enrichment**: a general EU goal that is seldom converted into specific implementation or monitoring, nor does this goal tend to figure prominently in national education systems;
- *to further the elaboration and modernization of the African languages*: this corresponds to EU language planning work (corpus planning,

terminology) for the eleven EU languages, and the allocation of funds for language engineering (language technology and software development), but such work strengthens dominant rather than minority languages;

• *to promote national economic development,* **economics**: this is basic to the entire EU operation, explicitly so in policies for the 'knowledge society', 'lifelong learning', the 'European research area', and a human capital approach to education. In EU policy overall, the links between national languages, international languages, and economics are relatively unexplored. *Laissez faire* policies are bound to strengthen those languages that are powerful in the national and international economy.

The clear affinities at the level of broad goals do not reappear when considering the second set of variables from South Africa, the fundamental assumptions on which language policy is based in 'the highly sensitive area of language practices and language usage'.[6] The assumptions relate to how languages are seen, no language being superior to any other, languages as resources and fundamental human rights, the duty of the state to develop language policies for a multilingual society as an integral part of general social policy, and the implementation of the citizen's language rights.

The language policies of EU member states are not articulated along similar lines. The policies in force can promote linguistic diversity at the national, sub-national, and international levels, or they can constrain it. Policies seldom refer to language rights, except as regards some 'regional' minorities. Some of these have been granted more rights in recent decades, whereas immigrant languages receive little support. The Declaration of Oegstgeest, in The Netherlands, 'Moving away from a monolingual habitus',[7] 30 January 2000 (see Appendix 4), approved at an international conference on regional, minority, and immigrant languages in multicultural Europe, makes specific recommendations for how all of these languages could be acknowledged as 'sources of linguistic diversity and enrichment'.[8] Specific proposals are made for using these languages in all public domains, for research and documentation, teacher training, and awareness raising. The recommendations are in the spirit of the South African endorsement of the state undertaking an obligation to promote multilingualism and the rights of the speakers of all languages. For these ideas to materialize throughout Europe would require a major change in language policy.

Table 1 in Chapter 3 lists many of the factors that are influencing the way English is expanding in the contemporary world, several of which account for language policy being politically sensitive and difficult to coordinate internationally. There are many additional factors that can influence the goals of language policy:

- the degree of linguistic homogeneity or heterogeneity within a state, past and present,
- the extent to which language rights are granted to linguistic minorities,
- whether the dominant national language is widely used in other countries,
- levels of literacy in the languages in a given territory,
- language technology and linguistic engineering (publications, software, databases) for each language, developed in either the private sector or in public services,
- the immobility of the status quo in education (teacher qualifications, curricular traditions),
- the degree of centralization of education, and control of content and budget,
- the extent to which people in the worlds of politics, academia, business, and minority affairs have articulated language policy concerns, and if so, whether there is any consensus on needs,
- the degree of public interest in language policy,
- the existence of expertise in language policy.

These factors are interconnected, and the list could be extended. Together the variables influence the linguistic climate of a given state or institution. This can be termed its 'linguistic culture', which is deeply influenced by the groundswell of beliefs, attitudes, myths, and associations with languages that accumulate over centuries.[9] As the forms of political and social collaboration of the EU are of recent origin, and as democratic participation and deliberation at the supranational level are still in the making, it is clear that new forms of supranational linguistic culture are evolving. These could be converted into new language policy goals, for instance greater sensitivity to linguistic diversity and international communication. Whether they do so or not will depend in part on how languages are seen in relation to economics.

Economics and language

Language policy and education function in a world which is increasingly dominated by market economies, even if exclusive reliance on market forces has shown itself to be theoretically, politically, and economically suspect.[10] The fact that many of the world's poor may be culturally and multilingually rich does not count on the balance sheets of states and transnational corporations. Analysis of the economics of language can clarify relationships between resources, allocations, and certain types of justice and efficiency, while reminding us that approaches in economics are not independent of value judgements. Nor is 'equity' an absolute standard but a principle requiring different goals and means in varying contexts. Less powerful languages can become victims of linguicide as much from economic forces, the 'laws' of the market, as state policies. In either case, linguistic human rights are violated when members of a minority group are not able to use their language so that they can reproduce themselves as a distinct cultural or ethnic group.

Money and language perform similar functions. *Money* is, for economists,[11]

1 a system of exchange,
2 a unit of account, a measure by which the value of goods and services is computed,
3 a store of value, in metal, paper or virtual form.

Each of these traits has a parallel in *languages* as

1 the medium for the exchange of ideas,
2 a system for analysing, structuring, and assessing the world,
3 a resource for storing cultural values.

Money is one element of economic policy, which has to do with the creation and distribution of value. Languages are a key constituent of social and cultural policies, and contribute in shaping the world. Linguistic capital is a significant form of cultural capital. Some forms of linguistic capital, privileged languages or forms of language, are more easily convertible into material resources and influence than others. Political crises occur when injustice and economic inequality are seen as correlating with distinct linguistic groups.

A national currency also has, like language, social and emotional dimensions to it. Well-established currencies engender strong attachment. The appeal is reinforced by the words and visual symbols portrayed on banknotes (the British monarch, national cultural luminaries, etc.). The euro can function as a measure of exchange, and a unit of account, but it has as yet little cultural value or appeal within the EU or outside it.

The imagery of Europe as an ongoing building project can be seen on the euro notes issued on 1 January 2002, which display a range of architectural styles, all projecting the buildings of 'Europe', and symbolizing the construction of Europe. Euro banknotes lack the clutter of words found on national banknotes. The appeal and legitimacy of the dollar, pound, and crown are reinforced by reference to the authority of the state, traditional values, and in the case of the USA, religion. The euro, by contrast, facilitates and follows the laws of the market, guaranteed by a bank that, unlike national banks, does not have the authority or emotional appeal of a state behind it. The launch of the euro therefore represented an act of faith, with fragile legitimacy. Linguistically a euro banknote (eurobill?) is restricted to the letters (in Latin and Greek script) of the issuing bank, and a single word, euro. The euro started life as 'Godless, stateless, and untrustworthy?'[12] Its banknotes are virtually language-less (whereas the European Central Bank conducts its affairs exclusively in English). However, the euro is also high politics, as it is being used as an instrument to create European economic and political union. The policy will only succeed if the euro generates emotional loyalty to Europe. The euro banknotes mark a shift from 'In God we trust', or 'In the monarch we trust', to 'In money we trust'.

Economic policies deal with 'the efficient allocation of scarce resources which have alternative uses', and the funding (by some form of taxation or contribution) of the allocation and distribution of resources, which should aim, so far as language policies are concerned, at ensuring fair and efficient results for speakers of different languages.[13] This is complicated by the degrees of economic power behind languages, for instance German as the EU-internal giant, and the Lilliputian Baltic languages, although the modest position of German at the supranational level suggests that the EU hierarchy reflects factors other than demography and the national economy. The position of English is strengthened because of its role in the global economy.

The distribution of resources to languages in EU institutions reflects these imbalances but may also serve to counterbalance some of them. Thus the EU envisages the same number of appointments for the

languages of the enlargement countries, irrespective of the demographic or economic power of each state. This is a defensible policy on
the grounds of equity, when linguistic diversity is regarded as a source
of value, as is reiterated in EU treaties and policy statements.

The language policies in force in European institutions correspond
to the first two functions of money, language for interactive exchange,
and language as a means of recording information and specifying value.
The precise value of any EU words can be interpreted and laid down
definitively in the European Court of Justice (see the section
'Languages and Eurolaw' pages 157–60). The third function, *languages
as a store of values*, is recognized when EU rhetoric supports the maintenance of cultural traditions and diversity. On the other hand the
existence of a hierarchy of languages in EU institutions, with French
and English at the top, could mean that the store of value embedded in
these languages is treated as greater than that of other languages.
Concepts from French and English are exported to other languages,
whereas the flow of ideas in the other direction is minimal. There is an
obvious risk of this when documents are initially drafted in French or
English, from which they are translated into other languages.
Widespread borrowing from English is a symptom of global americanization. It is presumably the fear of cultural and linguistic
homogenization in the internal affairs of the EU that led Fischer and
Védrine to warn against 'unilingualism' – which is probably a diplo-
matically coded word for the worldview of Anglo-American
globalization, and the fear that other languages and their speakers are
being downgraded to second-class languages and second-class citizens.[14]
If the EU can consistently allocate financial resources to counteract
such tendencies, this would exemplify how economic policies can facilitate and foster linguistic diversity.

The *cost of language learning* is considerable, if one considers the investment in institutions, teacher training, salaries, space on timetables, and
the effort made by the individual learner over a long period of time.
Education systems are increasingly oriented towards instrumental skills
and markets in which certain types of linguistic capital are perceived as
being a better investment than others. Foreign language learning
involves acquiring communicative skills and intellectual and intercultural
competence, cultural capital of the kind that the language policy makers
at the EU and the Council of Europe endorse: 'Going beyond the cultural to the intercultural, the goal is not to develop native-like
proficiency, but intercultural speakers, citizens able to mediate between
cultures within national, regional and European identities'.[15]

Some countries invest far more in foreign language learning than others. The marketability of English accords immediate benefits to the British and the Irish, as English opens many economic doors. British insularity has naively assumed that the importance of English globally made the learning of other languages unimportant.[16] As a result, children in school can opt out of foreign language learning at age 14, and few young people appreciate what sort of return they will get on a personal investment in learning foreign languages. Continental European countries have taken on the financial burden of ensuring that their nationals can communicate in English, and to a lesser extent French and other languages.

As less British investment goes into learning foreign languages than in their EU partner countries, one can regard Britain as having a competitive advantage, more time available in schools for other activities, and fewer material and personal resources committed. Whether there is any real advantage depends, of course, on many other factors that influence educational success, which regular OECD evaluations monitor. Two implications follow, however.

The first is that the advantages that accrue from the widespread use of English globally may be short-lived. Britain may be at a competitive disadvantage if British people have inadequate skills in foreign languages. It is predictable that as skills in English become more widespread, there will be a drop in the labour market value of English. Empirical research shows that skills in English are 'associated with significant earnings gains in the Swiss labour market', high competence resulting in up to 30 per cent more in earnings, for females as well as males, particularly in the German-speaking part of Switzerland. However, the economic value of English as compared with competence in other languages may well depreciate with time, when more people become proficient in English, particularly in English as a foreign language, while also being competent in other languages.[17] Monolingualism may well lead to an economic dead-end. (The unquantifiable non-material value of cultural and linguistic diversity is a separate issue.)

The second is that the global hierarchy of languages provides a major economic bonus for the British economy, through the strength of the English teaching industry. This provides services (language teaching, teacher training, consultancy, etc.) and goods (books, television series, etc.) in Britain and abroad, with the competitive advantage that books published for a vast English-using market can be produced more cheaply than others. It is ironical that a country that has a poor record in foreign language learning is a global leader in the teaching of English as a foreign or second language, in teaching methods, in curriculum development, and in language learning theory. This activity has been built up as a direct result of government policy since the 1950s, and has been of decisive importance in maintaining the position of English in post–colonial education systems.[18] It is also influential in the adult education market globally, and is increasingly in evidence in all parts of Europe. Successive British governments and language policy makers, aided and abetted by the media, have assumed that the more English expands, the better for British influence and earnings. Box 5.1 presents samples of official and media discourse on English. English is clearly not merely a lingua franca but also a *lingua economica*.

Box 5.1 Triumphant English

England will be 'the dominating force in international politics, the professed and confessed arbiter of liberty . . . the world's leading nation'. Britain has a new responsibility which means that 'we not only have a spiritual heritage of our own – a national soul – but that somehow this possession is incomplete unless shared with other nations'. A new career service is needed, for gentlemen teachers of English with equivalent status to 'the Civil Service, Army, Bar, or Church', an 'army of linguistic missionaries' generated by a 'training centre for post-graduate studies and research', and a 'central office in London, from which teachers radiate all over the world'. The new service must 'lay the foundations of a world-language and culture based on our own'.

R. V. Routh, *The diffusion of English culture outside England. A problem of post-war reconstruction*, Cambridge University Press, 1941

Within a generation from now English could be a world language – that is to say, a universal second language in those countries in which it is not already the native or primary tongue.

British Cabinet, *Report on the Teaching of English Overseas*, 1956[19]

A Ministry of Education – under nationalistic pressures – may not be a good judge of a country's interests . . . insofar as a second language becomes truly operative, the view that the mind takes will change . . . English, through its assimilations, has become not only the representative of contemporary English-speaking thought and feeling but a vehicle of the entire developing human tradition: the best (and worst) that has been thought and felt by man in all places and in all recorded times.

> I. A. Richards, *Anglo-American Conference on Teaching English Abroad*, 1961[20]

Britain's real black gold is not North Sea oil but the English language. It has long been at the root of our culture and now is fast becoming the global language of business and information. The challenge facing us is to exploit it to the full.

> British Council, *Annual Report*, 1987–88

If Europe is to have a future, it needs more than a common currency, a common foreign policy and a common set of laws. It must have a common language. That language can only be English.

> *Daily Mail*, 14 November 1991

The way of salvation for the French language is for English to be taught as vigorously as possible as the second language in all its schools . . . Only when the French recognize the dominance of Anglo-American English as the universal language in a shrinking world can they effectively defend their own distinctive culture . . . Britain must press ahead with the propagation of English and the British values which stand behind it.

> *The Sunday Times*, 10 July 1994

Britain is a 'global power with worldwide interests thanks to the Commonwealth, the Atlantic relationship and the growing use of the English language'.

> Malcolm Rifkind, British Foreign Secretary, reported in *The Observer*, 24 September 1995

> ... to exploit the position of English to further British inter-ests, as one aspect of maintaining and expanding the role of English as a world language into the next century ... Speaking English makes people open to Britain's cultural achievements, social values and business aims.
>
> The British Council, market research project
> *English 2000*, 1995
>
> English has in fact become the lingua franca of the European Union ... Almost every conceivable human opinion, almost any human sentiment, is expressed in English.
>
> Abram de Swaan, *Words of the world.*
> *The global language system*, 2001[21]

The widespread faith in the value of the British variant of English and of British methods for teaching it, in the profession known under various labels, English Language Teaching (ELT) and English for Speakers of Other Languages (ESOL), is founded on a number of fallacies, particularly about the assumed universal relevance of the native speaker as a teacher of English.[22] Foreign language teaching has evolved along very different lines in continental Europe. The assumed universal relevance of British ELT is increasingly being critiqued, not only for some of its unfounded pedagogical assumptions, but also because of the fundamentally ideological and political nature of foreign language education.[23]

If English were to be made the sole administrative language of the EU, which presupposes a political decision on this at the highest level, this would not only be to the benefit of the English teaching industry, it would also deliver a huge market in translation and interpretation services to the UK and Ireland, although they contain only a small proportion of the population of the EU. Any such decision would also tie EU institutions more closely to the culture of the dominant economic order, and serve to legitimate it.

In the linguistic market-place, the appropriate branding of languages is a significant asset, a productive resource that is convertible into power, material and immaterial resources.[24] Language policy decisions in each of the three areas of language planning, decisions on the status of languages (e.g. choice of working languages, registering a patent either in the local language or in a 'global' language), educational policy on which languages should be learned (acquisition planning), and investment in the corpus of a language (e.g. corporate investment in terminology software and language technology tools[25]) all have major economic consequences. Resources invested in this way represent an investment in production, as the languages chosen are used in discourse to create our world. Their use consolidates the power of the speakers of the languages chosen for all such purposes.

Linguistic human rights, or just language rights?

The task of guaranteeing respect for linguistic human rights involves ensuring that linguistic minorities enjoy the rights that majority groups take for granted for themselves. The human rights system was evolved to protect the victims of an oppressive state, and can be seen as a counterweight to market forces and forced assimilation. Human rights are absolute in the sense that no state can be justified in departing from them. There are rights for individuals and groups to maintain and develop their languages, and the state has a duty to implement them.

Although scores of human rights declarations and covenants since 1945 proclaim that discrimination on grounds of language is a human rights violation, it has been estimated that anything between 50 and 90 per cent of the world's languages are at risk from the forces of globalization and the nation-state.[26] For the maintenance and development of languages, educational linguistic rights, including the right to education through the medium of the mother tongue, are absolutely vital. The linguistic protection of national minorities rests, according to the High Commissioner on National Minorities of the OSCE (the Organisation for Security and Co-operation in Europe), on two human rights pillars (the abbreviations are explained below):[27]

> the right to non-discrimination in the enjoyment of human rights; and the right to the maintenance and development of identity through the freedom to practise or use those special and unique aspects of their minority life – typically culture, religion, and language.

The first protection can be found, for instance, in paragraph 31 of the Copenhagen Document, Articles 2(1) and 26 of the ICCPR, Article 14 of the ECHR, Article 4 of the Framework Convention, and Article 3(11) of the 1992 UN Declaration. It ensures that minorities receive all of the other protections without regard to their ethnic, national, or religious status; they thus enjoy a number of linguistic rights that all persons in the state enjoy, such as freedom of expression and the right in criminal proceedings to be informed of the charge against them in a language they understand, if necessary through an interpreter provided free of charge.

The second pillar, encompassing affirmative obligations beyond non-discrimination, appears, for example, in paragraph 32 of the Copenhagen Document, Article 27 of the ICCPR, Article 5 of the Framework Convention, and Article 2(1) of the 1992 UN Declaration. It includes a number of rights pertinent to minorities simply by virtue of their minority status, such as the right to use their language. This pillar is necessary because a pure non-discrimination norm could have the effect of forcing people belonging to minorities to adhere to a majority language, effectively denying them their rights to identity.

Copenhagen Document: Copenhagen Meeting of the Conference on the Human Dimension of the Conference on Security and Cooperation in Europe (CSCE), 1990

European Charter: (Council of Europe) European Charter for Regional or Minority Languages, 1998

ECHR: European Convention on Human Rights and Fundamental Freedoms, 1950

Framework Convention: (Council of Europe) Framework Convention for the Protection of National Minorities, 1998

ICCPR: UN International Covenant on Civil and Political Rights, 1976

ICESCR: UN International Covenant on Economic, Social and Cultural Rights, 1976

UN (Minorities) Declaration: UN Declaration on the Rights of Persons Belonging to National or Ethnic, Religious and Linguistic Minorities, 1992

In many of the post-1945 human rights instruments, language has been identified in the preambles as one of the most important characteristics of humans for human rights purposes, but in the binding clauses, and especially those relating to education, language often disappears completely or is subject to opt-outs, modifications, and alternatives. In effect, binding international and European Covenants,

Conventions, and Charters provide very little support for linguistic human rights in education.[28] The efforts of the OSCE reflect a change in the awareness of people working in preventive diplomacy (particularly in trouble spots in the former communist world), education, and human rights law: 'there is an increasing acknowledgement in legal circles that language not only can but must be respected and accommodated because of fundamental human rights principles'.[29]

The entry into force on 1 March 1998 of the European Charter for Regional or Minority Languages[30] is a step in this direction. The Charter is a comprehensive document, a standard-setting instrument that all states that are members of the Council of Europe are being encouraged to adhere to, even states that have been reluctant to admit the existence of minorities within their territory, such as France, Greece, and Turkey. A state can choose which languages it wishes to be covered by the Charter, and which paragraphs or sub-paragraphs it wishes to apply (a minimum of 35 is required). The opt-outs and alternatives in the Charter permit a reluctant state to meet the requirements in a minimalist way, which it can legitimate by claiming that a provision was not 'possible' or 'appropriate', or that numbers were not 'sufficient' or did not 'justify' a provision, or that it 'allowed' the minority to organize teaching of their language as a subject, at their own cost.

The Charter does not apply to immigrant languages. Nor does it apply to Sign languages, even though these fulfil the criteria for qualifying.[31] Sign languages are completely independent languages and have nothing to do with oral languages. Hopefully they will be the object of a separate Council of Europe initiative.

Despite its limitations, the Charter is a key point of reference for what happens to minority languages in each member state of the EU. It has clauses relating to all levels of the education system, to public services, and to the media. There is a monitoring process to ensure follow-up.

The Charter is not concerned with languages at the supranational level, where communication involves speakers of nationally dominant languages sharing new linguistic territory that is divorced from the nation-state. The human rights system functions on the principle of the state being responsible for the observance of rights within its jurisdiction. When states interact, it is up to them to agree on what language rights shall apply. Any such provisions would be in force as a result of articles in an international treaty, rather than by virtue of a human rights principle. This is the case with the Treaty of Rome and its successor treaties, in which there is a clause empowering the Council of Ministers to legislate on language use. The fact that the EU is a new type of political construction, and sovereignty is shared between the supranational and national levels, complicates the issue of language rights.

The human rights system is constantly being expanded, as consensus on new needs and principles evolves.[32] Language teachers' associations have campaigned for the right to learn a foreign language as a human right. This right is not contained in any universal human rights declaration. The right to learn the mother tongue and one of the official languages of the country of residence can be regarded as *necessary* linguistic rights. By contrast, the right to learn a foreign language can be seen as an *enrichment* right, one that can enlarge one's cultural and economic repertoire and horizons, rather than an inalienable human right. Enrichment rights assume that the mother tongue is not at risk, which is the case when minorities are forced or enticed into shifting language.[33]

The right to learn a foreign language is, however, creeping into various rights declarations. This can be seen in the Draft UNESCO Declaration on Cultural Diversity[34] of 23 October 2001:

> Culture should be regarded as the set of distinctive spiritual, material, intellectual and emotional features of society or a social group . . . it encompasses, in addition to art and literature, lifestyles, ways of living together, value systems, traditions and beliefs.

This Declaration has sections devoted to Identity, Diversity and Pluralism; Cultural Diversity and Human Rights; Cultural Diversity and Creativity; and Cultural Diversity and International Solidarity. The main lines of an action plan are identified in an Annex. Among the clauses referring to language are the following:

> All persons should therefore be able to express themselves and to create and disseminate their work in the language of their choice, and particularly in their mother tongue. . . . (Article 5)
>
> Safeguarding the linguistic heritage of humanity and giving support to expression, creation and dissemination in the greatest possible number of languages. (Annex, point 5)
>
> Encouraging linguistic diversity – while respecting the mother tongue – at all levels of education, wherever possible, and fostering the learning of several languages from the youngest age. (Annex, point 6)

These educational rights aim at preparing people for an international-izing world, in which multilingualism is increasingly necessary for access to the higher levels of the education system, and for employ-ment. This 'need' does not mean that foreign language learning can be regarded as a universal, inalienable human right, one that no govern-ment can violate. A formulation along the lines of 'Anyone has the right to learn any language', which figures in a draft Universal Declaration of Language Rights, primarily elaborated by Catalan orga-nizations and the international PEN club (the NGO that works for freedom of expression for authors), is scarcely likely to result in oblig-ations on any state. The Declaration has been submitted to UNESCO, which is now responsible for its further elaboration. Progress on all such declarations is invariably slow, and in the case of this proposal will meet resistance from many states.

What about communication rights? Could there be support in dec-larations of communicative rights for the right of representatives of EU member states to operate in the language of their choice in EU insti-tutions? The *People's Communication Charter*[35] is the work of journalists, communications experts, and non-governmental organizations from many countries, who are concerned about cultural globalization driven by commercial interests, and by the way governments tend to monop-olize the available channels of communication.[36] The Charter enumerates ways in which the right to be informed, to be heard, and to influence policy should be enshrined. It takes the principle of free-dom of speech into the age of technological media and mass communication networks, and seeks to encourage linguistic and cul-tural diversity. It recognizes the need for more active national and international policy-making to strengthen people's fundamental right to communicate. In its efforts to link up with civil society, and give voice to ordinary people, it is actually attempting to do what the EU claims that it now wishes to do, namely to involve ordinary people in dialogue with supranational government.

Rights are of little other than symbolic value unless the signatories clearly identify a duty-holder (which is the most obvious weakness of the People's Communication Charter), and if they cannot be enforced. In principle the language regime of EU institutions lives up to the requirements of linguistic human rights in relation to the use of eleven languages. EU citizens have the right to address EU institutions in any of the official languages of the EU (but not always: see the court cases reported on below), and to be replied to in the same language. The equality of the working languages of the EU should also mean that the individual's rights are respected in all EU activities. The significance of linguistic human rights in basic education, and the collective right of minorities to reproduce themselves and resist assimilation, are implicitly supported in EU declarations, such as the Resolution concluding the European Year of Languages (Appendix 2). Implementation is the sovereign concern of member states, whose domestic language policies are being influenced by europeanization and globalization, though probably not yet in ways that impact strongly on basic education or minority rights. The role of the Council of Europe and the EU is confined to endorsements of good practice in education, and modest cash injections that strengthen various types of language teaching and learning. The EU might consider demonstrating its commitment to multilingualism by formulating a Code of Good Multilingual Practice that fully respected fundamental principles for linguistic human rights in its own activities – and then following them.

Languages and Eurolaw

Disputes about the application or interpretation of European Community (EC), now European Union, law are decided by the European Court of Justice. There have been several cases involving language rights in recent years. It is worth summarizing the way the court has dealt with language issues in some detail, since this has implications for how the equality of languages is understood by those who decide on supranational Eurolaw.

In the case of *Kik v. Office for the Harmonisation in the Internal Market (Trade Marks and Designs)* (hereafter 'Office'), the European Court of Justice (Court of First Instance, case T-120/99, 12 July 2001) had to consider whether an EU institution, the Office, had the right to decree that even if an application for a Community trade mark can be filed in any EU official language, the 'languages of the Office shall be English, French, German, Italian and Spanish'. The case was brought by a lawyer specializing in intellectual property law in The Netherlands, with the support of the Greek government, who claimed that the Office regulation was in conflict with the right of EU citizens to communicate with EU institutions in any of the official languages. The Office was supported by Spain and the Council of the European Union. The applicant pleaded infringement of the principle of non-discrimination in Article 6 of the EC treaty (now, after amendment, Article 12 EC), since as a Dutch person she is at a competitive disadvantage as compared with those for whom the Office languages are a mother tongue, secondly that translations may not be perfect, and thirdly that the measure is in conflict with Regulation 1 (see Chapter 4, Box 4.3), which ought to apply to the Office. The Greek government argued along similar lines. The Spanish government argued that the restriction to five languages was functional. The Council argued that Regulation 1 'contains no fixed principle of Community law', and is not in force at the Office. It also argued (in §51 and §52 of the judgement) that 'there is no Community law principle of absolute equality between the official languages. Otherwise there could be no Article 217 of the EC Treaty (now Article 290 EC)'. The Council pleaded that the restriction to five languages was practicable and reasonable, and saved money.

The Court ruled that:

- a 'Regulation 1 is merely an act of secondary law . . . Article 217 of the Treaty enables the Council, acting unanimously, to define and amend the rules governing the languages of the institutions and to establish different language rules . . . the rules governing languages laid down by Regulation No 1 cannot be deemed to amount to a principle of Community law' (§58).
- The rules do not involve an infringement of the principle of non-discrimination (§59).
- The Office regulations relate to choice of a language when there is a dispute (opposition, revocation, invalidity) by another party, with whom there needs to be an agreement on choice of a procedural language, and that it was therefore 'appropriate and proportionate' that this should be one of 'the most widely known languages in the European Community' (§63).
- The right to communicate with EU institutions in any official language applies to the Parliament, Ombudsman, Council, Commission, Court of Justice, Court of Auditors, Economic and Social Council, and the Committee of the Regions, but not to other bodies, and therefore not the Office (§64).

For all these reasons, the action was dismissed. From this one can conclude that if the Council of Ministers at some point in the future decide to scrap Regulation 1, they would be fully entitled to do so (as the Legal Opinion of the European Parliament of 29 August 2001 also stated; see Chapter 4). At present this requires unanimity between the member states, but the general trend in the EU is towards qualified majority voting, following the principles for proportional voting in the

Council (see Appendix 3). One could therefore imagine that at some future point a restricted number of working languages might be decreed, for instance identifying two or three for use at all times other than in the final stages of enactment and promulgation of Eurolaw. This would represent a major policy reversal, but it is not unthinkable that the speakers of the 'big' languages would press for it.

In *Geffroy* and *Casino France* (Case C-366/98, 16 September 2000), the Court clarified an issue put to it by France (the Court of Appeal in Lyon) on the labelling of foodstuffs, and whether Community law permitted national stipulation of exclusive use of a particular language. Coca Cola, cider, and ginger beer exported from Britain and on sale in France were labelled exclusively in English. The Court ruled that Article 20 of the EC Treaty (after amendment, Article 28 EC) and Article 14 of Council Directive 79/112/EEC 'preclude a national provision from requiring the use of a specific language for the labelling of foodstuffs, without allowing for the possibility for another language easily understood by purchasers to be used or for the purchaser to be informed by other means'.[37] This seems to mean that national legislation can require use of a particular language, but should allow for the possibility of an additional language or for the same message to be transmitted non-verbally. The ruling is singularly unclear in the English translation (the case was heard in French), both as regards the principle enunciated and its application. How should whether a language is 'easily understood' be ascertained? The ruling appears to signify that a general requirement of imported goods needing to be in a specific national language is untenable, and that presenting a product in a set of diagrams or pictures might be an adequate way of informing the consumer.

In *Commission of the European Communities v. Italian Republic* (Case C-212/99, 26 June 2001), the case was brought because university staff of non-Italian origin employed at Italian universities are discriminated against, and deprived of pay and pension rights that they are entitled to under Italian law. The court found 'that, by not guaranteeing recognition of the rights acquired by former foreign-language assistants who have become associates and mother-tongue linguistic experts, even though such recognition is guaranteed to all national workers, the Italian Republic has failed to fulfil its obligations under Article 48 of the EC Treaty (now, after amendment, Article 39 EC)'. In 1983 the Court ruled that the teachers should have the same contracts as their Italian counterparts. In three judgements since then, the Italian state has been found at fault. As the Italian government has failed to act on these judgements, or to react to condemnation in the European

Parliament at three plenary sessions, 1500 foreign language lecturers in Italy have requested the Commission to impose sanctions on Italy to force it to comply.[38]

The human rights system was initially devised as a means of according rights to the individual and imposing duties on a state. A state can be accused of violating human rights at the European Court of Human Rights (which has nothing to do with the EU). The accountability of a supranational body is another matter, which the appointment of an EU Ombudsman seeks to address. The human rights system was not conceived of as potentially redressing the hierarchies of a global market in which internationally dominant languages impact on national languages. Court cases on such issues can be taken to the European Court of Justice, as the three very different recent cases show, where the Court acts at the interface between national law and Eurolaw. For a human rights approach to the languages of Europe to be pursued more actively in the affairs of the EU would require a major change of approach. To situate language rights principles within a wider concern with the global ecology of languages would be a good starting-point.

Towards an Ecology of Languages paradigm

Many of the dimensions in the contemporary tension between a globally expansionist language and alternatives to it are illuminatingly brought together in two paradigms that were initially proposed by a Japanese communications scholar, Yukio Tsuda. His work was impelled by anger about inequality in international communication. Native speakers of Japanese, whether ambassadors, scholars, or business people, experience that they simply have fewer rights than speakers of English in most contexts of international communication. Japanese culture is now also so strongly influenced by the west that the Japanese have become obsessed by 'Anglomania' and the need to learn English, though they are not very successful at doing so. English is taught ever earlier in the school system, and pre-school mothers 'are more proud of their children being able to speak English than . . . Japanese'.[39] Tsuda's sense of injustice led him to propose two language policy paradigms, for which he suggested six parameters. They have been elaborated in a more differentiated analysis by Tove Skutnabb-Kangas, who devised Table 3.[40] This has the merit of presenting an overarching conceptual framework within which many of the fundamental dilemmas and genuine complexities of language policy in a given context can be understood.

Table 3 The Diffusion of English and Ecology of Languages paradigms

1 monolingualism and linguistic genocide	1 multilingualism and linguistic diversity
2 promotion of subtractive learning of dominant languages	2 promotion of additive foreign/second language learning
3 linguistic, cultural, and media imperialism	3 equality in communication
4 americanization and homogenization of world culture	4 maintenance and exchange of cultures
5 ideological globalization and internationalization	5 ideological localization and exchange
6 capitalism, hierarchization	6 economic democratization
7 rationalization based on science and technology	7 human rights perspective, holistic integrative values
8 modernization and economic efficiency; quantitative growth	8 sustainability through promotion of diversity; qualitative growth
9 transnationalization	9 protection of local production and national sovereignties
10 growing polarization and gaps between haves and never-to-haves	10 redistribution of the world's material resources

Language policies in Europe do not adhere unambiguously to either of these paradigms. Nation-states have traditionally aimed at monolingualism (as in the Diffusion of English paradigm), whereas now there is much proclamation of multilingualism (as in the Ecology of Languages paradigm), though how this should be understood or implemented is less than clear.

Skutnabb-Kangas has demonstrated that the continuation of monolingualist assimilation strategies in the education of minorities falls within Articles II(e) and II(b) of the UN Genocide Convention (1948 UN International Convention on the Prevention and Punishment of the Crime of Genocide) and the definition of linguistic genocide in Article III(1) in the Final Draft of the Convention.[41] Article III was voted down in the UN General Assembly, but the definition was accepted by all UN member states.

Article II(e), *'forcibly transferring children of the group to another group'*; and
Article II(b), *'causing serious bodily **or mental** harm to members of the group'* (emphasis added).

Article III(1), *'prohibiting the use of the language of the group in daily intercourse or in schools, or the printing and circulation of publications in the language of the group'*.

If children are linguistically assimilated because they are not given education through the medium of their own languages and/or because the parents have been forced, or enticed through false arguments, to give up speaking their own languages to their children, the children are being forcibly transferred to a dominant language group; they risk suffering mentally, and the use of their language is prohibited. This is the subtractive learning of languages (point 2 in Table 3), aiming at monolingualism (point 1). The promotion of additive foreign and second language learning, now firmly endorsed by the EU and the Council of Europe, should apply both to majority group members and to linguistic minorities. This is a matter of equality (3) and human rights (7).

Linguistic imperialism (3) builds on an assumption that one language is preferable to others, and its dominance is structurally entrenched through the allocation of more resources to it. The dominance of English in contemporary Europe (for contributory factors, see Table 1) can constitute linguistic imperialism if other languages are disadvantaged, and are being learned or used in subtractive ways. This is one of the worries in commerce, science, culture, and the media in continental Europe, with domain loss as a symptom of linguistic imperialism. There is clear evidence of language teaching being encumbered by an Anglo-American set of values and norms in southern Europe,[42] and in the post-communist world.[43]

The myth that what the 'world' needs is a single language of international communication is patently false but fits into the mould of linguistic imperialism, americanization, and the homogenization of world culture (4).[44]

At their crudest, linguistic and cultural imperialism merge, as observed in Japan by an American political scientist, Douglas Lummis, who was appalled by the assumption of cultural superiority of native-speaker Americans. In an article entitled 'English conversation as ideology', he wrote that 'the world of English conversation is racist. . . . The expression "native speaker" is in effect a code word for "white" . . . their real role is not language teacher but living example of the American Way of Life'.[45] He recommends that the Japanese should start thinking of English as the language of Asian and Third World solidarity. When English study is transformed from a form of toadying into a tool of liberation, all the famous 'special difficulties' which the Japanese are supposed to suffer from will probably vanish like the mist. Language schools which employ only Caucasians should be boycotted. Japanese who want to study English should form study groups with Southeast Asians, and together work out a new Asian version of English that reflects the style, culture, history, and politics of Asia. And then if the Americans who come to Asia complain that they can't understand this new variety of English, they should be sent to language school.

The diffusion of whose English?

Work along the lines proposed by Lummis is currently under way in Asia.[46] The idea of a local form of English, distinct from a British or American variant, building on local needs, cultural norms, and intelligibility, is similar to a proposal for English as a Lingua Franca (ELF) in Europe. The assumption, in relation to Asian English and ELF, is that people from different cultures can interact freely in a language that is not a mother tongue, and that many of the subtleties and linguistic complexities of British and American English are irrelevant, so that time does not need to be wasted on teaching them.[47] ELF is an attractive idea if it facilitates equality in communication (3), and the maintenance and exchange of cultures (4), as well as the promotion of linguistic diversity (1, 8) and national sovereignties (9).

A similar vision of English as a democratic world language underpins the *Encarta World English Dictionary*, published by Bloomsbury in 1999, and in an electronic form by Microsoft. It attempts to cover all forms of English worldwide, and treats all of them as equally acceptable. In a short introductory article on 'World English' for the dictionary, Tom McArthur writes:

> No-one can even think today about who 'owns' the language or its many varieties. The English language has become a global resource. As such, it does not owe its existence – or its future – to any nation, group, or individual. Inasmuch as a language belongs to any individual or community, English is the possession of every individual and community that wishes to use it, wherever they are in the world. It is in effect as democratic and universal an institution as humankind ever possessed.[48]

It is true that English, like any language, is not good or bad intrinsically. Any language can serve noble or evil purposes. What is decisive is the uses to which individuals and groups put the language. On the other hand norms for the language, and who decides what is 'proper' English, are important issues, whoever is using it. Whether English is still an Anglo-American prerogative, or has been liberated from its origins, is a question that permeates a number of contradictory trends. These are of essentially two types. The first set can be seen as reinforcing the privileges of those for whom English is a mother tongue.

First, belief in the *special virtues of native speakers of English* is widespread. Announcements advertising employment in the EU, or in a body partly funded by the EU, frequently state a preference, or even a requirement, that the applicant should be a native speaker of English. The issue has been raised in questions in the European Parliament,[49] in the French Parliament,[50] and in the EU Commission by the Belgian Minister of Employment and Equal Opportunities, Laurette Onkelinx (25 January 2001), on the grounds that such ads are in conflict with a principle of non-discrimination in employment. Romano Prodi, and two Commissioners, those for Education and Culture, and for Employment, have responded by stating unambiguously that while job announcements can legitimately specify a particular level of linguistic proficiency, a requirement of mother tongue proficiency can be 'disproportionate in relation to the declared objective', and that the principle of linguistic non-discrimination under Eurolaw and Belgian law must be respected.[51] A similar complaint has been made about a job ad for a post at the Council of Europe, which has admitted that giving preference to a native speaker can amount to discrimination, and suggests that the criterion 'principal language of education' can function as an alternative to 'mother tongue'.[52] As this discrimination is still continuing, under cover of a requirement of 'English mother tongue or equivalent', an official complaint was made on 7 May 2002 by the President of the Universal Esperanto Association, Professor Renato Corsetti, to the EU Ombudsman, Jacob Söderman.[53] The complaint refers to 400 ads of this nature, and cases of discrimination against continental Europeans who have studied in Britain. It requests the Commission to admit that there is unjust discrimination in favour of native speakers, to cease funding any bodies guilty of this discrimination, and to work out solutions so that EU-funded bodies no longer discriminate on linguistic grounds.

Second, the recruitment of *native speakers as teachers of English* for jobs at all levels from the primary school to the university reflects a preference for those brought up speaking the language (which looks suspiciously like a throwback to English teaching by native speakers in Japan representing a way of life). There has been substantial recruitment through the US Peace Corps and various British recruitment agencies for teaching posts of this kind in several Asian countries, post-communist Europe, and to a lesser extent in the EU, here mainly in the private language school sector (which typically flourishes in southern Europe as a supplement to the teaching of English in schools).

Third, a number of politicians have floated the proposal that *English should be declared the second official language* of their country, apparently in the belief that if this is done, all their problems of learning English would be solved by act of parliament. The idea has been seriously considered in Japan and Korea, countries which have been influenced massively by the USA since 1945 (with US troops still stationed there). The EU Commissioner from Greece, Anna Diamantopoulou, came up with the same idea for her country in December 2001. She was forced, by the furore her remarks aroused (much of it of a crudely nationalist kind), to admit publicly that what she really meant was that all Greek schoolchildren should learn English at school.[54] This shows an abysmally low level of awareness on the part of a Commissioner about what an 'official' language is. In somewhat similar vein, the Danish Minister of Education in the early 1990s referred to English as the 'second mother tongue' of Danes. Most Greeks and Danes would regard these ideas as pretty irrelevant and ill-informed. One wonders whether it is asking too much to expect our political leaders to show some care and insight when making public statements about language policy.

Fourth, believers in *World English* tend to argue that the language belongs to its users, wherever they come from, and however they express themselves. Authorities on language write that 'the English language has already grown to be independent of any form of social control',[55] while also arguing that 'the foundation for World Standard Spoken English is already being laid around us',[56] claims that are manifestly incompatible. There is still a great deal of uniformity in *written* English worldwide, whereas *spoken* English is much more varied, and invariably signals something of the speaker's background. It is likely that the influence of global media corporations is such that if a single standard for the spoken language ever emerges, it is likely to be a North American one, or possibly some kind of BBC/CNN hybrid. The very notion of a 'standard' implies norms, and guardians of the standard, which makes a nonsense of the idea of complete freedom for the users of the language. One can use local forms for local purposes, but if communication is to function internationally, there has to be a more serious engagement with intelligibility and linguistic norms shared across cultures. A 'World Standard Spoken English' is bound to be based on Anglo-American mother tongue norms.

Underlying each of these instances of the way English is confirmed as a dominant language is an ideology of the pre-eminence of the native speaker, the model for other users of English, the language of global officialdom and world affairs in all key international domains. They fit snugly into the Diffusion of English paradigm, and an uncritical acceptance of the prevailing economic and linguistic world order.

There are, however, counter-arguments and trends that see English as an international language differently, and envisage a different focus in teaching and learning the language, one that would strengthen features of the Ecology of Languages paradigm.

1 Lingua Franca English. English is in active use as a lingua franca, by people for whom the language is not a mother tongue, in many contexts in Europe, but the basic research into charting such uses of English has barely begun.[57] Work is under way on vocabulary and pragmatic use of the language. A recent book on the phonology of English as an international language[58] explores the notion of a common core that is present in many forms of English, whether spoken as mother tongue or foreign language. The purpose is to elaborate more realistic pedagogic goals for learners of English, cutting out the unimportant subtleties of a prestige variant of native speaker English pronunciation. The focus is on accent addition rather than the elimination of foreign accent, a principle that has much in common with additive as opposed to subtractive learning of languages. Another recent book focuses on the role of communities for whom English is not the mother tongue in the establishment of 'world English' with multicultural identity.[59]

2 The fluent non-native as the learning target. People learning foreign languages are not on a route towards pretending to be native speakers. They need to be able to express themselves effectively in English with people from anywhere in the world. Teaching should build up this competence as rapidly and economically as possible. Those who advocate English as a Lingua Franca (ELF) seek to legitimate a shift away from native speaker norms towards equipping people to function effectively as non-native speakers. Teachers of ELF can then project themselves as authoritative users of English as a lingua franca rather than as less than perfect users of English as a native language.[60] The accident of birth, or at least of the language of upbringing, embedded in the term 'native speaker competence' ought to be unimportant as compared with professional qualifications. This applies particularly in teaching jobs, for which insight into the learner's culture and language ought to be a basic requirement for employment, one that well-qualified teachers of foreign languages are likely to have. Such people also have the benefit of having gone through the process of successfully learning the target language.

3 Native speakers as the cause of communication difficulties. Although native speakers have an edge in many types of intercultural communication, tend to talk more, and may succeed in influencing outcomes more, native speakers can in fact be the cause of communication problems (see Box 5.2). Native speakers have greater facility in speaking the language, but not necessarily greater sensitivity in using it appropriately. In many international fora, competent speakers of English as a second language are more comprehensible than native speakers, because they can be better at adjusting their language for people from different cultural and linguistic backgrounds. What is perhaps striking is that it is rare for such issues to be discussed, for instance how an international meeting or conference can be organized so as to give everyone, irrespective of mother tongue, a chance to contribute on a basis of equality.

Box 5.2   Inequitable international communication

British journalists frequently interview non-British people on radio or television. They make few if any allowances for the fact that the non-natives are expressing themselves and being spoken to in a foreign language. The tendency is to use complex, idiomatic language that presupposes a great deal of cultural and linguistic knowledge.

When a new Danish government was formed in December 2001, the Foreign Minister was interviewed shortly after his appointment on BBC World (17 January 2002) in London on a programme appropriately called 'Hard talk'. The Danish government had just formed a strategic alliance with an extremist right-wing party. The journalist was eminently well prepared for the interview, and the Minister found himself having to defend very dubious government policies. He speaks fluent but far from precise or 'correct' English, whereas his French is reported to be rather better than his English.

The British journalist frequently interrupted the Minister, and made many statements ending in a tag question (à la *It's like this, isn't it?*), with falling intonation, which is used in standard English when agreement by the interlocutor is expected. He used difficult vocabulary. For instance, the initial question involved a series of statements, ending up with *Isn't that rather disingenuous?* The journalist referred to a (female) Danish MP making a statement that basically admitted that the new government is following a racist agenda. The journalist commented that she *let the cat out of the bag*. This term was not understood, providing a clear instance of ineffective communication caused by the native speaker. The journalist then reformulated his question, and asked whether the Minister agreed with what this MP had said, to which he replied that he did not. The journalist then asked whether the MP was *speaking out of turn*, meaning without authority to do so. The Minister paused, and stated that she was speaking *out of tune*. This is not a fixed phrase in English, but one could hypothesize that there is some semantic overlap between *speaking out of turn* and *out of tune*, i.e. not sending the right signal.

The interlocutors reached some kind of understanding, but even if meaning has been 'successfully' negotiated, the new form produced by the user of English as a foreign language is not one that other users of English would wish to copy.

The interview as a whole was generally regarded in Denmark as having shown the Minister making a complete fool of himself. The programme aroused so much interest that it was shown several times on Danish television. Danish journalists had a field day commenting on the Minister's English. None raised the question of whether the communicative inequality, the asymmetrical communication, and the insensitive native speaker language was defensible.

4 A level linguistic playing-field. In the summer of 1996 I attended two international conferences, a Language Rights conference in Hong Kong,[61] and a language policy symposium in Prague as part of the Universal Esperanto Association 81st World Congress.[62] At the Hong Kong conference, English was virtually the sole means of communication. In the question time of one of the plenary sessions, a South African participant expressed surprise at why those whose competence in English was less than ideal, particularly Asians who had great difficulty in expressing themselves in English, accepted the unequal communication rights imposed on them by the conference organizers. The answer was that the organizers, mainly British, had not given the matter any thought, and the non-native speakers, from all over Asia, were too polite to protest. A couple of weeks later at the Esperanto symposium, it was amazing to experience participants from all over the world communicating confidently in a shared international language, among them a number of Asians who were manifestly at no disadvantage. As this event was my first experience of Esperanto in action (with interpretation provided for us non-Esperantists), it was a vivid and memorable way of seeing at first hand that Esperanto is not merely utopian but a reality for those who have chosen to make it part of their lives, domestic, national, and international. The juxtaposition of the experience of English working badly and inequitably – and for once this being discussed openly in public – and Esperanto working well provides appetising food for thought. The Esperanto option will be taken up in the next section.

Neither native speakers nor non-native speakers have a monopoly of sensitivity or competence in communication. Both can contribute to inequity in communication, but as the examples show, sometimes inequity is built into the structures and ideologies of international relations. The Diffusion of English paradigm ascribes to English a function as the default language, the universal norm, even though this gives its native speakers unfair advantages, and non-native speakers a substantial learning burden.[63]

I can see the following points in favour of an ELF approach:

- non-native speakers do interact effectively in English, using whatever competence they have in the language,
- communication involves negotiating meaning, and correctness in all details is less important than the capacity to reach understanding interactively,
- an excessive focus, in teaching English, on abstruse points of pronunciation or grammar may be a waste of limited teaching time,

- the term 'non-native' defines users of English as a foreign language negatively, in terms of what they are not, rather than positively – it therefore implies stigmatization and is discriminatory.

On the other hand, presumably the goal of users of English as a foreign language is to be as precise as possible, which means using vocabulary as it is presented in dictionaries, whether of English as a national language (Oxford, Webster) or as a World Language (Encarta). Good users of English as a second language evolve strategies for communicating effectively, and teaching should assist this, but teaching must also involve a great deal of exemplification of the language of rich, precise, error-free users of English, whether as a mother tongue or as a second language.

It is important in any analysis of communication to distinguish between use of the language in speech and in writing, which are very different tasks, and to distinguish between productive competence (speaking, writing) and receptive competence (listening, reading), which also make very different demands on users.

The issue of whether local forms of English are appropriate and correct, or errors, has not been resolved in the analysis of 'World Englishes', and is bound to complicate efforts to incorporate non-native uses of English as a teaching goal in Europe. Much learner-centred pedagogy already involves learners in creating their own learning, and building on their expanding competence, rather than being passive reproducers of knowledge selected and defined by others.

I will conclude this section with another anecdote that highlights these problems. When Salman Rushdie was due to travel to Denmark to receive a literary prize awarded by the EU in 1995, the Danish government initially cancelled the ceremony on the grounds that there was a security risk. After a few tumultuous days, they agreed to go through with the ceremony on a later date. At a press conference in Copenhagen, Rushdie asked why it was that the Danes were unable to guarantee his safety for a few hours on the first date. The Danish Prime Minister replied that he did not have the 'ability' to answer the question. If he had stated that he was not 'able', for security reasons, to do so, he would have avoided casting doubt on his own mental faculties. The tiny shift from adjective to noun makes all the difference.

I have been accused of native-speaker-centredness, when I reported on this 'error' in the English of a top Danish politician.[64] I referred to the Prime Minister's error creating an impression he did not intend, whereas a protagonist of ELF claims that native speaker correctness is an irrelevant criterion here, that ELF interlocutors would understand what the PM meant, and that the problems are in the eye of the native speaker beholder.[65] It is impossible to know which interpretation is valid, since how people reacted cannot be verified, but the contexts from which I have drawn the anecdotes in this chapter (politicians being interviewed or questioned, or chairing a meeting) are formal, with little scope for meaning negotiation. Many people may have a high tolerance threshold for users of ELF, but clearly the conditions for communication in high-level negotiations and in the media are often inequitable (it is grossly unjust to expect a Danish politician to have native-speaker English: see Box 5.2), and language use is of crucial importance. We should therefore be concerned with how communication can be made more democratic and effective.

A language for equality in communication?

There is a tendency for those not familiar with Esperanto to reject it without seriously investigating whether it might provide a more efficient and equitable solution to some problems of international communication, and contribute to making foreign language learning in schools more effective. This reflects ignorance, which Zamenhof, the founder of Esperanto, found an explanation for in Ovid: 'Ignoti nulla cupido' – one does not wish for what one is ignorant of.

It also reflects historical amnesia. At the League of Nations, founded to work for the avoidance of military conflagrations like the First World War, the suitability of Esperanto to function as the official language was seriously considered. Earlier in the twentieth century Esperanto had been of considerable interest to governments: no fewer than eleven were represented at the conference in 1910 of the Universal Esperanto Association. Between 1920 and 1924 the League of Nations considered reports of the experience of learning the language in 26 countries. Delegates of eleven states (Belgium, Brazil, Chile, China, Columbia, Czechoslovakia, Haiti, India, Italy, Persia, South Africa) recommended in 1920 that Esperanto should be learned in schools 'as an easy means of international understanding'.[66]

In September 1922 the League voted not to follow the recommendation of a committee to develop Esperanto as a working language of the organization. Thirteen states were in favour of such a solution: Albania, Belgium, China, Columbia, Finland, India, Iran, Japan, Poland, Romania, Czechoslovakia, South Africa, and Venezuela.[67]

There was fierce resistance to the idea of Esperanto becoming the key international language, particularly on the part of France, which did not wish to see any change in the role of French as the primary diplomatic language (at least in the western world). The existing world order might have been threatened not only by a neutral language but also by the pacifist utopian political beliefs embraced by some Esperantists.[68] The Esperanto option was rejected, a pattern that holds to this day, apart from some nominal recognition and consultative status at the UN and UNESCO.

There is a copious literature on Esperanto.[69] Among the most relevant sociolinguistic facts are that:

*   several thousand children worldwide are growing up (in over 2000 families) with Esperanto as one of their mother tongues,
*   fiction flourishes, novels and poetry in the original as well as in translation,
*   Esperanto is used as the medium for scientific conferences on many topics,
*   Esperanto can be learned much faster than other languages because of the regular, productive rules underlying it,
*   the simple, systematic grammar of Esperanto makes it easier for non-Europeans to learn than European languages,
*   proficiency in Esperanto enables its speakers to talk directly to people from a wide range of cultural and linguistic backgrounds,
*   interpersonal communication in Esperanto is symmetrical, irrespective of the mother tongue of the interlocutors, unlike much 'international' communication in a language connected to a nation-state,
*   Esperantists were persecuted by Stalin and Hitler,[70] but were tolerated in eastern European communist countries and in communist China,
*   lack of political or economic clout is of course the primary weakness of the language.

The Universal Esperanto Association is attempting to influence language policy in international organizations. The Manifesto approved at its 81st World Congress in Prague in 1996 enumerates a number of principles that the movement stands for. These cover democracy, global education (ethnic inclusiveness), effective education (better foreign language learning), multilingualism, language rights, language diversity, and human emancipation. The two most relevant ones in the present connection are these:

DEMOCRACY. Any system of communication which confers life-long privileges on some while requiring others to devote years of effort to achieving a lesser degree of competence is fundamentally antidemocratic. While Esperanto, like any language, is not perfect, it far outstrips other languages as a means of egalitarian communication on a world scale. We maintain that language inequality gives rise to communicative inequality at all levels, including the international level. *We are a movement for democratic communication.*

LANGUAGE RIGHTS. The unequal distribution of power among languages is a recipe for permanent language insecurity, or outright language oppression, for a large part of the world's population. In the Esperanto community the speakers of languages large and small, official and unofficial, meet on equal terms through a mutual willingness to compromise. This balance of language rights and responsibilities provides a benchmark for developing and judging other solutions to language inequality and conflict. We maintain that the wide variations in power among languages undermine the guarantees, expressed in many international instruments, of equal treatment regardless of language. *We are a movement for language rights.*

There are forces attempting to persuade the European Parliament to consider the Esperanto option seriously, and an increasing number of MEPs are reportedly interested in debate on such matters. A hearing was held in 1993,[71] and various petitions have been penned since then. Esperantists who happen to work within EU institutions are convinced that serious attention ought to be given to using the language, and have identified a number of options for consideration in language policy fora.[72]

The Joint Interpreting and Conference Service has been asked to explore the possible use of Esperanto as an 'intermediary' (i.e. pivot or relay) language for interpretation.[73] A preliminary answer by Neil Kinnock on behalf of the Commission refers to the absence of qualified interpreters and interpreter training for Esperanto, and constraints of cost when qualified interpreters are needed for the languages of present and future EU member states. These are valid points, practical hurdles that would need to be overcome as part of any longer-term strategy. Kinnock's response goes on to state that 'recourse to a language that is not used in everyday life would run the risk of not being able to convey the full range of messages and ideas communicated during meetings'. This reveals ignorance of the sociolinguistic realities of Esperanto, and is a perfect example of the prejudice that Esperanto tends to encounter. It is also disturbing that language policy issues are handled as part of a secret internal review procedure,[74] without the criteria underpinning the official response being made explicit.

In the long term the use of Esperanto as the sole relay language for interpretation and for document drafting would potentially result in major economic savings. It could contribute towards maintaining a healthier, less hierarchical ecology of the official languages of the EU. It could serve to strengthen the language rights of speakers of all these languages, and give a new purpose to the rhetoric of support for multilingualism. This is admittedly a scenario that could not be implemented overnight, but Eurocrats and language specialists who are used to operating multilingually would need only a modest investment of time and effort to be able to add Esperanto to their repertoire. The principle of an international language that facilitates symmetrical communication between people from different linguistic backgrounds, and that does not threaten other languages, ought to be an attractive one for the EU. Whether the political will for bringing this about could be found is an open question, but one that ought to be asked.

Chapter 6

Recommendations for action on language policies

We know what we are, we know not what we may be.
William Shakespeare, Hamlet, *IV. v. 43, 1600*

Words are no deeds.
William Shakespeare, Henry VIII, *III. ii. 154, 1612*

Whatever people say about the shortcomings of translation, it remains one of the most important and meritorious tasks in international communication.
Johann Wolfgang von Goethe, Kunst und Altherthum, *1828*

Real unity of cultures and species is found in their very diversity.
Ngũgĩ wa Thiong'o, 2000[1]

This book has attempted to follow Shakespeare in 'knowing what we are' in language policy in Europe, in understanding the complexity of the linguistic mosaic of Europe, past and present, the pressures on languages from trends in globalization, and the way europeanization is affecting the language ecology of Europe. To 'know what we may be' is an invitation to be visionary, to build on the vitality of the languages and cultures of Europe, and create conditions for the continued flowering of this cultural and linguistic diversity. 'Words are no deeds' is a reminder that proclamations and good intentions have to be converted into action.

Language policy for Europe must therefore address:

*   *sociolinguistic* realities, including 'big' and 'small' languages, nationally and internationally, the risk of severe loss of linguistic diversity, asymmetrical communication due to linguistic hierarchies, the native/non-native imbalance, the nature of English in a Europe of fluid national and supranational identities;

- issues of *cost*, in relation to the use and learning of a range of languages at the sub-national, national, and supranational levels;
- matters of *principle*, language as a human right, equity as a paramount concern in democratic communication structures, and criteria for a just and sustainable ecology of languages;
- issues of *practicability and efficiency*, how multilingualism can be managed in a wide spectrum of contexts, among them education, science, culture, and the media, and how interpretation and translation can function optimally in political life and commerce;
- issues of *political will* and power, the challenge of taking up the sensitive topic that language policy is, and the conversion of policy initiatives into legislation and policy implementation.

Let us begin with *worst-case scenarios*. Half a dozen, which may appear singly or in combination, are quite enough to show what needs avoiding:

- *laissez faire* at the national and supranational levels, linguistic nationalism, antagonism, and defensiveness lead to English 'triumphing' over all other European languages, speakers of which experience increasing marginalization, domain loss, attrition of their languages, and a loss of cultural vitality, and there is an intensification of the polarization between haves and have-nots locally, Europe-wide, and globally, that correlates closely with a consolidation of corporate power, and proficiency in English;
- English becomes the sole in-house working language in the affairs of the EU, resulting in a limiting, technocratic dumbing-down process, and evolution of a simplified, pidginized but unstable 'Euro-English' that inhibits creativity and expressiveness, whether English is used as a mother tongue or as a foreign language, a language that is spoken with so much imprecision that communication difficulties and breakdowns multiply;
- foreign language learning continues unchanged, with the result that this vast investment in schools remains relatively ineffective and unrewarding, elites become multilingual, others (apart from linguistic minorities) are *de facto* monolingual;
- the continued neglect of immigrant minority languages hinders a dynamic, multicultural integration process;
- language policy decisions continue to be taken by politicians and administrators without reference to the substantial body of

knowledge and experience that the research community globally has accumulated;

• the vast majority of the British and Irish end up as the under-qualified in a global economy in which bilingual competence is a minimum requirement for influential positions.

Then there are the *best-case scenarios*. A dozen can provide a glimpse of what language policies can do to stimulate linguistic vitality. Again, they can appear singly or in any combination:

• harmonious, complementary national and supranational identities evolve with full respect for language rights at each level;
• an infrastructure at national and supranational levels is built up, with the responsibility and power to ensure well-informed decision-making on language policy measures, to commission research and consultation exercises that bring together policy makers, administrators, and grassroots constituencies;
• in the corporate world, science, culture, the media, education, publications, and internet services, investment in English is systematically counterbalanced by an equivalent investment in another language;
• a much larger proportion of the population is educated successfully through a wider range of languages, for instance by children being taught through the medium of two languages, while a third language is learned well as a foreign language;
• encouragement of a number of widely used lingua francas rather than just one, and a variety of models of polyglot communication,
• much greater awareness, developed through enlightened policies in school, higher education, and the media, of the importance of languages for maintaining and intensifying cultural diversity and creativity;[2]
• more reciprocity in Europeans and non-Europeans learning each other's languages, in the reciprocal learning of majority and minority languages, and of neighbouring languages;
• the efficient and sensitive multilingual policies practised in EU institutions facilitate democratic consultation processes and promote a flourishing continent-wide European public sphere;
• adequate funding for acceptance of Esperanto as the sole pivot language for interpretation, and as the initial drafting language for all EU documents, results in a strengthening of all languages and more culturally sensitive dialogue between speakers of different languages;

- translation and interpretation function as valuable facilitators of cross-linguistic dialogue, bringing Goethe's awareness of their importance into the electronic, multi-media world;
- language policy implementation is based on incentives rather than sanctions;
- the vision of the real unity of cultures and species being in their diversity (Ngũgĩ wa Thiong'o) rather than in homogeneity becomes widely understood and practised.

We need now to sketch out what steps might be taken so that words become deeds. Specific recommendations are identified, and numbered consecutively, to facilitate follow-up. The recommendations derive from the analysis of earlier chapters, and are inspired by language policy formulation in many other contexts, national (the assessment of foreign language needs, and language and the economy, in several countries), regional (active minority language constituencies), and international (as in Council of Europe projects). Since europeanization entails the continuous merging of the national and the supranational, these levels need to be brought together.

Policies at the European level, whether on fishing stocks, food additives, or foot and mouth disease, are formed after proper consultation with the available scientific expertise. This does not happen in the field of language policy, where states cling to what they regard as the national interest, and politicians seem more interested in maintaining maximal freedom of manoeuvre than in commissioning serious study of the issues, and consultation with all the relevant constituencies. As a political scientist writes, when assessing the fluctuations in the implementation of bilingual education policies in Sweden, 'scientific "truths" are often subordinated to economic "truths"'.[3]

It is also likely that language issues have not been high among the priorities of governments, and that many public figures and journalists are woefully, but perhaps pardonably, ignorant in this area. The need for action has been stressed in a range of studies:

- The Nuffield Languages Inquiry in the United Kingdom, a comprehensive consultation exercise that resulted in a large number of findings and proposals, concludes baldly: 'The government has no coherent approach to languages . . . The scene remains a patchwork of often unrelated initiatives. There is no rational path of learning from primary school to university and beyond and investments in one sector are rarely exploited in another.'[4]

- The Haut Conseil de la Francophonie was more bombastic in describing the teaching of languages as 'a planetary defeat that needs to be remedied'.[5]
- The Dutch are often considered as among the best users of foreign languages in Europe, but a national survey concluded that the Dutch over-rate their competence in English, and 'are not fully convinced of the usefulness and necessity of a knowledge of foreign languages. The consequences of ongoing internationalization for our foreign languages are underestimated, even in trade and industry'.[6]
- A report by an independent consultant for the EU's LINGUA programme in 1993 concluded, after consultations in each member state: 'most Member States have not yet reached the position of defining their own strategy for languages in a coherent form'.[7]

At a time of political uncertainty about the 'construction' of Europe, and about the balance of powers between the Commission, the European Parliament, national governments, and the Council of Ministers, it is important to focus on the language dimension of europeanization. Irrespective of how these constitutional matters are determined in the first decade of the twenty-first century, and whether more accountability, transparency, and legitimacy are ensured, the language policy issues will continue to permeate and influence all EU activities. If more adequate and dynamic language policies are to be elaborated for the national and supranational levels, there has to be a much firmer framework to permit coordination of the collaborative efforts of teams of bureaucrats, experts, and politicians. There has to be serious reflection on how EU institutions, language teaching and learning, and research can contribute to this. The recommendations that follow address these issues. The broader political context of language policies is taken up in the concluding section of the chapter.

Recommendations

National and supranational language policy infrastructure

1   Academics and policy makers from eleven countries are convinced that 'Europe urgently needs a transparent public discussion on language policy with the aim of developing guidelines for European and national language policies. Therefore it is necessary

to set up forums . . . for developing a new European approach to the language issue in which as many players as possible should participate (from the political and economic arenas, the media, NGOs)' (Vienna Manifesto of June 2001, first recommendation: see Appendix 5[8]). There is a need for infrastructure and consultative procedures to facilitate this.

2   Dialogue between key stake-holders in language policy work, politicians, journalists, researchers, administrators in the national and EU civil service, non-governmental organizations (NGOs), and users of language services, is a prerequisite for more informed policy formation. It must draw on the existing scholarly evidence worldwide, which at present appears to have little impact on policy.

3   Each national government must have well-qualified civil servants specializing in language policy, with responsibility for integrating language policies in commerce, culture, education, research, the media, international relations, and in the supranational institutions of the EU system.

4   There is a need for an equivalent strengthening of the EU Commission with expertise in all aspects of language policy, and with a mandate to strengthen the 'general interest' in the sense of cross-cutting policies that ensure the vitality of languages globally.

5   The Vienna Manifesto also suggests (Recommendation 3) that 'All governments should use a fixed percentage of their GDP for promoting multilingualism in education, research, politics, administration and the economic sector.' Such a proposal could provoke a major rethink of the value of existing efforts and investment in this field, a reconsideration of goals and priorities, and fruitful dialogue between the public and private sectors.

6   A primary function of the national and supranational specialists would be to bring language policy higher up on relevant political, academic, and media agendas, to conduct awareness campaigns, and produce pamphlets that debunk common myths (about the excessive cost of EU language services, the need for a single 'world' language, monolingualism as something normal, or age being the most important factor in learning a foreign language) and dispel ignorance (about personal or societal bilingualism, language X having no grammar, or language Y too much) and prejudices (linguistic xenophobia, Esperanto not being a 'real' language), etc. They should also collect and disseminate information on good practice in multilingualism nationally (e.g.

Luxembourg maintaining its national language proudly but using French and German extensively in state affairs), and internationally (instances of national and international languages being in healthy equilibrium).

7 There should be urgent development of MA programmes in currently neglected language fields, particularly multilingualism, the sociology and ecology of languages, language rights, the auditing of language needs, language planning and policy, language and economics. A huge amount of scholarly literature has been produced in recent years, in virtually all parts of the world.[9] The related fields of applied linguistics and foreign language pedagogy, which tend to focus on the forms of language, and theories and practices of learning and teaching, are already well established in some countries.

8 MA and PhD degrees that are given the 'European' label should set a good example of multilingual practice by following criteria agreed on by the federation of university rectors and vice-chancellors, and in particular require that the programme of study is conducted in at least two languages, and evaluation undertaken by assessors from at least two EU countries.[10]

9 In-depth analysis of the relationship between economic policies and languages, at local/regional, national, and international levels, and the extent to which the education system is able to respond to changing needs, should be linked to studies of linguistic diversity and its maintenance, and to how economic policies for threatened languages can be not merely defensive but more proactive and preventive.

10 One of the concerns of specialists in language policy should be to ensure that the language factor is explicitly addressed in all policy fields where it may be relevant, rather than language being seen as something special and distinct, or only a matter for education, law, and commerce. At the other extreme, a narrow focus on language rather than its embedding in social and cultural contexts needs to be monitored, so as to avoid the risk of 'the medium becoming the message'.[11]

11 Measures are needed to counteract Hollywood dominance on the screen, so that cinemas and TV companies diversify culturally and linguistically in ways that promote exposure to a range of European cultures and languages. Policy needs to be shaped so as to ensure that such channels attract a broad public.[12]

12 Awareness campaigns should aim at informing the public about

languages in supranational affairs, language rights as human rights, arguments in favour of a diversification of the languages learned, big and small, and explaining how multilingualism connects with cultural and biological diversity and sustainability.[13]

13   A Language Policies Handbook should be elaborated that can serve as a source of inspiration for many routes to equitable communication, through sensitive policies that respect linguistic diversity, with examples of the provision of language services, including those for people with special needs, examples of how successful minority language policies can be undertaken, and suggestions for how guidelines for European and national policies could be formulated.

14   There is a need for networks that bring together the various associations concerned with individual languages, NGOs and para-statal bodies which have the interests of each of the EU official languages at heart (French, Swedish etc.), so as to coordinate strategy internationally.

EU institutions

15   There must be proper briefing for Members of the European Parliament on how the translation and interpretation services operate, since there is evidence that MEPs are 'ignorant about many aspects of what multilingualism involves'.[14]

16   There should be similar briefing for politicians, experts, and civil servants who work in member states and attend meetings in EU institutions on the principles underlying interpretation and translation, and the constraints that may account for complete, direct interpretation not always being provided.

17   A Code of Language Conduct in EU Institutions should be elaborated. This should aim at ensuring complete equality for everyone in EU interaction, irrespective of mother tongue. It should be monitored by the EU Ombud institution, which deals with specific complaints but aims at also ensuring good administrative practice, but has not yet been given a mandate for this.[15]

18   If the Council of Ministers were to consider any change in Regulation 1, for instance introduction of a *de jure* two-tier system according 'big' languages more rights than other languages, no decision should be taken before there has been an in-depth study of the consequences of any such decision for all the languages concerned, and study of alternative solutions. Such

studies would need to be based on prior identification of criteria and principles that should be followed when language regimes are being decided on.

19 Special attention should be paid to the implications of an increasing use of English for speakers of other languages. This is a significant issue for people based permanently in Brussels or Luxembourg, for those attending meetings there irregularly, and for European civil society as a whole. Policies that favour English, as a procedural language, or as a sole link language with applicant states, or in correspondence between EU institutions and member states, should not be adopted without proper analysis of the implications for speakers of each official language, and only after a transparent consultation process. Monitoring procedures should be implemented to ensure the rights of speakers of all official languages.

20 The EU must develop active policies that counteract linguistic discrimination. Employment in EU institutions, or in bodies funded by the EU, must at all levels require bilingual or multilingual competence. Recruitment must never discriminate in favour of native speakers of a language, either *de jure* or *de facto*. Myths about the superior merits of any language, or about assumed linguistic competence due to the accident of birth, need to be effectively dispelled.

21 There needs to be more coordination between the language services in EU institutions and national language policy authorities, covering such matters as the training of translators and interpreters, efforts to improve the quality and accessibility of texts, terminology, use of databases, citizen access, and users' experience of the language services and suggestions for improving these.[16]

22 There should be regular monitoring by EU insiders and outsiders of the operation of the system of working and procedural languages in EU institutions, and the availability or otherwise of texts in all languages when documents are sent out to the governments and citizens of member states. When the internet is used so as to make papers available early in the decision-making process, as part of a policy of ensuring greater transparency, it is essential that documents are available in all official languages simultaneously.

23 There needs to be regular monitoring of the functioning of EU language services when full interpretation is not provided, for

instance use of the SALT system, Speak All, Listen Three (i.e. interpretation is provided from all languages but only into English, French, and German), which some MEPs would like to see extended,[17] and of the efficacy of the system in Commission or Council meetings when some speak a foreign language.

24   Serious consideration should be given to the use of Esperanto as a bridging or pivot language for the spoken and written word in EU-internal communication, to calculating the economic costs in the short term for learning the language, and the longer-term economic savings that could result from implementation of an Esperanto-based system. In parallel there should be pilot studies and assessment of the implications for language learning in schools, when Esperanto is learned as the first foreign language, and as a bridge to learning others, where the research evidence is that this is likely to provide all learners with successful experience of a new language.

25   As lobbyism is a fact of Brussels life, there being over 2000 lobbying groups with a permanent office in Brussels, most of them representing commercial interests, but none specifically concerned with languages (with the exception of an office representing the interests of 'francophonie', and the EU-funded European Bureau for Lesser Used Languages), thought needs to be given to how language policy interests can be better covered by lobbies that should preferably receive funding from a variety of sources.

26   A number of specific recommendations for strengthening multilingualism in the EU are made under point 4 of the Vienna Manifesto (on working languages, consistent multilingualism, terminology, funding for translations, simultaneous interpretation, translation quality, teacher exchanges, research funding).

Language teaching and learning

27   The Vienna Manifesto makes specific proposals for how a reform of language teaching can result in a wider range of languages being learned more effectively (see the nine topics listed under point 5). These build on ongoing experience, a range of types of innovative and inspired foreign language learning that is already taking place in Europe.[18] This should be analysed more intensively prior to popularization in an accessible form for parents, teachers, and decision-makers.

28   Publications on language learning topics for the general public are needed. An admirable model of writing of this kind is *A parents' and teachers' guide to bilingualism*, by Colin Baker,[19] which is written entirely as responses to typical questions, grouped under section headings entitled Family questions, Language development questions, Questions about problems, Reading and writing questions, and Education questions (basic education, types of bilingual education, achievement and underachievement, language in the classroom).

29   Dissemination of good practice, sharing information on resources, teaching materials, software, methods of language learning, and internet facilities, is also now widely available. Many countries have national information centres, such as the Centre for Information on Language Teaching and Research, CILT, in London.[20] The exchange of experience across national borders should be intensified, as a supplement to the work of the British Council and the Goethe Institut (which function independently, though mainly state-funded), French linguistic advisers (who are attached to embassies), and other national language promotion bodies. These fund useful activities, but their role is to strengthen a particular national language (English, Spanish, . . .), and commercial interests are increasingly involved, education being a key field of activity for corporate globalization (as seen in Chapter 3).

30   As a means towards diversifying language learning, it has been suggested, often by French sources,[21] that the criterion of different linguistic families ought to guide a choice of two foreign languages in school, e.g. one Romance language and one Germanic language (or with enlargement, one Slavic language). The same argument might be advanced when and if the EU decides to consider formally restricting the number of working languages in its institutions. Diversification can alternatively be promoted if a geographical criterion is used, for instance the learning of the language of a neighbouring community (e.g. Czech or Hungarian in Austria). Another possibility is for minority and majority children to learn an immigrant language (as in the two-way programmes that are successful in the USA[22]). All of these lines of argument can contribute to ensuring that a range of languages is learned.

31   An increasing number of EU countries are experimenting with various types of bilingual education, and with the teaching of certain subjects through the medium of a foreign language.[23] Some

of the most successful results are achieved in Luxembourg, where education effectively makes most school-leavers trilingual in the mother tongue, French, and German.[24] Also extremely relevant as a model for imitation elsewhere are the 'European schools', intended mainly for EU employees, and that exist in six countries, in which the education is given in two languages and an additional foreign language is learned to a high level.[25]

32   If a wider range of languages is learned more successfully in school, there could be more reciprocity and diversity in students travelling for higher education in other member states. The schemes funded by the EU (ERASMUS, SOCRATES) can promote the learning of all EU official languages, but when students who do not specialize in a language go abroad for a term, or even a year, their stay may strengthen their competence in English rather than in, say, Dutch or Finnish. The figures for foreign students in Britain[26] show that study abroad is big business for Britain.

33   Higher education institutions should be encouraged to formulate a languages policy for their activities, covering teaching, research, publications, and professional development in a broad range of languages, and partnerships that can strengthen multilingualism[27] and plurilingualism.[28]

Research

A conference on European language policy organized by the European Cultural Foundation in 1998, involving academics, politicians, and administrators, was followed up by a report detailing a large number of research needs.[29] These have been incorporated into the set below, which builds on needs identified in early chapters.

34   Multi-disciplinary research should be undertaken of the use made of languages in EU institutions in the principal types of internal and external communication, as one means of providing a well-documented clarification of the hierarchies of languages in place.

35   There is a need for conceptual clarification of terms that are central to language policy and that tend to be used inconsistently, such as lingua franca, national language, international language, minority language, official language, and working language.

36   There should be a broad range of studies of multilingualism as it evolves in a changing Europe, which can be seen as four distinct areas: Domestic Europe in each country, Civil Europe

internationally, Institutional Europe (the EU), and Educational Europe. State-of-the-art reports should draw out present and predictable consequences of current language policies for the linguistic groups involved. This research could be connected to the study of domain loss and diglossia (functional differentiation between languages for different purposes), for which a refinement of research methods and approaches is needed, particularly in light of the fact that many contexts of use are fundamentally new because of technological innovation, and changing patterns of communication as a result of globalization and europeanization.

37 Research should analyse people's experience of foreign language learning, the collection of good practice in educational contexts that achieve positive attitudes to societal multilingualism. Key topics for multi-disciplinary analysis are language awareness, good strategies for language learning, and the potential for foreign language learning to be assisted by means of Esperanto. There should in general be a strengthening of scholarly input into decisions on the organization of language learning in schools. This should also include serious consideration of the importance of learning non-European languages.

38 Research is needed into the use and learning of English, not as a British or American language but as one for continental European purposes. This should build on a description of English as a lingua franca, and the relevance of this for the teaching of English. Micro-level analysis of the forms of English should be linked to study of macro-level questions, such as the special position of English in globalization and in European affairs, within the broader constellation of all languages in the European linguistic ecology.

39 Research should clarify, in the light of experience worldwide, which language policy issues lend themselves to rules and regulations (for instance language rights and duties), and which to recommendations and attitudinal change (for instance inducements that facilitate multilingual communication, awareness campaigns).

40 Many aspects of business communication are being studied (intercultural communication, branding, mergers, etc.) but little work addresses the implications in globalization of an increased use of English (e.g. as the in-house language) on language diversity and language maintenance. This should be explored, along with the relationship between corporate policies and EU law on language

use in a unified market. Would corporations wish for a European Language Union? As two-thirds of the interest organizations in Brussels represent business, and as access to the EU is 'systematically skewed in favour of employers, business, and capital',[30] it would be important to know more of corporate intentions.

41   There is a need for research into the cosmologies associated with particular languages, the 'linguistic culture' inherent in national language traditions, so as to clarify whether and why each national group understands language issues in specific ways, and what foundations there are, if any, for essentializing stereotypes, 'the Germans/Greeks/ . . . are like this'.

42   Serious efforts should be made to induce professional associations to develop and reflect on principles of good multilingual practice in their own affairs, at research conferences and in publications, so that debates and decisions on language policy can be based on solid information rather than subjective evaluation and opinion.

43   The coverage of language rights in international and national law should be scrutinized so as to identify gaps and limitations. Surveys should also assess how far linguistic human rights are respected.

44   There is a need for further research on language topics that have been barely touched on in this book, among them Sign languages, Romani, and a range of adult literacy needs.

45   A framework should be elaborated that provides for partnership between researchers and decision-makers at the national and supranational levels, so as to ensure better coordination in the identification of research needs and the dissemination of research results.

The integration of the language dimension into ongoing work to reform the EU system

European leaders are well aware that reform of its institutions and policies is needed, that enlargement cannot be implemented without major changes, and that the level of confidence in the EU among ordinary citizens is low. This can be seen in poor turn-out for elections to the European Parliament, and referenda in Denmark and Ireland that have gone against EU plans and their government's decisions and wishes. Critics of europeanization are divided between euro-sceptics working for 'less Europe' and those who hope for reform from within.

One of the means by which the Commission in Brussels has been attempting to improve this state of affairs is by instituting a rethink of how its institutions function, a review of European 'governance'. Twelve working groups of experts were involved in this, and a White Paper was published in July 2001.[31] Governance is defined as 'rules, processes and behaviour that affect the way in which powers are exercised at European level, particularly as regards openness, participation, accountability, effectiveness and coherence'. The key proposals are for

* more openness, more consultation and information at all stages of decision-making,
* better policies, regulation, and delivery, with a simplification of EU law, guidelines on the collection and use of expert advice, and use of an increased range of policy tools,
* more coherence in its relations with the outside world, in contributing to 'global governance',
* refocused institutions so that the Commission's executive responsibilities are clear and the EU's long-term objectives coherent.

One wonders when 'guidelines on the collection and use of expert advice' will begin to apply in the field of language policy. The acknowledgement in the White Paper that scientific experts play an increasingly significant role in preparing and monitoring EU decisions should open up for this. However, expertise in language policy tends to be fragmented, because of under-funding at the national and supranational levels, and because the existing professionalism is often restricted to fairly narrow specializations, or to the promotion of a single language. Funding for major research projects and networking at the European level, intended to build up a European Research Area, currently neglect the humanities and social sciences. Leaders in the research and university worlds have (as reported in Chapter 4) stressed the need to invest more in this area so as to counteract cultural and linguistic homogenization.

One of the White Paper's proposals is that 'The European institutions should jointly continue to develop EUR-LEX [the EU legislation database] as a single on-line point in all languages, where people can follow policy proposals through the decision-making process'.[32] It is good that greater transparency is understood as being equally important in all languages. However, a second wish, the laudable one of speeding up the legislative process, will create greater pressures on the translation service.

The governance mission was followed up at the meeting of the European Council in Laeken, Belgium in December 2001 at which plans for a 'Convention' of 100 planners, to work for a year from early 2002, were laid. Among their tasks is to consider many issues related to:

- a clearer allocation and definition of powers at the supranational and national levels,
- a simplification of EU processes,
- more democracy, openness, and efficiency,
- progress towards a European Constitution.

As communication (by means of language) is central to the whole exercise, one might expect some thought to be given to language policy, but this is unlikely to be a high enough priority when so many basic matters of power are at stake. But if one of the concerns of the demographically and economically small countries, one that leaders from Austria, Belgium, and Finland articulated early in 2002, is that their interests will suffer when the big boys gang up together, one cannot help wondering whether language rights is really a non-issue.

It is ironic that half of the budget for the Convention is being swallowed up by the costs of translation and interpretation. Perhaps this is no surprise to the members of the Convention, most of whom have been active in the EU system for several decades. There is a risk that this expense is seen as unjustified, and will contribute to myths about the expense of running institutions multilingually. As the figures in Box 4.1 show, these costs are a considerable proportion of the administrative budget of the EU, but a fraction of the overall budget. In absolute terms, per capita for EU citizens, the figures are modest, and a small price to pay for relative communicative equality.

The Convention has to tackle thorny issues of legitimacy and effectiveness, goals and banal rules, while attempting to create a framework for agreement on where the European project is leading. Some see the need for a leap into high politics, for instance by ensuring that military and economic affairs are run by a European security council, and a European monetary council,[33] because present arrangements are anarchic, and represent a hopelessly messy compromise between national and supranational interests. Others would like the few markers of supranationalism, a flag, an anthem borrowed from Beethoven, and a vote every five years for the European Parliament, to be quietly buried. These problems at the supranational level, of lack of political participation, and disillusionment with the political process, are not in fact that different in kind from the position at state level, except that a stronger degree of positive identification with the state has been built up over two centuries.

Serious attention to language policy issues in the Convention cannot be expected if I am right in my contention that there are serious unresolved tensions in European language policy, and that what is at stake is extremely complex when one explores the origins of European linguistic diversity and the pressures it is under from globalization trends in many domains. Conceptual fuzziness does not facilitate enlightened, well-informed policy decisions. The criteria to guide European language policy still need to be clarified and made explicit.

The language dimension of the EU has in fact been brought to the attention of the Convention, in a letter to its President, Valéry Giscard d'Estaing, on 5 June 2002, sent by a body called 'Le droit de comprendre' (The right to understand), which represents five Paris-based NGOs for the 'defence' and 'expansion' of French. The letter warns against the forces which are working for the acceptance of English as the sole working language of the EU, complains of a pretence of parity between three working languages (yes, this typical error), and states that representatives of several languages wish to provide input to the Convention. The letter rightly points out that the language issue is a key aspect of the EU project. One cannot expect a short letter to do more than raise the issue of language policy, but it is disturbing that the letter seems to be impelled more by frustration at the downgrading of French as the dominant language of EU institutions than by commitment to a principle of the equality of the eleven EU languages.

Whether the EU in its present form – with intensive interaction between Eurocrats, representatives of member states, and lobbies – is equipped to play an influential role in language policy is an open question, but it is extremely unlikely. The fact that the EU's achievements are confined to producing every few years a resolution on multilingualism that merely has advisory status, and funding for various schemes for international liaison and student mobility, shows that language policy has a low priority, and has been accorded only modest funding. It has evidently been too politically sensitive for more serious engagement at the supranational level. EU funding for research in the area, and the occasional report, has been minimal, and mostly concerned with regional minority languages. The few relevant activities fit into the pattern of nation-states competing for power and influence within the EU, burdened by the dead weight of linguistic nationalism and the different conceptual universes that have evolved over centuries. Within the four walls of its institutions the EU employs a significant number of people to work with languages, and has built up a sophisticated apparatus for translation and interpretation functions, but these people are specialists within a limited subset of the many issues that fall within language policy. They cannot be expected to be familiar with developments in the corporate or academic worlds in Europe and elsewhere, or with the evolving language policy scene within each member state. There is therefore a strong case for action at the national and supranational levels, along the lines of the recommendations put forward here, in the hope that some of the best-case scenarios may come about.

A separate issue is whether the activities of the EU institutions have much influence on communication throughout the member states. At one level, the influence of the EU is huge, since countless decisions affecting the lives of citizens are taken supranationally. On the other hand, communication between an EU body and the average citizen is minimal. At the mundane level of everyday interaction, the language policies recommended in Brussels, and the internal policies of EU institutions, have little impact, if any. By contrast, commercially driven globalization processes have a much more immediate and widespread impact on socially significant fields such as education, the media, and popular culture. These global trends will continue to impact on European economies, cultures, and languages. This strengthens the case for language policy formation that is grounded in human rights principles, and seeks to maintain the language ecology of Europe as a dynamic vital continuation of the cultural traditions that make Europe distinctive. There is little prospect of leadership on the maintenance of multilingualism from the sole global super-power, which is more likely to favour an English-only Europe. If inaction on language policy in Europe continues, at the supranational and national levels, we may be heading for an American English-only Europe. Is that really what the citizens and leaders of Europe want?

Appendix I

Linguistic diversity and multilingualism in the European Union

Council conclusions, 1995

1 The Council affirms the importance for the Union of its linguistic diversity, which is an essential aspect of the European dimension and identity and of the common cultural heritage.

2 It underlines the implications, be they democratic, cultural, social or economic, of such diversity. Linguistic diversity is also a source of employment and occupation and a factor of integration. It is an asset for the Union's influence in the outside world, since most European Union languages are used in a large number of non-member States.

3 The Council considers that the development of the information society offers new opportunities and presents new challenges for multilingualism and linguistic diversity.

4 Linguistic diversity is a component of the national and regional diversity of the cultures of the Member States referred to in Article 128 of the Treaty, and the Community must take it into account in its action under other provisions of the Treaty, including Articles 126 and 127, which cover education, vocational training and youth.

5 The Council emphasizes that linguistic diversity must be preserved and multilingualism promoted in the Union, with equal respect for the languages of the Union and with due regard to the principle of subsidiarity.

6 From the citizen's point of view, support for an integrated Europe will require an assurance that the languages of the Union will be taken into consideration and will require equal access to information, in conformity with Member States' internal law and with Community law.

7 In this context, the Council welcomes the Council Resolution of 31 March 1995 on improving and diversifying language learning

and teaching within the education systems of the European Union and the adoption of the SOCRATES, LEONARDO and YOUTH FOR EUROPE programmes.

8   It also takes note of the Commission's intention of submitting a communication on the language aspects of the information society, drawn up in response to the request by the Corfu European Council, which it will examine without delay.

9   The Council stresses the importance of taking the language dimension into account in the Union's external relations, particularly in the framework of Union programmes involving third countries.

10   The Council invites the Commission to take linguistic diversity and multilingualism into account in preparing Community actions or policies, and in implementing them.

11   The Council asks the Commission to make an inventory of the Community's policies and activities which take linguistic diversity and multilingualism into account, and to assess those policies and activities. It invites the Commission to report back within a year.

12   The Council asks the Commission to set up a working party of representatives of the Member States, appointed by the Member States, with responsibility for monitoring, without prejudice to the activities of the existing Committees and in liaison with them, whether linguistic diversity is being taken into account and multilingualism promoted in the Union's policies and activities, with due respect for Member States' national policies.

13   The Council would also reiterate the importance it attaches to the equality of the official languages and working languages of the Union's institutions, namely, Danish, Dutch, English, Finnish, French, German, Greek, Italian, Portuguese, Spanish and Swedish, in accordance with Regulation No 1/58, as amended, determining the languages to be used by the institutions of the Union. The Council recalls the particular status of Irish under Article S of the Treaty on European Union and the Treaty of Accession of Denmark, Ireland and the United Kingdom.

(Council meeting 1853, General Affairs, Luxembourg, 12 June 1995.)

Appendix 2

Draft Council Resolution on the promotion of linguistic diversity and language learning in the framework of the implementation of the objectives of the European Year of Languages 2001

THE COUNCIL OF THE EUROPEAN UNION,

Having regard to:

(1) The Council Resolution of 31 March 1995 on improving and diversifying language learning and teaching within the education systems of the European Union, according to which 'pupils should, as a general rule, have the opportunity of learning two languages of the Union other than their mother tongue(s)';

(1a) The responsibility of Member States for the content of teaching and the organisation of education systems and their cultural and linguistic diversity;

(2) The Commission's 1995 White Paper 'Teaching and learning: Towards the learning society';

(3) The Council conclusions of 12 June 1995 on linguistic diversity and multilingualism in the European Union;

(4) The Council Resolution of 16 December 1997 on the early teaching of European Union languages;

(5) The Presidency conclusions of the Lisbon European Council of 23 and 24 March 2000, which include foreign languages within a European framework for the definition of basic skills;

(6) The Decision of the European Parliament and of the Council of 17 July 2000 establishing the European Year of Languages 2001;

(7) Article 22 of the Charter of Fundamental Rights of the European Union of 7 December 2000, welcomed by the Nice European Council, which states that the Union shall respect cultural, religious and linguistic diversity;

(8) The Resolution of the Council and of the Representatives of the Governments of the Member States, meeting within the

Council, of 14 December 2000 concerning an Action Plan for Mobility which was approved by the Nice European Council;

(8a) The Council Decision of 19 January 2001 on Guidelines for Member States' employment policies for the year 2001 and in particular the horizontal objective concerning lifelong learning;

(9) The Report of the Education Council of 12 February 2001 on the concrete future objectives of education and training systems which was submitted to the Stockholm European Council and which explicitly includes improving foreign language learning as one of its objectives, and the Council conclusions of 28 May 2001 on the follow-up to be given to the Report;

(10) The Commission's 2000 Memorandum on lifelong learning that has given an impetus to a broad discussion, both at European level and in the Member States, on how to implement broad and coherent strategies for lifelong learning, inter alia in the field of language learning;

(11) The Recommendation of the European Parliament and of the Council of 10 July 2001 on mobility within the Community of students, persons undergoing training, volunteers, teachers and instructors;

(12) The activities developed by the Council of Europe in the field of the promotion of linguistic diversity and language learning.

Emphasises:

(1) (a) That the knowledge of languages is one of the basic skills that each citizen needs to acquire in order to take part effectively in the European knowledge society and therefore facilitates both integration into society and social cohesion; and that a thorough knowledge of one's mother tongue(s) can facilitate the learning of other languages;

(b) That knowledge of languages plays an important role in facilitating mobility, both in an educational context as well as for professional purposes and for cultural and personal reasons;

(c) That knowledge of languages is also beneficial for European cohesion, in the light of EU enlargement;

(2) That all European languages are equal in value and dignity from the cultural point of view and form an integral part of European culture and civilisation.

Recalls:

That the European Year of Languages 2001, organised in cooperation with the Council of Europe is stimulating the awareness of linguistic diversity and the promotion of language learning.

That the Report of the Education Council of 12 February 2001 on the concrete future objectives of education and training systems, which explicitly includes improving foreign language learning as one of its objectives, should be implemented via a detailed work programme to be defined in a joint report which the Council and Commission will present to the Barcelona European Council.

Reaffirms:

The objectives set out in Article 2 of the Decision of the European Parliament and of the Council of 17 July 2000 establishing the European Year of Languages 2001, with a view to the further implementation of these objectives.

Invites the Member States within the framework, limits and priorities of their respective political, legal, budgetary, educational and training systems:

(1)   To take the measures they deem appropriate to offer pupils, as far as possible, the opportunity to learn two, or where appropriate, more languages in addition to their mother tongues, and to promote the learning of foreign languages by others in the context of lifelong learning, taking into account the diverse needs of the target public and the importance of providing equal access to learning opportunities. In order to promote cooperation and mobility across Europe, the supply of languages should be as diversified as possible, including those of neighbouring countries and/or regions;

(2)   To ensure that study programmes and educational objectives promote a positive attitude to other languages and cultures and stimulate intercultural communication skills from an early age;

(2b) To promote the learning of languages in vocational training, thereby taking into account the positive impact of language knowledge on mobility and employability;

(3)   To facilitate the integration of non–native speakers in the educational system and in society as a whole, including through

measures to improve their knowledge of the official language(s) of instruction, respecting the languages and cultures of their country of origin;

(4) To promote the application of innovative pedagogical methods, in particular also through teacher training;

(4a) To encourage future language teachers to take advantage of relevant European programmes to carry out part of their studies in a country or region of a country where the language which they will teach later is the official language;

(5) To set up systems of validation of competence in language knowledge based on the Common European Framework of reference for languages developed by the Council of Europe, taking sufficient account of skills acquired through informal learning;

(6) To stimulate European co-operation in order to promote transparency of qualifications and quality assurance of language learning;

(7) To bear in mind the wealth of linguistic diversity within the European Community in the context of the above-mentioned objectives, and thus to encourage, inter alia, co-operation between official centres or other cultural institutions for the dissemination of the languages and cultures of the Member States.

Invites the Commission:

(1) To support the Member States in their implementation of the above-mentioned recommendations;

(2) To take into account, in this context, the principle of linguistic diversity in its relations with third and candidate countries;

(3) To draw up proposals by early 2003 for actions for the promotion of linguistic diversity and language learning while ensuring consistency with the implementation of the report on concrete future objectives of education and training systems.

(Draft of 23 November 2001, General Secretariat of the Council, 13795/01.)

Appendix 3

Declaration on the Enlargement of the European Union

Allocation of seats in the European Parliament, and weighted votes in the Council, in EU-27 compared to population size.

Member state	MEPs	Weighted votes	Population (millions)
Germany	99	29	83.029
France	72	29	59.551
Italy	72	29	57.681
United Kingdom	72	29	59.648
Poland	50	27	38.634
Spain	50	27	40.037
Romania	33	14	22.364
Netherlands	25	13	15.981
Belgium	22	12	10.258
Greece	22	12	10.623
Portugal	22	12	10.066
Czech Republic	20	12	10.264
Hungary	20	12	10.106
Sweden	18	10	8.875
Austria	17	10	8.151
Bulgaria	17	10	7.707
Denmark	13	7	5.352
Finland	13	7	5.176
Slovakia	13	7	5.415
Ireland	12	7	3.840
Lithuania	12	7	3.610
Latvia	8	4	2.385
Slovenia	7	4	1.930
Estonia	6	4	1.423
Cyprus	6	4	0.763
Luxembourg	6	4	0.443
Malta	5	3	0.395
Total	**732**	**345**	**483.707**

Appendix 4

Declaration of Oegstgeest (The Netherlands)

Moving away from a monolingual habitus

Art. 1   Taking into account:
- the intrinsic relation between multiculturalism and multi-lingualism in Europe, as expressed in the vitality of regional, minority and immigrant languages;
- the (outdated) Directive 77.486 of the Council of the European Communities on the schooling of children of migrant workers (1977);
- the Charter on Regional or Minority Languages of the Council of Europe (1992);
- the Framework Convention on National Minorities of the Council of Europe (1995);
- the Universal Declaration of Linguistic Rights (1996);
- the current support programme of the European Commission for measures to promote and safeguard regional or minority languages;
- the aims(*) of the European Year of Languages (2001), prepared by the Council of Europe;

affirmative conventions and action programmes on regional, minority and immigrant languages within the context of multicultural Europe should be based on a non-exclusive acknowledgement of the existence of all of these languages as sources of linguistic diversity and cultural enrichment.

Art. 2   The development of new programmes for regional, minority and immigrant languages should further enhance and strengthen the positive developments of principles and action programmes as referred to in Article 1.

Art. 3   European, national, regional and local action programmes should be set up to upgrade the status of regional, minority and immigrant languages in public domains, in particular the domains of:

(a)   education;
(b)   audiovisual media and the written press;
(c)   public libraries and information/Internet services;
(d)   translation and interpretation services;
(e)   books and translations;
(f)   occupational requirements.

Art. 4   Statistics on language use and language abilities offer highly relevant evidence on the degree to which languages function as core values of cultures, and should be considered as long-term complements to nationality and/or birth-country based statistics on the multicultural composition of (school) populations.

Art. 5   Language statistics on multicultural (school) populations should be considered as important tools for language planning in general, for educational planning in the domains of the learning and teaching of languages, and for sociolinguistic research.

Art. 6   Education in regional, minority and immigrant languages should be offered, supervised, and evaluated as part of the regular curriculum in preschool, primary and secondary education.

Art. 7   The range of regional, minority and immigrant languages to be offered in preschool, primary and secondary education should be based on the demographic composition of the school population and the expressed desire of parents and pupils.

Art. 8   Both primary and secondary school reports should contain information on the pupil's proficiency in regional, minority and immigrant languages, thus demonstrating that progress in these languages is conceived of as part of school success.

Art. 9   European, national, regional and local action programmes should be set up for regional, minority and immigrant languages with a focus on:

(a)   the development of curricula, learning methods and eval-
      uation tools;
(b)   the initial and post-initial training of teachers;
(c)   the cross-national exchange of methods, tests and teachers.

Art. 10   Information on the rationale and contents of the provisions
          mentioned under Articles 6 through 9 should be made avail-
          able in the range of languages under Article 7.

Art. 11   European, national, regional and local research programs on
          regional, minority and immigrant languages should be pro-
          moted, in order to contribute to our awareness and
          understanding of language diversity in multicultural Europe.
          The following priorities should be considered for such
          research programmes:
          •   municipal or larger-scale surveys on language use of mul-
              ticultural school populations;
          •   macro and micro studies on regional, minority and immi-
              grant languages in education;
          •   the status of regional, minority and immigrant languages
              in other public domains.

Art. 12   This declaration should be made public and brought to the
          attention of those European, national, regional and local insti-
          tutions and agencies that play an important role in the
          development of language policies.

Note(*)
The European Year of Languages 2001 has three major aims:
•   to increase awareness and appreciation among young people and adults, including
    parents, policy deciders and those responsible for language teaching, of the richness
    of Europe's linguistic heritage;
•   to celebrate linguistic diversity and to promote it by motivating European citizens
    to develop plurilingualism, that is, to diversify their learning of languages includ-
    ing less widely used and taught languages, whilst also protecting and encouraging
    multilingualism in European societies;
•   to encourage language learning on a lifelong basis, not only by creating awareness
    of its necessity, but also by providing sufficient information concerning ways and
    possibilities of learning, depending on regional and national situations and
    possibilities.

(Approved on 30 January 2000, at the international conference on
regional, minority and immigrant languages in multicultural Europe,
convened by the European Cultural Foundation, Amsterdam.)

Appendix 5

Vienna Manifesto on European Language Policies

The cost of monolingualism

In the framework of the 'European Year of Languages 2001', the Austrian Academy of Sciences organised the conference 'The Cost of Multilingualism – Globalisation and Linguistic Diversity' in Vienna from 7 to 9 June 2001. Special emphasis was placed on the subject of multilingualism in the humanities and sciences. Scholars from 11 countries worked out the below principles and recommendations for the development of a European language policy that has to be supplemented by measures at national and regional levels:

Principles

(a) Only if Europe's linguistic diversity is preserved and promoted will the project of European integration succeed. On the one hand, it is impossible to make foreign language skills a prerequisite for exercising democratic rights. On the other hand, mutual understanding is indispensable for living together.

(b) There is no contradiction between using a *lingua franca* (predominantly English) in some spheres of work and actively practising multilingualism in other areas. Very often the cost of multilingualism is overestimated.

(c) It is a sine qua non for building a European identity to assure citizens that their mother tongues will form part of it. In some cases understanding will not be possible without a *lingua franca* (e.g. English) but European communication processes should not rely exclusively on it. The introduction of a 'leading' European language would mean to favour the native speakers of this 'single language' politically and economically. This fact would result in political conflicts with unforeseeable consequences.

Many cultural achievements of Europe are closely linked to the achievements of specific languages and intellectual traditions. If these languages and achievements are no longer used, this would mean a depletion and loss of Europe's cultural diversity.

To stop practising multilingualism would have serious consequences: necessary investments would no longer be made into these languages, important skills and knowledge (e.g. in the area of translation) would be lost and valuable intellectual heritage would become inaccessible.

(d) It is the task of schools, universities and institutions of advanced training on the one hand, and of governments on the other hand to safeguard multilingualism. These sectors have to interact and create instruments to make multilingualism possible and to enhance its status. A vital element in this process is to preserve and use the existing wealth of languages by placing more emphasis on minority and migrant languages in the general educational system than in the past.

Recommendations

1. Europe urgently needs a transparent public discussion on language policy with the aim of developing guidelines for European and national language policies.

    Therefore it is necessary to set up forums responsible for language-policy-related aspects of enlargement and for developing a new European approach to the language issue in which as many players of society as possible should participate (from the political and economic arenas, the media, NGOs).

2. The foundations of this new approach are as follows:
    (a) the right of all citizens to learn and use their own national and minority languages,
    (b) the right of all citizens to learn at least two foreign languages in compulsory school education,
    (c) the duty of all governments to encourage and promote foreign language learning even beyond school education,
    (d) the duty of all governments to promote multilingual undertakings, institutions, homepages and the like by tax relief and bonus systems (e.g. in contract award processes) or similar measures,
    (e) the duty of all governments to organise in an exemplary way the establishment, access and utilisation of public terminology

resources and to promote standardisation activities by different measures (incentive systems, legal provisions).

3. All governments should use a fixed percentage of their GDP for promoting multilingualism in education, research, politics, administration and the economic sector.

4. The European Union is called upon to implement multilingualism in its own practices in a more credible way,
    *   by extending the working language regime, e.g. based on the principle of European regions,
    *   by using the Internet to achieve a greater diversity of languages,
    *   by implementing recommendations providing for the support of multilingual media, journals and abstract services,
    *   by involving national and sector-specific terminology resources, including those of the private sector,
    *   by early use and standardisation of these terminology resources at all stages of the legislative process and by providing a transparent explanation of the terms and concepts used in all legal documents,
    *   by supporting the translation of project applications, research projects, publications by publishing houses and of scientific texts published in journals,
    *   by re-considering the practice of simultaneous interpretation,
    *   by a greater reliability of document translations,
    *   by an exchange of language teachers, even at the elementary school level,
    *   by increasing funds for research in the area of multilingualism (focused research).

5. By reforming traditional foreign language teaching it would become possible to offer a wider range of languages in the educational system within a shorter period. Therefore a reform of foreign language education must be an integral part of a European language policy. Key aspects of this reform are for example:
    *   early beginning of foreign language education, with a special emphasis on neighbouring languages and contact languages
    *   greater flexibility in the order of languages
    *   using foreign languages as working languages, while reducing the duration of traditional foreign language education

- using intensive courses in foreign language education at school instead of extensive forms of learning during several years
- using multimedia e-learning resources (above all technical languages)
- promoting receptive multilingualism
- developing curricular multilingualism by using the synergy effects of the second and the third foreign language
- modifying the training of foreign language teachers: the philological model should be replaced by training experts in multilingualism or language and subject coordinators
- promoting stays and teaching assignments abroad of teachers and taking adequate measures to avoid disadvantages in terms of insurance and pension schemes.

6. The candidate countries should be encouraged to make the promotion of foreign language learning and the preservation of their own national and minority languages in their educational systems and in academia an integral part of their national language policies.

   As a result of enlargement, the European Union will have to give more consideration to the previously neglected Slavonic languages and Hungarian in language teaching, research, its language policy and terminology resources and to explore new approaches to the current informal internal working language regimes.

Multilingualism in the humanities and sciences

7. As regards the humanities and sciences, measures have to be taken to ensure that national languages other than English domineering as a *lingua franca* in academia will be preserved and further developed. At least in the humanities and arts, this is a crucial prerequisite for preserving academic cultures with their specific knowledge gains.

   This means
   - to promote the bilingualism and multilingualism of scholars
   - to develop a multilingual academic culture, e.g. by supporting multilingual abstract services and technical journals, by multilingual teaching and by supporting the translation of academic publications
   - to promote doctoral theses and theses required of candidates

wishing to qualify for lecturing at a university written in the respective national (technical) language

- not to base the evaluation of academic achievements on evaluation standards such as a citation index that clearly favours one *lingua franca* but, on the contrary, to encourage multilingual publications (particularly in so-called 'national' fields of knowledge such as history and linguistics).

8. The ability of adequate linguistic action is a prerequisite for an effective multilingualism in the humanities and sciences. To this end it is necessary to investigate multilingual discourse communities including receptive multilingualism and synergy effects between related languages as well as the development of adequate training programmes for (fledgling) scholars.

(29 June 2001)

Notes

1 The risks of *laissez faire* language policies

1 This remark was made at an informal lunch at the University of Roskilde, Denmark.

2 At the Round Table on 'Social and economic factors promoting and inhibiting linguistic diversity', Innsbruck, 10–12 May 1999; see Council of Europe, *Linguistic Diversity for Democratic Citizenship in Europe*, 2000, 63–77.

3 Official Journal of the European Communities, C 364/1, 18.12.2000, or <http//www.europarl.eu.int/charter/default_en.htm>.

4 *Boswell on the grand tour*, ed. F .A. Pottle, 1953, 285, in *The Oxford Book of Literary Anecdotes*, ed. J. Sutherland, London: Futura, 1977, 145.

5 *The Independent*, 4 December 2001.

6 <http://www.euro-ombudsman.eu.int/letters/en/20020307–1.htm>.

7 *The Independent* of 31 May 2001 reported that graduates with foreign language skills earn more than others. Research in Switzerland also points in the same direction; see Chapter 5, and F. Grin, 'Market forces, language spread and linguistic diversity', in *Language: a right and a resource. Approaching linguistic human rights*, ed. M. Kontra, R. Phillipson, T. Skutnabb-Kangas and T. Várady, Budapest: Central European University Press, 1999, 169-86.

8 See note 2.

9 In a letter of 10 September 1956, cited in *Jawaharlal Nehru. An anthology*, ed. S. Gopal, Delhi: Oxford University Press, 1980, 525.

10 The complexity of languages in India is richly documented; see, for instance, E. Annamalai, *Managing multilingualism in India. Political and linguistic manifestations*, London and New Delhi: Sage, 2001.

11 <http://agence.francophonie.org>.

12 See the English summary of the parliamentary Committee on the Swedish language, <http://kultur.regeringen.se/propositionermm/sou/pdf/engelska.pdf>, which lists an action programme of 80 measures for implementation. The substantial report was published in spring 2002, and distributed widely with a view to legislation in 2003 and implementation in 2004. For a presentation of language policy issues in Sweden in English, see *Managing multilingualism in a European nation-state: challenges for Sweden*, ed. S. Boyd and L. Huss, Clevedon: Multilingual Matters, 2001.

13 How you speak is a significant marker of social class in English. When

George Orwell wrote about the link between class and accent in his essay, 'The English people', he cited Wyndham Lewis's observation that the English working class are 'branded on the tongue' (see *The collected essays, journalism and letters of George Orwell*, ed. S. Orwell and I. Angus, vol. 3, *1943–45*, Harmondsworth: Penguin, 1970, 19). This is similar to Bernard Shaw's obervation in 1914 that 'it is impossible for an Englishman to open his mouth without making some other Englishman despise him' (Preface to *Pygmalion*, Harmondsworth: Penguin 1986, 5). Branding in the modern, marketing sense has the opposite meaning, i.e. a purely positive ascription.

14 Such is the prestige of English-medium schools; and the neglect of schools using Indian languages, that 'even slum dwellers prefer to send their children to English medium schools', E. Annamalai, in *English and language planning: A Southeast Asian contribution*, ed. T. Kandiah and J. Kwan-Terry, Singapore: Times Academic Press, 1994, 261–77. The sacrifices of these parents are very unlikely to lead to educational success.

15 <http://europa.eu.int/comm/education/languages/lang/european languages.html>.

16 Ibid.

17 The *New Shorter Oxford English Dictionary*, 1993, states that the term came into English from German in the middle of the twentieth century. It defines subsidiarity as 'the principle that a central authority should have a subsidiary function, performing only those tasks which cannot be performed effectively at a more immediate or local level'.

18 <http://www.eurolang2001.org/eyl/common/content//R1+R2Listmult Rev.pdf>.

19 <http://www.eblul.org>.

20 COM(95) 590, of 29 November 1995.

21 <http://www.eurolang.net>.

22 See *Languages: the next generation. The Final Report and Recommendations of the Nuffield Languages Inquiry*, 2000. <www.nuffield.org>.

23 Other parts of the world have far greater linguistic diversity. Europe accounts for only 3 per cent of the world's languages.

24 See Eurobarometer Report 54 of 15 February 2001 for a representative study of foreign language competence in all member states. These reports are on <http://europa.eu.int/comm/dg10/epo/eb.html>.

25 C. Karlsson, *Democracy, legitimacy and the European Union*, Uppsala: Acta Universitatis Upsaliensis, Skrifter utgivna av Statsvetenskapliga föreningen, 2001; M. Bond and K. Feus (eds), *The Treaty of Nice explained*, London: The Federal Trust for Education and Research, and Kogan Page, 2001.

26 Thomas E. Schmidt, 8 August 2001.

27 T. Skutnabb-Kangas and S. Bucak, 'Killing a mother tongue – how the Kurds are deprived of linguistic human rights', in *Linguistic human rights: overcoming linguistic discrimination*, ed. T. Skutnabb-Kangas and R. Phillipson, Berlin: Mouton de Gruyter, 1994, 347–70.

28 For detailed analysis of state policies, see chapter 5 of T. Skutnabb-Kangas, *Linguistic genocide in education – or worldwide diversity and human rights?*, Mahwah, NJ: Lawrence Erlbaum, 2000.

29 The classic work is R. L. Cooper, *Language planning and social change*, Cambridge: Cambridge University Press, 1989.

30 One of the most reliable sources for such statistics is the Ethnologue database of the Summer Institute of Linguistics, which currently lists 6809 languages, of which 230 are in Europe. <http://www.ethnologue.com/>.

31 See J. Fishman, 'Rethinking language defense', in *Rights to language. Equity, power and education*, ed. R. Phillipson, Mahwah, NJ: Lawrence Erlbaum, 2000, 23–7.

32 The reference is to the traditional British nursery rhyme:
> Humpty Dumpty sat on a wall,
> Humpty Dumpty had a great fall,
> All the king's horses
> And all the king's men
> Couldn't put Humpty together again.

The *Oxford Dictionary of Nursery Rhymes*, ed. I. and P. Opie, Oxford: Oxford University Press, 1951, notes that equivalent rhymes exist in other European cultures, including 'Lille Trille', 'Boule, Boule', 'Wirgele, Wargele', etc. Lewis Carroll's fictionalized Humpty Dumpty in his 'nonsense' stories about Alice reflects the author's familiarity with semantic and philosophical theory.

33 The most central journals are *Journal of Sociolinguistics, International Journal of the Sociology of Language, Language Policy, Language Problems and Language Planning, Sociolinguistica, World Englishes, Journal of Language, Identity, and Education*. Journals in the field of applied linguistics also publish an increasing number of articles on language policy topics. For a select bibliography listing many titles in German and English, and a selection in Dutch, Esperanto, French, Italian, and Russian, see 'Sprachenpolitik in Europa, Auswahlbibliographie', D. Blanke and J. Scharnhorst, in *Sprachenpolitik in Europa*, ed. D. Blanke, *Interlinguistische Informationen*, 6, Berlin, October 2001. See also *L'Europe parlera-t-elle l'anglais demain?*, Actes du colloque international de Bordeaux organisé par le Goethe Institut et l'INTIF (3 mars 2001), ed. R. Chaudenson, Paris: Institut de la Francophonie, l'Harmattan.

34 Emma Wagner of the EU Translation Service, personal communication, 12 October 2001.

35 This is an authentic example from the professional journal of the Danish higher education staff union, *Magisterbladet*, 2, 31 January 2002, 34. The entire sentence is much more comprehensible if you understand Danish, for instance 'as a link' corresponds to 'in conformity with'.

36 One typical example: when Peter Nelde, from Belgium (who has a superb command of several languages), recommends the book *Language and minority rights. Ethnicity, nationalism and the politics of language*, by Stephen May, Harlow: Pearson Education, 2001, after the Table of Contents of the book itself, he writes that it covers the 'major concerns of language politics, policy and planning', and stresses its importance for 'the fast developing interdisciplinary discourse on the implementation of language politics'.

37 <http://www.scilt.stir.ac/uk>.

38 The Podestà Report, draft of 27 June. See coverage in *Le Monde* of 9 August 2001, also reported in the English edition published by *The Guardian Weekly*: 'The enlargement of the Union raises the problem of equality between languages', 16–22 August 2001.

39 A prime example is the editorial 'Organic is healthier' in *The Daily Telegraph*

of 16 August 2001. Another is Ian Black's 'EU learns to conduct its business with an English accent', *The Guardian Weekly*, 4–10 April 2002.

40 See critical discussion of this in P. A. Kraus, 'Political unity and linguistic diversity in Europe', *Archives Européenes de Sociologie*, XLI/1, 2000, 138–63, and C. Karlsson, *Democracy, legitimacy and the European Union*, 74–5.

41 It is possible that the Germans also boycotted meetings in Sweden in 2000, but if this in fact happened, there does not appear to have been publicity or press coverage about the issue.

42 For statistics on languages and their speakers, see Box 1.1 and Appendix 3.

43 'Ich bin auch der Meinung, dass Deutsch principiell dieselben Rechte haben sollte wie die anderen grossen Sprachen. Es is nur ein praktisches Problem, weil sich das Sprachenproblem in der Union ohne Plan entwickelt hat. Wir müssen diese Frage zusammen lösen', *Berliner Zeitung,* 18 October 1999.

44 For details of the allocation of seats in the European Parliament after enlargement, the weighting of votes in the Council, and both of these as compared to population size, see Appendix 3, reproduced from Bond and Feus, op. cit.

45 *Animal Farm* (1945) traces the transition from a society established on liberal principles, enshrined in commandments such as 'All animals are equal', to a totalitarian society in which 'Some animals are more equal than others'. Orwell's later novel, *1984*, portrays a world in which the meaning of words is deliberately corrupted so as to produce a conformist society and make 'all other modes of thought impossible'; see the Appendix that expounds the Principles of Newspeak (Penguin, 1949, 241).

46 Reported by S. Montgomery, cited in J. Swales, 'Language, science and scholarship', *Asian Journal of English Language Teaching*, 8, 1998, 1–18.

47 Cited in M. Holroyd, *Bernard Shaw. The one-volume definitive edition*, London: Chatto and Windus, 1997, 660.

2 European languages: families, nations, empires, states

1 *Tacitus on Britain and Germany*, a new translation of the 'Agricola' and the 'Germania' by H. Mattingly, West Drayton: Penguin, 1948, 61.

2 This is the second verse of a poem dedicated to Ludvig Holberg, 1684–1754.

3 A. Meillet, *Les langues dans l'Europe nouvelle*, Paris: Payot, 1928 (first edition 1918), 1–2.

4 Ogden was the principal architect of Basic English, a simplified form of English intended to serve as an international auxiliary language and a route to English proper. BASIC is an acronym for British American Scientific International Commercial English. See R. W. Bailey, *Images of English. A cultural history of the language*, Cambridge: Cambridge University Press, 1992, 208–11.

5 The Declaration of the European Council at the summit of EU member state leaders and the Commission, held at Laeken, Belgium, December 2001.

6 See the detailed examples of Europe understood as referring to a place, a political unit, ethnicity, and language (toponyms, politonyms, ethnonyms, and linguonyms) in T. Skutnabb-Kangas, *Linguistic genocide in education – or*

worldwide diversity and human rights?, Mahwah, NJ: Lawrence Erlbaum, 2000, 177–95.

7   This is particularly true of all continents other than Europe, which have far greater linguistic, cultural, and biological diversity. These mutually reinforcing diversities tend to be denser, the closer one is to the equator. See <www.terralingua.org> and Skutnabb-Kangas, op. cit.

8   See R. Phillipson, *Linguistic imperialism*, Oxford: Oxford University Press, 1992, 31.

9   Genesis XI, 1–9.

10 George Steiner, speech in Oviedo, Asturias, Spain; see <http://www.fpa.es/ing/premios/discursos/2001chy.html>.

11 The sentence occurs in the Lord's Prayer, part of the Sermon on the Mount, in Matthew VI, 11. The citation is from the 'Authorized Version', also known as the King James Bible, of 1611.

12 E. V. Rieu, *The four gospels*, Harmondsworth: Penguin, 1952.

13 Matthew IV, 4. The text continues 'but by every word that proceedeth out of the mouth of God'.

14 Cited in *The Guardian Weekly*, 27 December 2001–2 January 2002.

15 Ibid.

16 See Skutnabb-Kangas, op. cit., 172–77.

17 See P. Schlesinger, 'Europeanness: a new cultural battlefield', in *Nationalism*, ed. J. Hutchinson and A.D. Smith, Oxford: Oxford University Press, 1994, 320.

18 'It's a crime. Euro-law wrongly defines terrorism', *Le Monde Diplomatique*, English edition, February 2002, 13.

19 In 'Culture', *The conduct of life*, 1860.

20 This phenomenon has been studied; see C. Grünbaum, *Nordisk Språkforståelse – at ha och mista* (Reciprocal comprehension in the Nordic languages – a vulnerable possession), Oslo: Nordisk Språkråd (The Language Council of the Nordic languages), 2001. Practical manuals for each language group also exist.

21 Cited in *English. History, diversity and change*, ed. D. Graddol, J. Swann and D. Leith, London: Routledge, for the Open University, 1996, 93–4.

22 From the biographical sketch of Noah Webster in *Webster's Third New International Dictionary of the English Language*, Chicago: Encyclopedia Britannica, 1966. This dictionary aims at coverage of the entire English-speaking world rather than solely the USA. National independence has been succeeded by global norm-setting.

23 L. L. Cavalli-Sforza, *Genes, peoples and languages*, London: Penguin, 2001, 36.

24 Interview with Joseph Ki-Zerbo, born in 1922 in Burkina Faso (then Upper Volta), Director of the Centre for the Study of African Development, Ouagadougou, *News from the Nordic Africa Institute*, January 2002, 17–19. <www.nai.uu.se>.

25 Cavalli-Sforza, op. cit., 99. D. Lasagabaster, 'Bilingualism, immersion programmes and language learning in the Basque country', *Journal of Multilingual and Multicultural Development*, 22/5, 2001, 401–25.

26 Cavalli-Sforza, op. cit., 23.

27 Ibid., 159–66.

28 Ibid., 128.

29   See the introduction to *Encyclopedia of the Languages of Europe*, ed. G. Price, Oxford: Blackwell, 1998.

30   See *The history of the idea of Europe*, P. den Boer, P. Bugge and O. Wæver, London: Routledge for the Open University, 1993, and G. Delanty, *Inventing Europe: Idea, identity, reality*, Basingstoke: Macmillan, 1995.

31   M. Bernal, *Black Athena: The Afroasiatic roots of classical civilization*, vol. 1, *The fabrication of Ancient Greece, 1785–1985*, London: Vintage, 1991, 317.

32   Ibid.

33   B. Russell, *On education*, London: Unwin, 1926 (revised edn 1960, 31).

34   Quoted in T. Crowley, *The politics of discourse. The standard language question in British cultural debates*, Basingstoke: Macmillan, 1991, 71–2.

35   Quoted in Bernal, op. cit., 305.

36   Cited in J. A. Hodson, *Imperialism, a study*, London: Allen & Unwin, 1902, 158.

37   Quoted in F. Colonna, *Instituteurs algériens: 1883–1939*, Alger: Office des publications universitaires, 1975, 40.

38   Cited in Skutnabb-Kangas, *Linguistic genocide in education – or worldwide diversity and human rights?*, 382.

39   In the 1950s my own education involved compulsory Latin from age 8 to 16. My elder brother also learned Greek at the same school.

40   G. Viswanathan, *Masks of conquest. Literary study and British rule in India*, New York: Columbia University Press, 1989.

41   Bernal, op. cit., 288.

42   *Tacitus*, op. cit., 72.

43   Bernal, op. cit.

44   There is a vast literature on nationalism. The language dimension is covered in depth in S. Wright, *Community and communication. The role of language in nation state building and European integration*, Clevedon: Multilingual Matters, 2000; the experience of each state is covered in S. Barbour and C. Carmichael (eds), *Language and nationalism in Europe*, Oxford: Oxford University Press, 2000.

45   O. Korsgaard, 'The controversy between Grundtvig and Goldschmidt', in *Images of the world. Globalisation and cultural diversity*, Copenhagen: Danish Center for Culture and Development, 2001, 84–9.

46   This notion is particularly associated with B. Anderson, *Imagined communities: Reflections on the origins and spread of nationalism*, London: Verso, 1983. Other influential writers such as E. Gellner, *Nations and nationalism*, Oxford: Blackwell, 1983, and A. D. Smith, *National identity*, Harmondsworth: Penguin, 1991 stress other factors. S. May, *Language and minority rights. Ethnicity, nationalism and the politics of language*, Harlow: Pearson Education, 2001 is a multi-disciplinary study that argues for a rethinking of national identity that accommodates minority language rights.

47   E. Renan, *Qu'est-ce qu'une nation?*, Paris, 1882, in Hutchinson and Smith, op. cit., note 17 above.

48   J. W. Tollefson, 'Language rights and the destruction of Yugoslavia', in *Language policies in education. Critical issues*, ed. J. W. Tollefson, Mahwah, NJ: Lawrence Erlbaum, 2002, 179–99.

49   R. Phillipson, M. Rannut and T. Skutnabb-Kangas, 'Introduction', in

Linguistic human rights: overcoming linguistic discrimination, ed. T. Skutnabb-Kangas and R. Phillipson, Berlin: Mouton de Gruyter, 1994, 1–22.

50 The technical term used by linguists for such languages is polycentric. English has 'centres' in the UK, USA, Australia, India, etc.

51 Welsh has been more successfully consolidated than have other British minority languages. The name of the Welsh nationalist party, Plaid Cymru, literally 'the party of Wales', has entered the vocabulary of English.

52 The law had to be modified during the drafting stage, when the French Constitutional Court decreed that some of the provisions about the private use of language were in conflict with a principle of freedom of speech.

53 Y. Marek, 'The philosophy of the French language legislation: internal and international aspects', in *Language legislation and linguistic rights*, ed. D. Kibbee, Amsterdam: John Benjamins, 1998, 341–50.

54 See Skutnabb-Kangas, op. cit. (note 6 above), 557.

55 Many aspects of the African and Asian experience are covered in Ngũgĩ wa Thiong'o, *Decolonising the mind. The politics of language in African literature*, London: James Currey, 1986, and A. Pennycook, *English and the discourses of colonialism*, London: Routledge, 1998. For comparison of the role of language in the French and British colonial traditions, see Phillipson, op. cit., ch. 5 (note 8 above).

56 Quoted in A. Haigh, *Cultural diplomacy in Europe*, Strasbourg: Council of Europe, 1974, 33.

57 Page 73 in the reprint published in Paris by arléa, 1991.

58 Meillet, op. cit., 251 (note 3 above).

59 This was stated in several articles in *Le Monde* by Jacques Toubon, the Minister for Culture and Francophonie.

60 See J. A. Fishman, *In praise of the beloved language: a comparative view of positive ethnolinguistic consciousness*, Berlin: Mouton de Gruyter, 1997.

61 Citations on pages 5 and 7 of B. B. Kachru, *The alchemy of English. The spread, functions and models of non-native Englishes,* Oxford: Pergamon, 1986.

62 Research conducted by Philip Seymour of the University of Dundee, and reported on in several British newspapers on 5 September 2001.

63 These figures are from Wollin, cited in B. Melander, 'Swedish, English and the European Union' in *Managing multilingualism in a European nation-state*, ed. S. Boyd and L. Huss, Clevedon: Multilingual Matters, 2001, 13–31.

64 See Bailey, op. cit., 209 (note 4 above).

65 See Phillipson, op. cit., ch. 6.

66 J. Habermas, 'A constitution for Europe?' *New Left Review*, 11, September–October 2001, 5–26.

67 Ibid.

68 Introduction to *Roots of the right. Readings in fascist, racist and elitist ideology*, series editor G. Steiner, London: Jonathan Cape, 1970. There were thinkers of this ilk throughout Europe.

69 E. M. Forster, 'What I believe', in *Two cheers for democracy*, Harmondsworth: Penguin, 1965, 78.

70 This paragraph and the following one draw heavily on information in E. Holm's book *The European anarchy. Europe's hard road into high politics,*

Copenhagen Business School Press, 2001. Holm is an academic who was economic adviser to the Danish Prime Minister for many years before and after Denmark's accession to the EU, and has held high office in the EU.

71 J. Spring, *Education and the rise of the global economy*, Mahwah, NJ: Lawrence Erlbaum, 1998, ch. 4.

72 See Holm, op. cit., 274.

73 See M. Billig, *Banal nationalism*, London: Sage, 1995.

74 For discussion in the light of political theory, see C. Karlsson, *Democracy, legitimacy and the European Union*, Uppsala: Acta Universitatis Upsaliensis, Skrifter utgivna av Statsvetenskapliga föreningen, 2001, 183–4.

75 The charter was elaborated by the European Movement in Germany, and endorsed at Lübeck on 28 October 1995.

76 'For every five people who voted for New Labour, seven voted for someone else, and a further eight voted not at all'; A. Rawnsley, *Servants of the people. The inside story of New Labour*, London: Penguin, 2001, 504.

77 G. Monbiot, *Captive state. The corporate take-over of Britain*, London: Macmillan, 2000; and Rawnsley, op. cit.

78 Henning Koch, Professor of Constitutional Law, University of Copenhagen, personal communication. He is director of a project that is studying these different legal cultures.

79 See M. Garre, *Human rights in translation. Legal concepts in different languages*, Copenhagen Business School Press, 1999, 144–54.

80 P. van Ham, 'European integration and the postmodern condition', *Foreign Affairs* 80/5, September/October 2001, 2–6.

81 This is not to deny its 'global' reach. It is marketed as being printed in 24 cities worldwide, and delivered to homes and offices in over 180 countries.

82 <http://europa.eu.int/comm/dg10/epo/eb/eb55/eb55.html>.

83 Report in *The Guardian Weekly*, 15–21 November 2001.

84 R. Griffiths, 'Reflections on the history of European IGCs (Intergovernmental Conferences)', in *The Treaty of Nice explained*, ed. M. Bond and K. Feus, London: The Federal Trust for Education and Research, and Kogan Page, 2001, 57–74.

3 Global trends impacting on European language policy

1 Cited in R. Phillipson, *Linguistic imperialism*, Oxford: Oxford University Press, 1992, 136.

2 Ibid.

3 <http://europa.eu.int/comm/dg10/epo/eb.html>.

4 Speech in Oviedo, Asturias, Spain; see <http://www.fpa.es/ing/premios/discursos/2001chy.html>.

5 Word of support for the Follow-up Committee, *Universal Declaration of Linguistic Rights*, Barcelona, <http://www.troc.es/dudl>.

6 R. Rosen, P. Digh, M. Singer and C. Phillips, *Global literacies. Lessons on business leadership and national cultures. A landmark study of CEOs from 28 countries,* New York: Simon & Schuster, 2000.

7 Eurobarometer Report 54, *Europeans and Languages*, 15 February 2001.

8 G. Nunberg, 'A weakness that can easily be translated', *The Washington Post*, 9 December 2001.

9 M. Reynolds, 'Why are the British such poor language learners? Sociolinguistic issues', <http://www.phon.ucl.ad.uk/home/dick/ec/EcmflRey/Abs.htm>.

10 See C. Baker, *A parents' and teachers' guide to bilingualism*, Clevedon: Multilingual Matters, 1995; C. Baker and S. Prys Jones, *Encyclopedia of bilingualism and bilingual education*, Clevedon: Multilingual Matters, 1998; and T. Skutnabb-Kangas, *Linguistic genocide in education – or worldwide diversity and human rights?*, Mahwah, NJ: Lawrence Erlbaum, 2000, ch. 8.

11 This provocative metaphor was launched by Tove Skutnabb-Kangas and has entered mainstream sociolinguistics. See the thematic number entitled 'Monolingualism is curable' of *Sociolinguistica*, the International Yearbook of European Sociolinguistics, 11, 1997.

12 Introduction to the brochure 'Mercator Information Networks, a resource for European languages'.

13 The position and power of English has been subjected to a great deal of analysis in books and periodicals; see, for instance, *Ideology, politics and language policies. Focus on English*, ed. T. Ricento, Amsterdam: John Benjamins, 2000. The constellation idea is central to the work of A. de Swaan, e.g. in *Words of the world*, Cambridge: Polity, 2001.

14 The term 'linguicism' was coined by Skutnabb-Kangas; see op. cit., 369 ff.

15 D. Cameron, *Verbal hygiene*, London: Routledge, 1995.

16 K. D. McRae, *Conflict and compromise in multilingual societies: Switzerland* (1983); *Belgium* (1986); *Finland* (1987), Waterloo, Ontario: Wilfred Laurier University Press.

17 See 'Introduction', R. Phillipson, M. Rannut and T. Skutnabb-Kangas, in *Linguistic human rights. Overcoming linguistic discrimination*, ed. T. Skutnabb-Kangas and R. Phillipson, Berlin: Mouton de Gruyter, 1994, 1–22.

18 J. Edwards (ed.), *Language in Canada*, Cambridge: Cambridge University Press, 1998.

19 J. Lo Bianco, *National policy on languages*, Commonwealth of Australia, Canberra: Australian Government Publishing Service, 1987.

20 The Language Plan of Action for Africa, approved at the Organization for African Unity in Addis Ababa, 1986, is reproduced as an Appendix in LANGTAG, *Towards a national language plan for South Africa*. Summary of the Final Report of the Language Plan Task Group (LANGTAG), 1996. <www.sacs.org.za/gov/arts&cul//docs/langrep.htm/>.

21 See the LANGTAG Report, op. cit. See also the contributions by Alexander, Desai, and Heugh in *Rights to language. Equity, power and education*, ed. R. Phillipson, Mahwah, NJ: Lawrence Erlbaum, 2000.

22 The *Financial Times* of 3 December 2001 reports that a survey in 2001 undertaken for the Community of European Management Schools, an alliance of academia and multinational corporations, concluded that a company's inability to speak a client's language can lead to failure to win business because it indicates a lack of effort.

23 Renamed as the World Terrorist Organization by activists at Seattle in 1999 because their policies deny millions the right to life and livelihood.

24 See <http://www.globalpolicy.org/socecon/tncs/2001/0926oplet.htm> for resistance, with the involvement of Members of the European Parliament.

25 G. Monbiot, *Captive state. The corporate takeover of Britain*, London: Macmillan, 2000.

26 R. Chaudenson, *Mondialisation: La langue française a-t-elle encore un avenir?* (Globalization: Does the French language have a future?), Paris: Institut de la Francophonie, and Didier, 2000, 169.

27 This topic is explored in an admirable study, D. Graddol, *The future of English?* London: The British Council, 1997.

28 Reported in *Børsens Nyhedsmagasin* 19, 28 May 2001.

29 Figures quoted in C. Tongue, 'New digital technologies – a threat or opportunity for European cinema?', *Cine Citta*, March 2001.

30 Denmark received 33 million euros in 1991–2001. The proportion of Zentropa's films exported to other EU countries rose in this period from 10% to 40%. *Europa-Kommissionens nyhedsbrev* (newsletter), Copenhagen, June 2002, 5.

31 G. Therborn, *European modernity and beyond. The trajectory of European societies, 1945–2000*, London: Sage, 1995, 224.

32 D. Schiller, 'Globe with a logo', *Le Monde Diplomatique* (English edition), May 2001, 15.

33 Cited ibid.

34 C. Hamelink's vivid image. See 'Human rights: the next fifty years', in *Rights to language. Equity, power, and education*, ed. R. Phillipson, Mahwah, NJ: Lawrence Erlbaum, 2000, 62–6, and *Media Development*, 1999, vol. 4, also the webpage of the World Association of Christian Communication, <www.wacc.org.uk>.

35 Burston Marsteler, cited in 'Anti-spin activist John Stauber penetrates America's lie machine', M. Manekin, *Westchester County Weekly*, August 23–29, 2001.

36 J. Pilger, 2001. <http://pilger.carlton.com/print/67484>.

37 Cited in R. Phillipson, *Linguistic imperialism*, 7.

38 Ibid., chs 6 and 7.

39 P. Bourdieu, *Contre-feux 2. Pour un mouvement social européen* (Counter-fire 2. For a European social movement), Paris: Raisons d'agir, 2001, 96–7.

40 In 'Campaign 2000: Promoting the national interest', cited in the Danish daily paper *Information*, 14 June 2001.

41 M. T. Klare, 'America's military revolution', *Le Monde Diplomatique* (English version), July 2001, 4–5.

42 P. S. Golub, 'America's imperial longings', *Le Monde Diplomatique* (English version), July 2001, 2–3.

43 Monbiot, op. cit., 331.

44 J. Mander, 'The rules of corporate behaviour', in *The case against the global economy – and for a turn toward the local*, ed. J. Mander and E. Goldsmith, San Francisco: Sierra Club Books, 1996, 309–22.

45 Cited in Monbiot, op. cit., 332.

46 Ibid., 333–4.

47 Ibid., 335–6.

48 Reported ibid., 288. G. Muttitt and C. Grimshaw, *Degrees of involvement. An examination of the relationship between the upstream oil and gas industry and UK higher education institutions,* Corporate Watch, 2000.

49 See 'The fat cats directory', ch. 6 of Monbiot, op. cit.

50   <http://www.britishcouncil.org>.
51   'What you need to know about marketing English language courses', <http://www.britishcouncil.org/english/marketing.pdf>.
52   <www.number-10.gov.uk/news.asp?Newsld=392>.
53   See figures for Finland in H. Haarman and E. Holman, 'The impact of English as a language of science in Finland', in *The dominance of English as a language of science. Effects on other languages and language communities*, ed. U. Ammon, Berlin: de Gruyter, 2001, 229–60.
54   *Financial Times*, 3 December 2001, 'Schools learn the value of English'.
55   B. Brock-Utne, 'Ny universitetslov en trussel mot norsk kultur' (New university law a threat to Norwegian culture), *Dagbladet*, 16 January 2002. The Norwegian Language Council and the University of Tromsø protested against this change.
56   Quoted in the *Guardian Weekly*, 16–22 November 2000.
57   <www.scienceacross.org>. As part of this 'Science across the world' scheme, the British Council administers a North–South school linking project: links are supposed to be 'equal and reciprocal', a criterion that presumably refers to the exchange of information rather than use of languages other than English.
58   Cited in Monbiot, op. cit., 329.
59   <http://kultur.regeringen.se/propositionermm/sou/pdf/engelska.pdf>. A summary in English.
60   Summarized in S. A. Feld, 'Language and the globalization of the economic market: the regulation of language as a barrier to free trade', *Vanderbilt Journal of Transnational Law*, 1998, 31, 153–202.
61   My copy of the three-volume Webster's *Third New International Dictionary of the English Language*, the 1966 edition (published by Encyclopaedia Britannica in Chicago), includes *The Britannica World Language Dictionary*, which 'comprises a list of about 6,000 most commonly used words in English with their closest equivalents in French, German, Italian, Spanish, Swedish, and Yiddish'. The implication is that educated Americans of that period were able to make use of several languages.
62   J. M. Swales, 'English as "Tyrannosaurus Rex"', *World Englishes* 16/3, 1997, 373–82.
63   C. Durand, *La mise en place des monopoles du savoir* (The creation of monopolies of knowledge), Paris: l'Harmattan, 2002.
64   See P. Jarvad, *Det danske sprogs status i 1990'erne, med særligt henblik på domænetab* (The status of the Danish language in the 1990s, particularly as regards domain loss), Copenhagen: Dansk Sprognævn (Danish Language Council), 2001. Similar reports exist for the other Nordic languages.
65   B. Brock-Utne, 'The growth of English for academic communication in the Nordic countries', *International Review of Education*, 47, 3/4, 2001, 221–33. The figures are from the University of Oslo in 1997.
66   The book was published in 2001 by Mouton de Gruyter in Berlin. See my fairly detailed review in *Journal of Language, Identity, and Education,* vol. 1/2, 2002, 163–9.
67   This point is made by the Belgian contributor, R. Willemyns. Diglossia is a technical term for functions being performed in two different languages, e.g. high-status ones in classical Arabic and low-status ones in demotic

Arabic. European examples of diglossia include Swiss German being used in most speech in Switzerland, and High German in writing and some formal spoken contexts; or Scots being used in speech in Scotland, whereas standard English is the norm in writing and in formal speech, with a Scottish accent. Willemyns reports (339–40) that the concept diglossia was used in French Hellenistic studies 1890–1930, and that a thick volume by G. Cohen, *Pour une sociologie du langage,* was published in 1964.

68 Figures (for 1995) range from 3% in Finland, through 2.3% in France and Germany, to 0.6% in Portugal and Greece.

69 These proposals are all contained in the Vienna Manifesto 'The cost of monolingualism' of 29 June 2001, approved at a conference convened by the Austrian Academy of Sciences and attended by scholars from 11 countries. The Manifesto is available in English, French, German, and Greek.

70 H. Daun (ed.), *Educational restructuring in the context of globalization and national policy,* New York and London: Routledge Falmer, 2002.

71 See, for instance, the *Reviews of National Policies for Education* series (e.g. covering higher education in Finland 1995, Sweden 1995), published by the OECD in Paris. On the way OECD promotion of science and technology has impacted in Québec, and the measures taken by the government there to strengthen French, see A. Martel, 'When does knowledge have a national language? Language policy-making for science and technology', in *The dominance of English as a language of science,* ed. U. Ammon, 27–57.

72 As presented in each number of *ESF Communications,* published twice a year, and available from <www.esf.org>.

73 *ESF Communications* 44, Spring 2002, 17. This number reproduces four articles on European science policy from *Nature,* 18 January 2002, 295, 443–6.

74 *ESF Communications* 43, Summer 2001, 9.

75 *ESF Communications* 43, Summer 2001, 16.

76 Bent Preisler conducted a representative national survey of competence in English, as well as a more detailed study of its use in several sub-cultures; see *Danskerne og det engelske sprog* (Danes and the English language), Frederiksberg: Roskilde Universitetsforlag-Samfundslitteratur, 1999; and 'Functions and forms of English in a European EFL country', in *Standard English: the widening debate,* ed. T. Bex and R. J. Watts, London: Routledge, 1999, 239–67.

77 Of a population of just over 5 million in Denmark, around 1 million are classified as poor readers in OECD studies; see Jarvad, op. cit., 15–22 (note 64 above).

78 <www.scandinavian.net> and <www.sas.dk> for Denmark.

79 Thanks to Poul Christensen, head of communications, SAS Denmark.

80 G. Nunberg, 'Will the internet always speak English?', *The American Prospect,* 11/10, March 27 to April 10, 2000. <http://www.prospect.org/print/V11/10/nunberg-g.html>.

81 This was the case of the EUROTRA programme, in the 2nd Framework Programme for Research and Technological Development, 1982. Language engineering was also included in later Framework Programmes.

82 See the Newsletter of the Nordic Research Academy (in Scandinavian languages) of December 2001, on <www.norfa.no>.

83 See Preisler's studies, note 76 above.

84   A trenchant denunciation by M. Grenfell, cited in Reynolds, op. cit. (note 9 above).

85   I am indebted to Albert Raasch of the University of Saarbrücken for this concept.

86   My analysis of the problems of German in Denmark draws on an unpublished conference paper, 17 November 2001, by Per Øhrgaard, Professor of German at the University of Copenhagen, and a paper 'At kommunikere professionelt med sine naboer' (Communicating professionally with one's neighbours) by Henning Gade, an attaché at the Danish Embassy in Berlin, in Proceedings of the Conference in Copenhagen, 3 November 2000 on *Videregående sproguddannelser – er der brug for reformer?* (Foreign languages in higher education – is reform needed?), Humanistisk Uddannelsesråd (The Educational Council for the Humanities), Copenhagen, 2001. The Goethe Institut has organized language policy conferences in several countries about the status and learning of EU languages.

87   H. Glück, *Das Deutsche als Fremdsprache in Europa vom Mittelalter bis zum Barock*, Berlin: de Gruyter, 2001.

88   B. Brock-Utne, *Whose education for all? Recolonizing the African mind?* New York: Falmer, 2000.

89   See <http://europa.eu.int/scadplus/leg/en/lvb/l29001.htm>.

90   K. Feus, 'Substantive amendments - the Treaty of Nice explained', in *The Treaty of Nice explained*, ed. M. Bond and K. Feus, London: The Federal Trust for Education and Research, 2001, 27–53.

91   See <www.eurocult.org>.

92   European Cultural Foundation, *Which languages for Europe?* Report of the conference held at Oegstgeest, the Netherlands, 8–11 October 1998. Amsterdam: European Cultural Foundation, 1999. The only follow-up was in the less contentious but equally disputed area of minority language rights; see G. Ekstra and D. Gorter (eds), *The other languages of Europe. Demographic, sociolinguistic and educational perspectives*, Clevedon: Multilingual Matters, 2001, from which Appendix 4 is taken.

93   For a summary see <www.eurolang.net/news.asp?id=596>, which shows how the original draft was watered down into a more vague pronouncement.

94   For EU Commission actions, see <http://europa.eu.int/comm/education/languages/commactions.html>.

95   Figures quoted in Reynolds, op. cit. (note 9 above).

96   M. Barlow and H. Robertson, 'Homogenization of education', in Mander and Goldsmith, op. cit. (note 44 above), 60–70.

97   See 'Communications' from the US government to the WTO, Council for Trade in Services, S/CSS/W/23, 18 December 2000.

98   Australia: S/CSS/W/110 of 1 October 2001; New Zealand: S/CSS/W93 of 26 June 2001.

99   Barlow and Robertson, op. cit., 70.

100 D. Rosenthal, 'Examinations abroad', *CAM*, Easter, 31–2.

101 COM(95), 29 November 1995.

102 Ibid., 51.

103 Ibid., 44–6.

104 T. McArthur, *The English languages,* Cambridge: Cambridge University Press, 1998, and the journals *English Today*, and *World Englishes*.

105 This is similar to the way in which 'second language' is used in immigrant language learning. For a child who speaks Kurdish or Panjabi at home in Britain, English is not a foreign language but the language of the wider community, and the second in order of learning.

106 See details of 'Janua Linguarum, La porte aux langues, Gateway to languages' on <http://www.chez.com/jaling/> and at the Council of Europe's Centre for Modern Languages in Graz, Austria, <http://jaling.ecml.at/>.

107 Quotations from the executive summary of *Languages: the next generation*, the final report and recommendations of the Nuffield Languages Inquiry, 2000, <http://www.nuffield.org>.

108 These are regularly surveyed in the abstracting journal *Language teaching* and in Council of Europe publications.

109 See *Common European framework of reference for languages: Learning, teaching, assessment*, Cambridge: Cambridge University Press for the Council of Europe, 2001. See <http://book.coe.int/>.

110 *Linguistic diversity for democratic citizenship in Europe*. Proceedings, Innsbruck 10–12 May 1999, Strasbourg: Education Committee, Council for Cultural Co-operation, Council of Europe, 2000. For a brief summary of the Modern Languages Projects and policy instruments, see the article by J. Shiels in Bulletin 7 of the European Language Council, on <http://www.fu-berlin.de/elc>.

111 <http://europa.eu.int/comm/education/languages/actions/index.html/>.

112 <http:/www.euroclic.net/>.

113 Information from Sylvia Vlaeminck, Head of the Language Policy Unit, 18 January 2002.

114 C. Blondin, M. Candelier, P. Edelbos, R. Johnstone, A. Kubanek-German, and T. Taeschner, Report for DG 22, European Commission, 21 November 1997.

115 'Les langues vivantes contribueront de façon spécifique à la maitrise de la langue nationale et de la lecture'. Speech on 29 January 2001, <http://www.education.gouv.fr/discours/2001/dlangviv.htm/>.

116 <http:/www.fu-berlin.de/elc>.

117 <www.dialang.org>.

4 Languages in EU institutions

1 M. Abélès, 'Multiculturalism and multilingualism in the European institutions', in *Which languages for Europe?*, Amsterdam: European Cultural Foundation, 1999, 111–18. <www.eurocult.org>.

2 M. Cutts, *Clarifying Eurolaw*, High Peak: Plain Language Commission, 2001. <www.clearest.co.uk>.

3 G. Lenaerts, 'A failure to comply with the EU language policy: A study of the Council archives', *Multilingua*, 20/3, 2001, 221–44.

4 N. Labrie, *La construction linguistique de la Communauté européenne*, Paris: Champion, 1993.

5 V. Mamadouh, 'Institutional multilingualism: an exploration of possible reforms', in *Which languages for Europe?*, 119–26.

6 B. McCluskey (acting Director-General, Translation Service, European

Commission), 'Practical steps to cope with the language consequences of EU enlargement'. Speech to the congress of the Bundesverband der Dolmetscher and Übersetzer e.V., Landesverband Bayern, 25 November 2001.

7   N. Fairclough, *Critical discourse analysis*, London: Longman, 1995; and for an application, N. Fairclough, *New Labour, new language*, London: Routledge, 2000.

8   P. Bourdieu, *Language and symbolic power*, Cambridge: Polity Press, 1991, 45 (translation of *Ce que parler veut dire: l'économie des échanges linguistiques*, Paris: Fayard, 1982).

9   COM(2001) 428 of 25 July 2001. <http://europa.eu.int/comm/governance/areas/index_en.htm> p. 8.

10 Commissioners are required by the Treaties to 'be completely independent in the performance of their duties' (Article 213, EC, earlier Article 157), this supposedly ensuring that they stand above national concerns and work for the general European interest. This interest has clearly not been general enough in the past, if it is now admitted that the EU has to change in the direction of greater transparency, openness, and legitimacy. See C. Karlsson, *Democracy, legitimacy and the European Union*, Uppsala: Acta Universitatis Upsaliensis, Skrifter utgivna av Statsvetenskapliga föreningen, 2001.

11 J. Fischer, speech at Humboldt University, Berlin, 12 May 2000, 'Vom Staatenforbund zur Föderation' (From an association of states to a federation). L. Jospin, speech to Foreign Press Association, Paris, 28 May 2001.

12 L. Friis, *Den europæiske byggeplads. Fra fælles mønt til europæisk forfatning* (The European building site. From a common currency to a European constitution), Copenhagen: Centrum, 2001; Erik Holm, *The European anarchy. Europe's hard road into high politics*, Copenhagen Business School Press, 2001.

13 See A. Musolff, 'Cross-language metaphors, the European family in British and German public discourse', in *Language across boundaries*, ed. J. Cotterill and A. Ife, British Association for Applied Linguistics, and London: Continuum, 2001.

14 'A multilingual community at work', September 2001, <http://europa.eu.int/comm/translation>.

15 Annexe IV.2 of 'L'interprétation de conférences face à l'élargissement. Une stratégie pour le SCIC à l'horizon 2004' (Conference interpretation vis-à-vis enlargement. A strategy for the SCIC forward to 2004). Draft Consultation Document, Commission, 13 November 2001. SCIC is the Service Commun Interprétation – Conférences.

16 <http://www.europa.eu.int/eurodicautom/>.

17 Information provided by the Communication Team, Translation Service of the Commission, 21 November 2001.

18 <http://www.europa.eu.int/comm/translation/bulletins/matters/2/feature.htm>.

19 E. Wagner, S. Bech, and J. M. Martínez, *Translating for the European Union institutions*, Manchester: St. Jerome, 2002.

20 List and figures from 'Conference interpreting and enlargement. A strategy for the Joint Interpreting and Conference Service in the lead up to 2004, Communicated to the Commission by Vice-President Kinnock', 10 December 2001.

21 H. Tonkin, 'Language hierarchy at the United Nations', in *Vers un agenda*

linguistique: regard futuriste sur les nations unies, Towards a language agenda: futurist outlook on the United Nations, ed. S. Léger, Ottawa: Canadian Centre for Linguistic Rights, University of Ottawa, 1996, 3–28.

22   <http://www.spainun.org/pages/viewfull.cfm?ElementID=1853>,   21 December 2001.

23   Tonkin, op. cit., 14.

24   'A multilingual community at work', September 2001, <http://europa.eu.int/comm/translation>.

25   Thanks to Svend Bech for this authentic example.

26   B. Melander, 'Swedish, English and the European Union', in *Managing multilingualism in a European nation-state*, ed. S. Boyd and L. Huss, Clevedon: Multilingual Matters, 2001, 13–31.

27   Op. cit. note 24.

28   '. . . dans une seule des trois langages de travail des institutions communautaires', '. . . in einer einzigen der drei Arbeitssprachen der Gemeinschaftsinstitutionen'. Intriguingly, the German Foreign Minister is identified as Joschka Fischer in the German text, and Joseph Fischer in the French text.

29   This is a fairly literal translation of Prodi's text: 'Diese Grundsätze sind eine wesentliche Voraussetzung dafür, dass die kulturelle und sprachliche Vielfalt unseres Kontinents im europäischen Aufbauwerk voll zum Ausdruck kommt'; 'Ces principes sont essentiels pour que la construction européenne soit une réalité prenant pleinement en considération la diversité culturelle et linguistique de notre continent.'

30   M. Schlossmacher, *Die Amtsprachen in den Organen der Europäischen Gemeinschaft* (Official languages in the institutions of the European Community), Frankfurt am Main: Peter Lang, 1996. 'Amtsprache' does not correspond exactly to 'official language'.

31   C. Quell, 'Language choice in multilingual institutions: a case study at the European Commission with special reference to the role of English, French and German as working languages', *Multilingua* 16/1, 1997, 57–76.

32   Wagner, Bech, and Martínez, op. cit., 142.

33   David O'Sullivan, Secretary-General of the European Commission, in Wagner, Bech, and Martínez, 142.

34   Theo van Els has mooted the idea, and reports that when Denmark negotiated accession in 1972, Danes suggested a French + English + no mother tongue solution; see 'The European Union, its institutions and its languages. Some language political observations', Lecture, University of Nijmegen, 2000.

35   'Language regime in the European Parliament', Legal Opinion, SJ-0224/01 of 29 August 2001. The text also exists in French.

36   <http://europa.eu.int/comm/agriculture/external/enlarge/countries/czech/finance/mafa_en.pdf>.

37   Melander, op. cit.; Schlossmacher, op. cit.; Quell, op. cit.

38   This example is from C. Piron, *Le défi des langues: du gâchis au bon sens* (The languages challenge: from waste to common sense), Paris: l'Harmattan, 1994. Piron was a UN interpreter for many years, and is very critical of the system of interpretation and translation. See my review of the book in *Language in Society*, 26/1, 1997, 143–7.

39   Colette Flesch, former Foreign Minister of Luxembourg, and long-time

Eurocrat, Director-General of the Translation Service; <http://europa.eu.int/comm/translation/en/ftfog/flesch.htm>.

40 Flesch, ibid., gives three reasons: the French version of the 'acquis communautaire' was the sole point of reference, key posts were occupied by French speakers, and British newcomers made use of French, as a sign of their European credentials.

41 F. Stark, *Deutsch 2000*. Materialen zur Fernsehdokumentation, citing work by Pfeil and Hemblenne. Bayerischer Rundfunk: <http://www.br-online.de>, then search for Deutsch 2000.

42 For analysis of translation issues, see Wagner, Bech, and Martínez, op. cit. The Eurodicautom database provides the following equivalents for 'acquis communautaire': Danish 'gældende fællesskabsret', English 'community patrimony', German 'EG-Besitzstand, gemeinschaftlicher Besitzstand, einschlägiges Gemeinschaftsrecht', etc. The website of the Translation Service has advice on suitable translation equivalents at <http://europa.eu.int/comm/translation/en/ftfog/>.

43 Y. Gambier, quoted by A. Pym, 'The European Union and its future languages: questions for language policies and translation theories', *Across Languages and Cultures*, 1/1, 2000, 1–18.

44 A. Karker, *Dansk i EF – en situationsrapport om sproget* (Danish in the EC – a report on the state of the language), Copenhagen: Nordisk Språksekretariats Skrifter, 16, Gad, 1993; reviewed by C. Henriksen in *Nys*, 19, 1994, 113–24. <http://europa.eu.int/comm/translation/theory/karker.htm>.

45 Abélès, op. cit., 114 (note 1 above).

46 See Wagner, Bech, and Martínez, op. cit., 72.

47 See the report of a speech at the London School of Economics by Peter Hain, Minister for Europe, reported in *The Independent*, 4 December 2001.

48 <http://www.justitie.regeringen.se/klarsprak>. This concern figures prominently in the parliamentary report on language policy, <http://kultur.regeringen.se/propositionermm/sou/pdf/engelska.pdf>, 2002.

49 <http://europa.eu.int/comm/sdt/en/ftfog/index.htm>.

50 E. Wagner, 'The "Fight the Fog" campaign at the European Commission', in *Bättre språk i EU* (Better languages in the EU), Report from a conference in Brussels, 29 November to 1 December 1998, Oslo: Nordic Language Council, 2000, 76–83.

51 Ibid.

52 M. Cutts, *Clarifying Eurolaw*, Plain Language Commission, 2001. <www.clearest.co.uk>.

53 Ibid., 10–11.

54 The Strategy Paper was adopted as a Commission document on 20 March 2002.

55 From the brochure 'A multilingual community at work. The European Commission's Translation Service' (see note 24 above).

56 From 'Multilingualism: the key to success', website of the Joint Interpreting and Conference Service, <http://europa.eu.int/comm/scic/multi/multi_en.htm>.

57 The Consultative Document of the Commission 'A strategy for the Translation Service: perspectives for 2002 and beyond', of 15 December

2001. I am tempted to guess that the original document was written in French, and that this is a translation. It describes translation as 'an intellectual activity requiring highly qualified staff'. Translation requires a good deal of brain power, and is therefore 'intellectually demanding', but calling it an 'intellectual activity' rings false in English, particularly as intellectuals are highly respected in France but barely tolerated in Britain.

58 Stark, op. cit. (note 41 above), quoting Hans von der Groeben.

59 F. Coulmas, 'The status of German: some suggestions for future research', *International Journal of the Sociology of Language,* 83, 1990, 171–85. See also the papers in *Sprachenpolitik in Europa – Sprachenpolitik für Europa,* ed. S. Sporrer and M. Weber, Materialen zum Internationalen Kulturaustausch, Stuttgart: Institut für Auslandsbeziehungen, 1997.

60 'A multilingual community at work', 1999 version.

61 'A multilingual community at work', 2001.

62 McCluskey, op. cit. (note 6 above).

63 A multilingual community at work, 2001.

64 See the internal paper 'Catégorisation', of 6 June 2001, listing and classifying ten types of document for translation. This is in an English version as Annex 5 of 'A strategy for the Translation Service. Consultative document of the Commission', 19 November 2001, with figures for the proportion of work in each category.

65 P. Muntigl, G. Weiss, and R. Wodak, *European Union discourses on un/employment. An interdisciplinary approach to employment policy-making and organizational change,* Amsterdam: John Benjamins, 2000.

66 Op. cit. note 57 above.

67 Ibid.

68 'Conference interpreting and enlargement. A strategy for the Joint Interpreting and Conference Service in the lead up to 2004', European Commission, 10 December 2001.

69 See for instance the website of the extremely successful Centre for Language Technology, based at the University of Copenhagen, Denmark, <http://www.cst.dk/>.

70 <http://agence.francophonie.org/dernieres/quoideneuf.cfm?qho_id=1100>. 'Un plan pluriannuel d'action pour renforcer le français au sein de l'Union européenne', 11 January 2002.

71 I have been sent a good deal of internal correspondence by EU employees that laments the way languages other than English are marginalized. This information has to be treated confidentially and anonymously.

72 Étude préliminaire d'évaluation de la qualité des prestations fournies par le SCIC en matière d'interprétation. Rapport de fin de mission, 22 October 2001. 799 delegate informants, 707 reports from interpreters.

73 Permanent Representatives of member states request interpretation, and have the right to decide when it is or is not required. It ought to be possible to analyse the criteria that determine these pragmatic language policy decisions, and to incorporate this information into multilingual profiles of users of the interpretation services as a contribution to longer-term policy formation.

74 J. Pool, 'Optimal languages regimes for the European Union', *International Journal of the Sociology of Language* 121, 1996, 159–79.

5 Towards equitable communication

1   R. Centassi and H. Masson, *L'homme qui a défié Babel* (The man who defied Babel), Paris: Ramsay, 1995.

2   Speech, 14 February 1923, reported in *The Times* of London, 16 February 1923.

3   Word of support for the Follow-up Committee, *Universal Declaration of Linguistic Rights*, Barcelona, <http://www.troc.es/dudl>.

4   M. Ramphele, *A life*, Cape Town: David Philip, 1995, 2nd edn 1996, 209. Ramphele has doctorates in medicine and anthropology, was imprisoned and banned under apartheid, has been Deputy Vice-Chancellor of the University of Cape Town, and currently works for the World Bank.

5   *Language and politics. Northern Ireland, the Republic of Ireland, and Scotland*, ed. J. M. Kirk and D. P. Ó. Baoill, Belfast Studies in Language, Culture and Politics 1, 2000; and *Linguistic politics. Language policies for Northern Ireland, the Republic of Ireland, and Scotland*, ed. J. M. Kirk and D. P. Ó. Baoill, Belfast Studies in Language, Culture and Politics 3, 2001; <www.bslcp.com>.

6   LANGTAG, *Towards a national language plan for South Africa*. Summary of the Final Report of the Language Plan Task Group (LANGTAG), 1996.

7   'Habitus' is from the work of Pierre Bourdieu, and means the ideas or mindset associated with a particular activity.

8   For the papers given at this conference, see *The other languages of Europe. Demographic, sociolinguistic and educational perspectives*, ed. G. Ekstra and D. Gorter, Clevedon: Multilingual Matters, 2001.

9   H. Schiffman, *Linguistic culture and language policy*, London: Routledge, 1996.

10 In Australia, faith in an economic gospel in the 1990s reversed some of the policies that supported multilingualism and multiculturalism in the 1980s; see M. Clyne, 'Promoting multilingualism and linguistic human rights in the era of economic rationalism and globalization', in *Rights to language: equity, power and education*, ed. R. Phillipson, Mahwah, NJ: Lawrence Erlbaum, 2000, 160–3.

11 E. Holm, *The European anarchy. Europe's hard road into high politics*, Copenhagen Business School Press, 2001, 149 ff.

12 B. Theret, 'Hard cash. Euro: Godless, stateless, and untrustworthy?', *Le Monde Diplomatique* (English version, with *The Guardian Weekly*), December 2001, 11.

13 F. Grin and F. Vaillancourt, 'On the financing of language policies and distributive justice', in *Rights to language*, ed. R. Phillipson, 102–110.

14 This fear is articulated by Mr Defraigne, the 'chef de cabinet' of Pascal Lamy, the EU Commissioner for Trade, in an interview on 13 March 2002 for an internal magazine for EU translators, *Verba Volant*.

15 J. Sheils, 'Council of Europe language policy', Council of Europe, *Linguistic diversity for democratic citizenship in Europe*, 2000, 129–36.

16 The report 'Language learning', published by the Department of Education and Skills on 12 February 2002, admits that government policy towards foreign languages has been 'half-hearted', and promises change, mainly by means of an increased effort in primary schools.

17 It is particularly the work of François Grin that has integrated classic eco-
    nomic approaches to the study of language groups and language compe-
    tence with sociolinguistic variables and a concern for diversity; see 'English
    as economic value: tools, facts and fallacies', *World Englishes*, 20/1, 2001,
    65–78.

18 R. Phillipson, *Linguistic imperialism*, Oxford: Oxford University Press, 1992;
    A. Pennycook, *The cultural politics of English as an international language*,
    Harlow: Longman, 1994.

19 See Phillipson, op. cit. 147–52.

20 Ibid., 164–9.

21 Cambridge: Polity Press, 174, 192.

22 Phillipson, op. cit., ch. 7; P. Medgyes, *The non-native teacher*, London:
    Macmillan, 1994; G. Braine (ed.), *Non-native educators in English Language
    Teaching*, Mahwah, NJ: Lawrence Erlbaum, 1999.

23 'Recent trends in ELT ... are promoted as neutral rather than as cultural,
    ideological and political inscriptions. Specific approaches, methods and
    techniques are construed as "universal goods" rather than as cultural prod-
    ucts ... appropriate teacher training programmes for language teachers
    who are required to contribute to the development of linguistic and cul-
    tural pluralism in Europe. Until pedagogical and social practices of those
    involved in the "business" of language teaching and learning consistently
    aim at securing the polyphony of Europe, such an aim will be difficult to
    achieve.' B. Dendrinos, *The politics of ELT*, Athens: University of Athens
    publications, 2001, 213.

24 For analysis of power and language, and how some languages are treated as
    handicaps rather than convertible resources, see T. Skutnabb-Kangas,
    Linguistic genocide in education – or worldwide diversity and human rights?,
    Mahwah, NJ: Lawrence Erlbaum, 2000, 405–8.

25 e.g. Sys Bundgaard, 'Nordea's cooperation with DANTERM on language
    technology tools', *LSP and professional communication*, 1/2, 2001, 85–92, a
    description of the policies of a Nordic bank, Nordea, in developing the
    software for its staff in four countries to handle translation for internation-
    al communication.

26 S. A. Wurm (ed.), *Atlas of the world's languages in danger of disappearing*, Paris:
    UNESCO, 2nd edn, 2001; Skutnabb-Kangas, op. cit.

27 M. van der Stoel, Report on the Linguistic Rights of Persons Belonging to
    National Minorities in the OSCE area, + Annex. Replies from OSCE
    Participating States. The Hague: OSCE High Commissioner on National
    Minorities, 1999, 8–9. The relevant sections of most of the human rights
    instruments cited here, and the entire text of the European Charter for
    Regional or Minority Languages, are reproduced in the Appendix of
    Linguistic human rights: overcoming linguistic discrimination, ed. T. Skutnabb-
    Kangas and R. Phillipson, Berlin: Mouton de Gruyter, 1994.

28 M. Kontra, R. Phillipson, T. Skutnabb-Kangas, and T. Várady, (eds),
    Language: A right and a resource. Approaching linguistic human rights, Budapest:
    Central European University Press, 1999; Skutnabb-Kangas op. cit.

29 F. de Varennes, 'Tolerance and inclusion: the convergence of human rights
    and the work of Tove Skutnabb-Kangas', in *Rights to language*, ed. R.
    Phillipson, 67–71.

30 News and details of Council of Europe instruments can be checked at
    <http://conventions.coe.int/treaty/EN/cadrenews.htm> and <http://
    conventions.coe.int/treaty/EN/cadreprincipal.htm>. The Draft Universal
    Declaration of Linguistic Rights is at <http://www.linguistic-
    declaration.org>. Many materials and documents on language and law can
    be downloaded from the Mercator Linguistic Law and Legislation site:
    <http://www.troc.es/ciemen/mercator/index-gb.htm>.

31 V. Krausneker, *Sign Languages in the minority languages policy of the European
    Union,* MA thesis, 1998, University of Vienna.

32 The Commission on Human Rights of the UN has special rapporteurs on
    key areas, for instance the Right to Education; see the reports of Katarina
    Tomaševski on this, <www.rwi.lu.se>.

33 T. Skutnabb-Kangas and R. Phillipson, 'Linguistic human rights, past and
    present', in Skutnabb-Kangas and Phillipson (eds) 1994, op. cit., 71–110.

34 <www.unesdoc.unesco.org/images/0012/001234/123405e.pdf>.

35 Reproduced in C. Hamelink, *Trends in world communication. On disempower-
    ment and self-empowerment,* Penang: Southbound, and Third World
    Network, 1994; <www.waag.org/pcc>.

36 C. Hamelink, 'Human Rights: the next fifty years', in Phillipson, op. cit.,
    62–6.

37 A second ruling was that Eurolaw did not 'preclude a national provision
    from requiring that the labelling of foodstuffs and the labelling methods used
    must not mislead the purchaser or consumer, particularly as to the charac-
    teristics of those foodstuffs', a point that choice of language is not central to.

38 *European Voice,* 13–19 December 2001, 4.

39 Y. Tsuda, 'Hegemony of English vs. Ecology of Language: building equal-
    ity in international communication', in *World Englishes 2000,* ed. L. E.
    Smith and M. L. Forman, Honolulu: University of Hawai'i, 1997, 21–31.

40 Skutnabb-Kangas, op. cit. (note 24 above), 657.

41 Ibid., ch. 5. On seeing languages as problems, rights, or resources, see the
    Introduction to Kontra et al., op. cit.

42 B. Dendrinos, 'The conflictual subjectivity of the periphery ELT practi-
    tioner', in A.-F. Christidis (ed.),'*Strong' and 'weak' languages in the European
    Union. Aspects of linguistic hegemonism.* Proceedings of an international con-
    ference, Thessaloniki, 26–28 March 1997. Thessaloniki: Centre for the
    Greek Language, 2 vols, 1999, 711–17.

43 M. Kontra, 'English linguistic and cultural imperialism and teacher training in
    Hungary', in Report on the 2nd ELT Conference on Teacher Training in the
    Carpathian Euro-region, Debrecen, Hungary, 25–27 April 1997. Budapest:
    British Council, English Language Teaching Contacts Scheme, 1997, 83–8.

44 David Crystal's book *English as a global language,* Cambridge: Cambridge
    University Press, 1997, has been impelled by a belief that multilingualism is
    desirable, but in an ideal world 'everyone would have fluent command of a
    single world language' (p. viii). My reasons for finding the book tri-
    umphalist and Eurocentric are explained in a review article, 'Voice in glob-
    al English: unheard chords in Crystal loud and clear', *Applied Linguistics,*
    20/2, 1999, 265–76.

45 D. Lummis, 'English conversation as ideology', in *Essays on Language,* ed. Y.
    Kurokawa, Tokyo: Kirihara Shoten, 1977, 1–26.

46   A. Kirkpatrick (ed.) *Englishes in Asia: Communication, identity, power and education*, Melbourne: Language Australia, 2002.

47   B. Seidlhofer, 'Closing a conceptual gap: the case for a description of English as a lingua franca', *International Journal of Applied Linguistics*, 11/2, 2001, 133–56; A. James, 'English as a European lingua franca: current realities and existing dichotomies', in *English in Europe: the acquisition of a third language*, ed. J. Cenoz and U. Jessner, Clevedon: Multilingual Matters, 2000, 22–38.

48   In like vein, the influential British applied linguist, Henry Widdowson: 'How English develops in the world is no business whatever of native speakers in England, the United States, or anywhere else. They have no say in the matter, no right to intervene or pass judgement. They are irrelevant. The very fact that English is an international language means that no nation can have custody over it.' In 'The ownership of English', *TESOL Quarterly*, 28/2, 1994, 377–81.

49   Parliamentary questions asked by Bart Staes, MEP from The Netherlands, E-1682/01 of 23 May 2001, and E-2900/01 of 9 October 2001. For an overview of parliamentary questions, see <http://lingvo.org/de/2/16/>.

50   <http://www.langue-francaise.org/Textes_ politiques/Myard25_06_01.html>.

51   Response by Rob Cornelissen on behalf of Prodi, 14 May 2001 (EMPL/E/US/hl CI(Prikatel) D(01) 53692); by Mme Diamantopoulou on 21 February 2001 (E-4100/00FR); and by Mme Reding of 5 July 2001 (E-1356/01) on behalf of the Commission; see <http://www.lachambre.be/qrva/50/pdf/061.pdf>. See the letter written on behalf of the Director General for Enlargement, Günther Verheugen, of 8 November 2001, reference ELARG/EL D(2001)/15292, addresssed to Scipo Prikatel, admitting discrimination in the advertising of a post at the Information Centre for Phare/Tacis.

52   Letter from Walter Schwimmer, Secretary General of the Council of Europe, 27 November 2001, to Scipo Prikatel.

53   <www.euro-ombudsman.eu.int>. For the press communiqué about the complaint or further details, contact komunikadcentro@esperanto.org.

54   Information from Professor Vassiliki Dendrinos, Athens, personal communication.

55   Crystal, op. cit., 139.

56   Ibid. 137.

57   Seidlhofer, op. cit.

58   J. Jenkins, *The phonology of English as an international language*, Oxford: Oxford University Press, 2000.

59   J. Brutt-Griffler, *World English. A study of its development*, Clevedon: Multilingual Matters, 2002.

60   Seidlhofer, op. cit, 152.

61   P. Benson, P. Grundy, and T. Skutnabb-Kangas (eds), Language Rights. Special Issue of *Language Sciences*, 20/1, 1998.

62   M. Fettes and S. Bolduc (eds), *Towards linguistic democracy*, Rotterdam: Universala Esperanto Asocio, 1998.

63   This argument is integrated with related economic and cultural arguments in the global restructuring of highly mobile labour in P. van Parijs, 'The ground floor of the world: on the socio-economic consequences of

linguistic globalization', *International Political Science Review*, 21/2, 2000, 217–33.

64 Seidlhofer, op. cit., analysing examples from R. Phillipson and T. Skutnabb-Kangas, 'Englishisation: one dimension of globalisation', in *English in a changing world, AILA Review*, 13, 1999, 17–36, ed. D. Graddol and U. Meinhof.

65 It is arguable that my worries about blurring the distinction between language policy and language politics in Chapter 1 fall into the same category.

66 U. Lins, *Die gefährliche Sprache. Die Verfolgung der Esperantisten unter Hitler und Stalin* (The dangerous language. The persecution of Esperantists under Hitler and Stalin), Gerlingen: Bleicher Lins, 1988, 49–61.

67 C. Piron, *Le défi des langues. Du gâchis au bon sens* (The languages challenge: from waste to common sense), Paris: L'Harmattan, 1994.

68 In the autumn of 1915 Zamenhof wrote an article entitled 'After the Great War – an appeal to diplomats', a kind of political testament. He propounded four principles (Centassi and Masson, op. cit., 329–31, note 1 above):

  1 All countries belong to their inhabitants and those who have settled there (naturalized). No people should, within a country, exercise rights or have duties which are superior or inferior to those of other peoples.

  2 Everyone has the inalienable right to use the language of his/her choice and to practise whatever religion they prefer.

  3 The government of each country is responsible for all injustices committed (by it/in its name) before a permanent European Tribunal constituted with the consent of all the European countries.

  4 No country and no province should bear the name of a people but rather a name which is geographically neutral and freely accepted by all the other peoples.

69 P. Janton, *Esperanto: language, literature, and community*, Albany: State University of New York Press, 1993 (translated from the French); H. Tonkin (ed.), *Esperanto, interlinguistics, and planned language*, Lanham, MD: University Press of America, 1997; S. Fiedler and L. Haitao (eds), *Studoj pri interlingvistiko. Studien zur Interlinguistik,* Festschrift für Detlev Blanke, Dobrichovice, Praha: Kava-Pech, 2001; <www.esperanto.org>.

70 Lins, op. cit.

71 'Das Kommunikations- und Sprachenproblem in der Europäischen Gemeinschaft - in wie weit könnte eine Plansprache zu seiner Lösung beitragen?', European Parliament, Brussels, 29 September 1993, organized by the Hanns Seidel Foundation.

72 H. Erasmus, 'Das Sprachenproblem in Europa', in S. Fiedler and L. Haitao (eds), op. cit., 70–6. Erasmus is a member of the Working Group on the Language Problems of the European Union: erasmusz@worldonline.nl.

73 Written Parliamentary question by Maurizio Turco, E-0075/02, of 14 January 2002. Neil Kinnock's response is dated 12 March 2002.

74 The response states that unspecified 'external partners in university and academic circles' were consulted. It would have been possible to involve scholarly opinion of a different persuasion.

6 Recommendations for action on language policies

1 Ngũgĩ wa Thiong'o, 'Writing for diversity', in *Rights to language: equity, power, and education*, ed. R. Phillipson, Mahwah, NJ: Lawrence Erlbaum, 2000, 97–101.

2 Inspired by the language awareness courses referred to in Chapter 3, etymology as a foundation for courses for intercultural, historically informed understanding, etc.

3 I. Municio-Larsson, 'Science and policy – when does science matter?', in Phillipson, op. cit., 127–31.

4 *Languages: the next generation*. The final report and recommendations of the Nuffield Languages Inquiry, London: The Nuffield Foundation, 2000. <www.nuffield.org>.

5 Summary, Annual Report, *L'état de la francophonie dans le monde 1994*, Paris: Haut Conseil de la Francophonie, 1995.

6 T. van Els, *Horizon Taal: National Action Programme on Foreign Languages. Recommendations and policy reactions*, Enschede: Ministry of Education and Science, 1992, 35.

7 R. Savage, *Policies for foreign language teaching in the member states of the European Union*. Report prepared for the European Commission, Task Force Human Resources, Education, Training & Youth, Brussels, 1994.

8 The German original text refers to 'die Entwicklung eines europäischen Gesamtsprachenkoncepts'.

9 Some relevant journals and books are referred to in Chapter 1. There is an increasing flow of reference works such as the *Concise encyclopedia of sociolinguistics*, ed. R. Mesthrie, Oxford: Pergamon, 2001, and *Sociolinguistics. A handbook of the science of language and society*, ed. U. Ammon, K. Mattheier, P. Nelde and P. Trudgill, Berlin: de Gruyter, 2nd edn 2002; and introductory textbooks such as the *Handbook of language and ethnic identity*, ed. J. A. Fishman, New York and Oxford: Oxford University Press, 1999, and *Language planning, from practice to theory*, R. B. Kaplan and R. B. Baldauf, Clevedon: Multilingual Matters, 1997.

10 There is some experience of the European doctorate at the Universities of Aalborg (Faculty of Technology) and Roskilde (Department of Geography and International Development Studies) in Denmark. In effect an additional 'European' diploma is awarded, over and above the national one, on the strength of residence, thesis supervision, and examination involving two EU countries. The European MA in Human Rights, coordinated by the University of Venice and involving many universities, is primarily in English but requires reading proficiency in French as well. This is a 'weak' form of bilingual degree.

11 This warning is expressed by Colin Williams in 'Language, territory and political context in Europe', in *Which languages for Europe?*, Amsterdam: European Cultural Foundation, 1999, 45 ff. He draws on the experience of strengthening Welsh in recent decades.

12 There is relevant experience on TV with Euro-news, which is disseminated in national languages, and one multilingual channel in Australia.

13 L. Maffi (ed.), *On biocultural diversity. Linking language, knowledge and the environment*, Washington, DC: The Smithsonian Institution Press, 2001.

14   The Cot committee of the EP on 'Multilingualism in light of enlargement', which reported on 19 April 1999, was surprised how ignorant MEPs were and recommended proper briefing.

15   Since 1995, when this institution was created, there have been over 7000 complaints, over 1000 of which have been investigated. See statements by Jacob Söderman on <www.euro-ombudsman.eu.int>.

16   One could envisage Eurodicautom being made available in a simplified version for the general public, a multilingual corpus-based tool projecting EU experience.

17   Michiel van Hulten, MEP for The Netherlands, cited in E. Wagner, S. Bech, and J. M. Martínez, *Translating for the European Union institutions*, Manchester: St Jerome, 2002, 137.

18   This is regularly reviewed in the abstracting journal *Language teaching*, and in Council of Europe publications; see <http://book.coe.int>.

19   Published by Multilingual Matters, Clevedon, UK, in 1995, which also publishes a quarterly *Bilingual Family Newsletter*, and many works relating to multilingualism, including an *Encyclopedia of bilingualism and bilingual education*, Colin Baker and Sylvia Prys Jones, 1998.

20   <www.cilt.org.uk>.

21   e.g. C. Hagège, *Le souffle de la langue*, Paris: Odile Jacob, 1992.

22   See Baker and Prys Jones, op. cit., 518 ff.

23   These are well documented in Sweden (<www.skolverket.se/studier/... r/material/skolvpubl/sprint.shtml>) and Finland.

24   N. Lebrun and H. Baetens Beardsmore, 'Trilingual education in the Grand Duchy of Luxembourg', in *European models of bilingual education*, ed. H. Baetens Beardsmore Clevedon: Multilingual Matters, 1993, summarized in Baker and Prys Jones, op. cit., 526.

25   See Baker and Prys Jones, op. cit., 527–32, and *Multilingualism for all*, ed. T. Skutnabb-Kangas, Lisse: Swets and Zeitlinger, 1995, which extracts general principles of multilingual education from the European school experience.

26   Figures for foreign students in Britain by country of origin, December 2000 (source: HESA Student Record): Greece, 28,640; Germany, 13,390; France, 12,500; Ireland, 12,220; Spain, 7,290; Italy, 6,080; Sweden, 4,060; Finland, 2,540; Netherlands, 2,470; Belgium, 2,400.

27   The European Language Council has elaborated a reference document, 'Universities and language policy in Europe', suggesting how multilingualism might be strengthened. The ELC conference in Berlin in June 2001 drew up a declaration, 'Language studies in higher education: a key contribution to European integration', which lists ways in which universities might be encouraged to take on more responsibility for multilingualism. <http.//www.fu-berlin.de/elc>.

28   In French a distinction is often made between plurilingualism and multilingualism, meaning competence in more than one language at the individual and the societal levels, but this usage has never caught on in English.

29   V. Mamadouh, 'Concluding remarks', in *Which languages for Europe?*, Amsterdam: European Cultural Foundation, 1999, 155–71.

30   C. Karlsson, *Democracy, legitimacy and the European Union*, Uppsala: Acta Universitatis Upsaliensis, Skrifter utgivna av Statsvetenskapliga föreningen, 2001, 88.

31 COM(2001) 428 of 25 July 2001; <http://europa.eu.int/comm/governance/areas/index_en.htm>.
32 Ibid., p. 12.
33 E. Holm, *The European anarchy: Europe's hard road into high politics*, Copenhagen: Copenhagen Business School Press, 2001.

Index

Estonia, Estonian 33–4, 92, 111, 199
ethnic conflict 67
euro 10, 26, 51, 54, 146
Eurobabble 3, 101
Eurobarometer study 8, 59, 66, 136
Eurodicautom 57, 114
Eurolaw, Community law 118, 123, 125–6, 128, 131, 157–160, 164, 187, 189, 193
European Bureau for Lesser Used Languages 10, 63, 184
European Charter for Regional or Minority Languages 92, 153–4, 200
European Coal and Steel Community 53
European Central Bank 28, 146
European Commission 4, 8, 29, 85, 91, 93, 97, 100, 103, 105–138, 158–9, 164, 179–80, 184, 194–198, 200
European Council 4, 8, 29, 91, 100, 103, 109, 132, 157, 190, 193–4
European Court of Justice 8, 53, 79–80, 109, 112, 115, 119, 123, 126, 147, 157–60
European Cultural Foundation 91, 186, 202
European Economic Community 53, 118–19
European Language Council 99–100
European Parliament 4, 8, 19, 29, 91–2, 96, 100. 106, 108–9, 112–13, 115, 117, 120–2, 131, 136, 158, 164, 173, 179, 182, 184, 188, 190, 195–8
European Round Table of Industrialists 70, 76
'European schools' 186
European Science Foundation 84–6

European Trade Mark Office 11
European Year of Languages 10–11, 92, 96, 98, 100, 124, 157, 195–8, 200–3
executives, language competence 62

films 72–3, 87
Fight the Fog 127–8, 135
Finland 16, 21, 49, 67, 83, 112, 126, 171, 190, 199
Finnish 33–4, 49, 81, 83, 111–13, 117, 119–20, 131–2, 135, 186, 194
Finns 61, 66, 136; Finland Swedes 111
Fischer, Joschka 20, 110, 121, 123, 128, 147
Fishman, Joshua 16, 48, 83
foreign language learning 11, 15, 17, 19, 89, 93, 95–9, 101–2, 142, 147, 151, 156, 161, 172, 176, 179–81, 184–7, 195–8, 201–2, 204–6
Forster, E.M. 52
France 6, 16, 21, 37, 42, 45, 48, 52–3, 72, 83, 90–4, 96, 101, 133, 154, 159, 164, 172, 199
francophonie 6, 133, 179, 184
French 21, 24, 28, 31, 33, 45–50, 54, 57–8, 62, 67–8, 70–1, 82–3, 93–4, 97, 112–13, 115–17, 119–22, 125–7, 130–6, 141, 147, 150, 157, 159, 181, 184–6, 191, 194
French empire 37, 47, 49
French Revolution 36, 42, 75

Gaelic 31, 42, 44
genocide, linguistic 49, 161
German 21–2, 24, 31, 33, 38, 43–4, 49–50, 54, 62, 71–2, 79–80, 82–3, 89–90, 93–4, 112–13, 115, 119–22, 124,